T0320154

The Economics of COVID-19

To Nisreen, Danny, Ryan and Ivy

The Economics of COVID-19

Implications of the Pandemic for Economic Thought and Public Policy

Imad A. Moosa

Adjunct Professor of Finance, Faculty of Finance and Banking, Ton Duc Thang University, Vietnam

Edward Elgar
PUBLISHING

Cheltenham, UK • Northampton, MA, USA

Published by
Edward Elgar Publishing Limited
The Lypiatts
15 Lansdown Road
Cheltenham
Glos GL50 2JA
UK

Edward Elgar Publishing, Inc.
William Pratt House
9 Dewey Court
Northampton
Massachusetts 01060
USA

A catalogue record for this book
is available from the British Library

Library of Congress Control Number: 2021946157

This book is available electronically in the **Elgar**online
Economics subject collection
http://dx.doi.org/10.4337/9781800377226

ISBN 978 1 80037 721 9 (cased)
ISBN 978 1 80037 722 6 (eBook)

Printed and bound by CPI Group (UK) Ltd, Croydon, CR0 4YY

Contents

Figures

Tables

Preface

COVID-19 has become an international household name as the virus spread from Wuhan to all corners of the world. The new virus, SARS-CoV-2, was identified in China in January 2020, and on 11 January the first death case was recorded in Wuhan. On 20 January 2020, the first confirmed cases outside mainland China were detected in Japan, South Korea and Thailand. On 30 January 2020, the WHO described the situation as a 'public health emergency of international concern', and on 11 March 2020 a pandemic was declared. The pandemic was still raging in April 2021, with some countries experiencing two or three waves. By 10 April 2021, the virus had infected more than 135 million and killed over 2.9 million worldwide. In the US alone, the death toll was over 574,000. In the UK, the virus had infected 4.37 million and killed over 127,000. One can only wonder why it is that the two countries ranked the top two in terms of the global health security index (US and UK) end up as the number one and number six most severely affected countries.

The pandemic is a public health–economic crisis that has affected every aspect of our lives. Economic activity has been disrupted severely, and millions of people lost their jobs. Governments worldwide reacted in a Keynesian fashion by resorting to the public purse and taking measures that break every rule in the neoliberal handbook. The crisis is viewed both as a challenge and an opportunity: a challenge in terms of responding appropriately and adequately, and an opportunity to put things right. For example, the pandemic has forced governments to provide accommodation for the homeless when this problem had been persistently ignored by putting it at the bottom of the list of priorities, or by claiming that the solution is unaffordable. Unfortunately, the pandemic has also been taken as an opportunity by governments to pursue their agendas as they kept on glorifying the military, expanding mass surveillance (hence enhancing the electronic concentration camp), ruling by decree, and abusing civil liberties and human rights. The pandemic has led to the rise of fascism, populism and nationalism. The pandemic has forced a rethinking of the prevailing economic principles and policies based on those principles.

This book deals with all of these issues. I started developing interest in the economics of COVID-19 while under lockdown in my home city of Melbourne. My initial interest was in the effect of social distancing on the severity of COVID-19, and for that I developed a statistical measure of severity, which is described in Chapter 2. Subsequently, I started to research the effect of population density on infection and mortality rates. This research was expanded to investigate the determinants of the severity of COVID-19 by considering demographic factors, preparedness, the quality of the healthcare system, the timing and severity of non-pharmaceutical interventions, international tourist arrivals, and others. By May 2020, I felt that I had accumulated adequate knowledge to be able to write this book, with the primary objective of demonstrating that COVID-19 is to a large extent a neoliberal pandemic caused and spread by blind adherence to market forces. This is why the pandemic is an opportunity to rethink the free market doctrine and principles of neoclassical economics that have shaped economic policy in the past 40 years.

Writing this book would not have been possible without the help and encouragement I received from family, friends and colleagues. My utmost gratitude must go to my wife, Afaf, who bore most of the opportunity cost of writing this book and helped with the drawing of diagrams. I would also like to thank my colleagues and friends, including John Vaz, Kelly Burns, Vikash Ramiah, Liam Lenten, Brien McDonald and Nirav Parikh.

In preparing the manuscript, I benefited from the exchange of ideas with members of the Table 14 Discussion Group, and for this reason I would like to thank Bob Parsons, Greg O'Brien, Greg Bailey, Bill Breen, Paul Rule, Peter Murphy, Bob Brownlee, Jim Reiss and Tony Pagliaro. My thanks also go to friends and former colleagues who live far away but provide help via means of telecommunication, including Kevin Dowd (whom I owe intellectual debt), Razzaque Bhatti, Ron Ripple, Bob Sedgwick, Sean Holly, Dan Hemmings, Ian Baxter, Basil Al-Nakeeb and Mike Dempsey. Last, but not least, I would like to thank Alex Pettifer, the editorial director of Edward Elgar, who encouraged me to write this book.

Naturally, I am the only one responsible for any errors and omissions that may be found in this book. It is dedicated to my daughter, Nisreen, my son, Danny, my grandson, Ryan, and my granddaughter, Ivy.

Imad A. Moosa

April, 2021

Abbreviations and acronyms

ABC	Australian Broadcasting Corporation
ABS	Australian Bureau of Statistics
AD	aggregate demand
AEI	American Enterprise Institute
AIDS	Acquired Immunodeficiency Syndrome
AS	aggregate supply
ATM	automated teller machine
BA	British Airways
BBC	British Broadcasting Corporation
BCBS	Basel Committee on Banking Supervision
BIS	Bank for International Settlements
BMJ	British Medical Journal
BOP	Balance of Payments
CARES	Coronavirus Aid, Relief, and Economic Security (Act)
CCTV	closed-circuit television
CDC	Center for Disease Control
CEO	chief executive officer
CFO	chief financial officer
CGE	computable general equilibrium
CNBC	Consumer News and Business Channel
CNN	Cable News Network
COVID	Coronavirus Disease
CPI	consumer price index
DC	District of Columbia

DJIA	Dow Jones Industrial Average
ECB	European Central Bank
EIU	Economist Intelligence Unit
EPA	Environmental Protection Agency
EU	European Union
EVD	Ebola Virus Disease
FAO	Food and Agriculture Organization
FDR	Franklin Delano Roosevelt
FIRE	finance, insurance and real estate
FTT	financial transactions tax
GDP	gross domestic product
GFC	global financial crisis
GHS	global health security
GST	goods and services tax
HIV	human immunodeficiency virus
ICA	International Currency Association
ICU	intensive care unit
IFAD	International Fund for Agricultural Development
IFPRI	International Food Policy Research Institute
ILO	International Labour Organization
IMF	International Monetary Fund
IP	intellectual property
IR	international relations
IRR	incidence rate ratio
LAS	long-run aggregate supply
LSE	London School of Economics
LTCM	Long-Term Capital Management
MA	Massachusetts
MEC	marginal economic cost
MERS	Middle East Respiratory Syndrome
MHB	marginal health benefit

MIT	Massachusetts Institute of Technology
MP	Member of Parliament
NASA	National Aeronautics and Space Administration
NASDAQ	National Association of Securities Dealers Automated Quotations
NATO	North Atlantic Treaty Organization
NBC	National Broadcasting Company
NBER	National Bureau of Economic Research
NESA	National Electronic Security Alliance
NHS	National Health Service
NPI	non-pharmaceutical intervention
NPR	National Public Radio
NTI	Nuclear Threat Initiative
OECD	Organisation for Economic Co-ordination and Development
OPEC	Organization of the Petroleum Exporting Countries
ORF	Observer Research Foundation
OTC	over-the-counter
PIN	personal identification number
PNAS	Proceedings of the National Academy of Sciences
PPE	personal protective equipment
PPP	Paycheck Protection Program
PPP	public–private partnership
QE	quantitative easing
RFC	Reconstruction Finance Corporation
SARB	South African Reserve Bank
SARS	Severe acute respiratory syndrome
SAS	short-run aggregate supply

SBS	Special Broadcasting Service
SEIR	susceptible-exposed-infected-recovered
SIPRI	Stockholm International Peace Research Institute
SIR	susceptible-infected-recovered
SSRN	Social Science Research Network
TRIPS	Trade-Related Aspects of Intellectual Property Rights
UBI	universal basic income
UHC	universal healthcare (or universal health coverage)
UK	United Kingdom
UN	United Nations
UNDP	United Nations Development Programme
UNESCO	United Nations Educational, Scientific and Cultural Organization
UNOCHA	United Nations Office for the Coordination of Humanitarian Affairs
UNWTO	United Nations World Tourism Organization
US	United States
VA	Virginia
VAT	value added tax
WFP	World Food Programme
WHO	World Health Organization
WTI	West Texas Intermediate
WTO	World Trade Organization
ZLB	zero lower bound

1. The economics and epidemiology of epidemics and pandemics

1.1 THE RISE OF COVID-19: EPIDEMIC TO PANDEMIC AND PERHAPS ENDEMIC

The COVID-19 pandemic, also known as the coronavirus pandemic, is caused by severe acute respiratory syndrome coronavirus 2 (SARS-CoV-2). The virus is primarily spread between people as a result of close contact via small droplets produced by coughing, sneezing and exhaling. Infection may also occur when people touch a contaminated surface (fomite) and then touch their faces, enabling the virus to reach the respiratory system via nose, mouth or eyes. According to a systematic review of the scientific literature, face touching occurs at least twice as frequently as the often-cited figure of 23 times an hour (Rahman et al., 2020).

The World Health Organization (2020a) describes the transmission of the virus as follows: 'Transmission of SARS-CoV-2 can occur through direct, indirect, or close contact with infected people through infected secretions such as saliva and respiratory secretions or their respiratory droplets, which are expelled when an infected person coughs, sneezes, talks or sings.' The WHO also refers to airborne transmission, which is caused by the dissemination of droplet nuclei (aerosols) that remain infectious when suspended in air over long distances and time. Moreover, the virus has been detected in biological samples, including the urine and faeces of some patients – however, the WHO suggests that no published reports confirm transmission through faeces or urine.

In December 2019, a cluster of pneumonia cases with unknown source were recorded in the city of Wuhan, China. These cases were reported to the WHO on 31 December 2019. The new virus was identified in January 2020, and on 11 January, Chinese state media reported the first known death from an illness caused by the virus, which had infected dozens of people. The 61-year-old man who died was a regular customer at the wet market in Wuhan. On 20 January 2020, the first confirmed cases outside mainland China were detected in Japan, South Korea and Thailand. The first confirmed case in the US was declared the following day, as a man in his 30s developed symptoms after returning to

Washington State from a trip to Wuhan. On 23 January, the Chinese authorities closed off Wuhan by cancelling planes and trains leaving the city, and suspending buses, subways and ferries within the city. On 30 January, amid thousands of new cases in China, a 'public health emergency of international concern' was officially declared by the WHO. This is a formal declaration of 'an extraordinary event which is determined to constitute a public health risk to other States through the international spread of disease and to potentially require a coordinated international response', formulated when a situation arises that is 'serious, sudden, unusual or unexpected'. The situation 'carries implications for public health beyond the affected state's national border' and 'may require immediate international action' (World Health Organization, 2019a).

On 11 February 2020, the WHO proposed an official name for the disease caused by the coronavirus, COVID-19, an acronym that stands for 'Coronavirus Disease 2019'. The name makes no reference to any of the people, places, or animals associated with the virus, which was intentional to avoid stigma (recall that Donald Trump always referred to the coronavirus as the 'China virus'). One month later, on 11 March, the WHO declared a pandemic, producing big losses in stock markets worldwide. On 14 April, the International Monetary Fund warned that the global economy was headed for its worst downturn since the Great Depression. The IMF predicted that the world economy would contract by 3% in 2020, a reversal from its earlier, pre-pandemic forecast that the world economy would grow by 3.3%. That happened as countries scrambled to implement public health measures, with dire economic consequences.

By early May 2020, a backlash was building against China for its alleged mishandling of the crisis. Australia called for an inquiry into the origins of the virus. In Britain and Germany, new questions were raised about the advisability of using the Chinese tech-giant Huawei for new 5G systems. President Trump continued to blame China for the outbreak and sought ways to punish the 'communist state'. The word 'reparations' became popular as the fingers pointed to China as the cause of the pandemic, either through mishandling and misinformation or because the virus had been accidently released from a lab in Wuhan.

Conspiracy theories began to emerge, some blaming China and others blaming the US for the pandemic. In February 2021, a fact-finding mission of the WHO investigating the virus's origins concluded a visit to Wuhan. On that occasion, Dr. Peter Embarek of the WHO said that it was 'extremely unlikely' that the coronavirus leaked from a lab in Wuhan, and that it was more likely that the virus had jumped to humans from an animal (Talmazan and Smith, 2021). The speculation that the virus was either manufactured at or accidentally leaked from a lab at the Wuhan Institute of Virology was partially fuelled by former US president Donald Trump.

On 13 May 2020, Dr. Mike Ryan, the head of the WHO's health emergencies program, said that the virus may become 'just another endemic virus in our communities' and that 'this virus may never go away'. He also tamped down expectations that the invention of a vaccine would provide a quick and complete end to the global crisis. Starting with an outbreak in Wuhan, COVID-19 has progressed from an epidemic to a pandemic, and it will perhaps remain as endemic (World Health Organization, 2020b). In February 2021, *Nature* published the results of a survey showing that 'scientists expect the virus that causes COVID-19 to become endemic, but it could pose less danger over time' (Phillips, 2021).

1.2   SOME PRINCIPLES OF INFECTIOUS DISEASES

Infectious diseases, which are ever present amongst us, are spread by either bacterial or viral agents (otherwise, the agents can be fungi or parasites). It is normal to observe infection cases below an expected threshold, but every now and then communities experience an outbreak, a new strain or a new disease that has a significant impact at either a local or global level. An outbreak is a greater-than-anticipated increase in the number of cases in a particular area – it can also be a single case in a new area. The terms describing an infectious disease are often used interchangeably in an erroneous manner. For example, distinction between the words 'pandemic', 'epidemic' and 'endemic' is blurred, particularly because the description of each of these terms changes as the underlying disease becomes more or less prevalent over time. The differences may refer to the spread and the rate of growth of new cases.

While the level of disease occurrence can be described in many ways, it is primarily defined by two measurable factors: (i) the pattern and speed by which a disease moves (the reproduction rate); and (ii) the size of the susceptible population (the critical community size). The terms may suggest that a specific threshold may be used to declare an outbreak, epidemic, or pandemic, but the distinction is often blurred, even among epidemiologists who are cautious about how they describe a disease event so that it is placed in the appropriate context. Certain terms can incite undue panic. One such example is the Zika outbreak of 2016, which triggered alarm in the US when a locally acquired disease occurred in 218 individuals in Florida and six people in Texas. Even with HIV, a disease that has spread across much of the planet, the term 'pandemic' has been increasingly replaced by 'epidemic', given the widespread distribution of effective treatment and declining rates in some previously hyper-prevalent regions. On the other hand, as influenza becomes more virulent year after year, public health officials commonly refer to seasonal outbreaks as pandemics, particularly given the 2009 H1N1 outbreak that affected 60 million people in the US, resulting in 274,304 hospital admissions and 12,469 deaths.

Humanity has always encountered pandemics. The HIV/AIDS pandemic has killed over 30 million people since 1982. The 541 AD Plague of Justinian killed 25–50 million people in one year. The Black Death (Bubonic Plague) killed more than 75 million people during the period 1347–1351, perhaps more if the count includes (in addition to Europe) those who died in the Middle East, China and India. The Spanish flu pandemic of 1918 killed well over 50 million people in one year. The smallpox pandemic of the 20th century claimed more than 300 million lives. The ongoing tuberculosis pandemic continues to kill over 1.5 million people every year. It appears that the likelihood of pandemics has increased over the past century because of global travel and integration, urbanisation, changes in land use, and greater exploitation of the natural environment. It is likely that these trends will continue and intensify.

1.3   SOME PRINCIPLES OF EPIDEMIOLOGY

Epidemiology is the branch of medicine that deals with the incidence, distribution and control of diseases. The role of epidemiology is to determine disease prevalence (the proportion of people affected within a population) and incidence (the occurrence of a disease over a specific period of time). This information is vital for the direction of an appropriate public health response.

A basic tool of epidemiology is the epidemiological curve (or epi curve), which shows the numbers of new cases over time. The spread of a contagious disease does not follow an exponential curve, in the sense that cases do not rise exponentially over time, except at the beginning. What happens in reality is that new cases rise rapidly, peak, and then decline. During the spread of the disease, some patients (most patients in the case of COVID-19) recover, some (tragically) die, and uninfected people start taking measures to reduce the infection rate.

Figure 1.1 shows a typical epi curve, with intervals describing the growth of new cases. The investigation interval is initiated by investigating infection (in humans or animals anywhere in the world) that is judged to have potential implications for public health. The recognition interval starts with the identification of increasing numbers of human cases or clusters of infection anywhere in the world, particularly when the characteristics of the virus indicate greater potential for human-to-human transmission. The initiation interval begins when cases are confirmed anywhere in the world, with demonstrated efficient and sustained human-to-human transmission. The acceleration interval is indicated by a consistently increasing number of cases. The deceleration interval is indicated by a consistently declining number of cases. The preparation interval is characterised by low pandemic activity, although outbreaks might continue to occur in certain regions. This interval involves preparing for potential additional waves of infection.

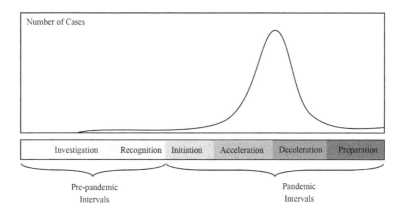

Figure 1.1 A typical epi curve

The simplest epidemiological model is the SIR model, which belongs to the family of compartmental models used for the mathematical representation of infectious diseases. According to this model, the population is assigned to three compartments: S (susceptible), I (infected) and R (recovered or dead). The susceptible include everyone who is not infected yet or is disease free. The infected, who carry the virus, are capable of infecting other people. Those who recover or die do not infect anyone else. Because the number of deaths is negligible with respect to the total population, R may be considered as the recovered only. People may move from one compartment to another: a susceptible person becomes infected, then recovers. Since the dynamics of an epidemic are faster than the dynamics of birth, the model is represented by following set of differential equations:

$$\frac{dS}{dt} = -\frac{\beta IS}{N} \tag{1.1}$$

$$\frac{dI}{dt} = \frac{\beta IS}{N} - \gamma I \tag{1.2}$$

$$\frac{dR}{dt} = \gamma I \tag{1.3}$$

where t is time, β is the rate at which the disease is transmitted from an infected to a susceptible, γ is the reciprocal of the average duration of recovery, and $N = S + I + R$. In this model, the basic reproduction rate (R_0) is the expected number of cases generated directly by one case in a population where all individuals are susceptible to infection. It is calculated as

$$R_0 = \frac{\beta}{\gamma} \tag{1.4}$$

The model is dynamic, in the sense that the number in each compartment changes over time. With time, the number of susceptible falls rapidly as more of them are infected (a change from S to I). In Figure 1.2, we can see how S, I and R change over time, in accordance with the set of differential equations. A modified version is the SEIR model, which has a fourth compartment, the exposed, who have already contracted the disease but the virus is still in the incubation period. In other words, the exposed are those who carry the virus without showing any symptoms.

1.4   ECONOMIC AND FINANCIAL CONSEQUENCES OF PANDEMICS

Pandemics lead to a significant increase in morbidity and mortality over a wide geographical area, in the process causing economic, social and political disruption. Economic damage can be caused through several channels, including short-term fiscal shocks and long-term negative shocks to economic growth. Individual behavioural changes, such as fear-induced aversion to workplaces and other public gathering venues are a primary cause of negative shocks to economic growth. Some pandemic mitigation measures can cause significant

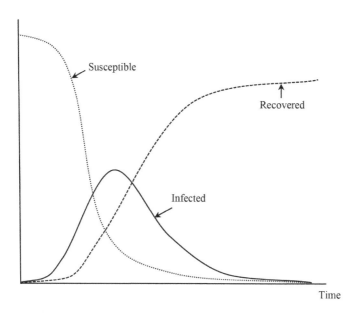

Figure 1.2   Prediction of the SIR model

social and economic disruption. In countries with weak institutions and political instability, pandemics can aggravate political stress and tension. In these contexts, outbreak response measures, such as quarantines, have sparked violence and tension between states and citizens.

A sizeable outbreak can overwhelm the healthcare system, limiting the capacity to deal with routine health issues, which aggravates the problem. Beyond shocks to the healthcare system, both the ill and their caretakers are forced to miss work, or if they go to work they are less effective, driving down productivity. Fear of infection can result in the closure of schools, factories, commercial establishments, means of transportation and public service venues, which disrupts economic and social activity. During a severe pandemic, all sectors of the economy (agriculture, manufacturing and services) face disruption, potentially leading to shortages, rapidly rising prices of staple goods and economic stress for households, firms and governments.

The direct fiscal impacts of pandemics are generally small relative to the indirect damage inflicted on economic activity and growth. Typically, the effect of aversive behaviour (such as the avoidance of travel, restaurants and

public spaces, as well as prophylactic workplace absenteeism) exceeds the
direct effect of absenteeism associated with morbidity and mortality. Negative
effects on economic activity are driven directly by the reduction in the labour
force caused by sickness and mortality and indirectly by fear-induced behavioural changes. In reference to the 2014 Ebola epidemic in West Africa, the
World Bank (2014) notes the following:

> Fear of association with others … reduces labor force participation, closes places
> of employment, disrupts transportation, motivates some governments to close land
> borders and restrict entry of citizens from affected countries, and motivates private
> decision makers to disrupt trade, travel, and commerce by canceling scheduled
> commercial flights and reducing shipping and cargo services.

The indirect economic impact of pandemics has been quantified primarily
through computable general equilibrium simulations. The simulations conducted by Burns et al. (2006) indicate that a severe pandemic could reduce
world GDP by roughly 5%. Country-specific estimates tell the same story.
Smith et al. (2009) demonstrate that the impact of an influenza pandemic on
the UK depends on the severity of the pandemic, such that a low-severity
event could reduce GDP by up to 1%, whereas a high-severity event could
reduce GDP by 3–4%. Thomas et al. (2015) show that economic disruption
in low-income countries could be even greater – for example, the Ebola
pandemic was so devastating for Sierra Leone that the growth rate went down
to −2% compared to 9% in the pre-Ebola period. The UNDP (2015) presents
a comprehensive analysis of the economic impact of the Ebola pandemic by
using the Solow–Swan growth model to analyse the macroeconomic impact of
a temporary shock on the labour force and capital accumulation.

   Table 1.1 provides a summary of some studies estimating the economic
losses due to pandemics and epidemics, real and imaginary. The 1918–19
influenza pandemic produced six percentage points loss in GDP growth,
according to Barro et al. (2020) and 18% decline in manufacturing activity
per year according to Correia et al. (2020). SARS produced a 0.1% decline
in global GDP, according to Lee and McKibbin (2004), and 1–2 percentage
points of Chinese growth, according to Hai et al. (2004). The losses that can
be produced by a 1918-type pandemic have been estimated by Arnold et al.
(2006), Burns et al. (2006) and Fan et al. (2016). Fan et al. (2016) consider
the economic loss due to a pandemic by including the intrinsic value of lives
lost, finding that the bulk of the expected annual loss from pandemics is driven
by the direct cost of mortality, particularly in the case of low-probability,
high-severity events. On the other hand, Arnold et al. (2006) estimate the
loss in annual GDP growth to be 4.25%, of which 2.25% is attributed to the
supply-side effect and 2% to the demand-side effect.

Table 1.1   Estimated economic effects of epidemics/pandemics

Study	Epidemic/Pandemic	Economic Losses
Lee and McKibbin (2004)	SARS, 2003	0.1% in global GDP in 2003
Hai et al. (2004)	SARS, 2003	1–2 percentage points of Chinese GDP growth
Burns et al. (2006)	A 1918-type pandemic	3.1% in annual global GDP growth
Arnold et al. (2006)	A 1918-type pandemic	4.25% in annual GDP growth (2.25% from the supply side and 2% from the demand side)
Keogh-Brown et al. (2010)	An H1N1 pandemic	1.4–6% in annual GDP growth
World Bank (2014)	Ebola, 2014–16	2.1% GDP growth in Guinea, 3.4% in Liberia, 3.3% in Sierra Leone in the first year of the epidemic
Fan et al. (2016)	A 1918-type pandemic	0.4–1% of GDP per year due to ex ante prospects of a pandemic, 86% of which is due to mortality and 14% to lost income
Global Preparedness Monitoring Board (2019)	A 1918-type pandemic	4.8% of annual global GDP
Barro et al. (2020)	Influenza pandemic, 1918–19	Six percentage points of GDP growth
Correia et al. (2020)	Influenza pandemic, 1918–19	18% decline in manufacturing activity per year

The adverse economic effects of pandemics are intertwined with their social and political effects. Price-Smith (2009) refers to evidence suggesting that pandemics can have significant social and political consequences, creating clashes between states and citizens, eroding state capacity, driving population displacement, and heightening social tension and discrimination. Diamond (2009) argues that severe pandemics have been associated with significant social and political upheaval, driven by mortality shocks and the resulting demographic shifts. As an example, he refers to deaths arising from the introduction of smallpox and other diseases to the Americas, which led directly to the collapse of many Indigenous societies.

Epidemics and pandemics can amplify existing political tensions and spark unrest, particularly in fragile states with legacies of violence and weak institutions. During the 2014 West Africa Ebola epidemic, steps taken to mitigate the transmission of the disease (such as the imposition of quarantines and curfews) were viewed with suspicion by segments of the public and opposition political leaders. According to McCoy (2014), this led directly to riots and violent clashes with security forces. Tension between previously warring factions in Liberia, which re-emerged early in the epidemic, were linked to threats to healthcare workers as well as attacks on public health personnel and facilities. Quarantine in opposition-dominated regions was delayed because of concerns that it would be seen as politically motivated. Incumbent politicians in Guinea, Liberia and Sierra Leone were accused of leveraging the crisis and mitigation measures to enhance political control while opposition figures were accused of hampering disease response efforts (International Crisis Group, 2015). Even though growing tensions did not lead to large-scale political violence or instability, they did complicate public health response efforts with further economic and social consequences. The UNDP (2015) reports on various effects of Ebola, suggesting that it has threatened the social fabric that glues society together.

The pandemic and the associated hardships have changed people's consumption habits; many have had to eat less than before the EVD outbreak. There is evidence that the EVD is eroding the age-long communal behaviours of the people including attendance at ceremonies, adjustment in burial rights and less caregiving to family and community members. Feelings of distrust between communities and between the people and their governments are still strong.

Large-scale outbreaks of infectious disease have direct and consequential social impacts. For example, widespread public panic during disease outbreaks can lead to rapid population migration. Barrett and Brown (2008) note that even though the 1994 outbreak of plague in Surat (India) caused only a small number of reported cases, fear led some 500,000 people (roughly 20% of the city's population, including a disproportionately large number of clinicians) to flee their homes. Toole and Waldman (1990) argue that sudden population movements can have destabilising effects, and migrants face elevated health risks arising from poor sanitation and nutrition, as well as other sources of stress. Migration also poses the risk of further spreading an outbreak. Furthermore, outbreaks of infectious disease can lead to the stigmatisation of already vulnerable social groups, as they get blamed for the disease and its consequences. For example, Siu (2015) tells a story about how Africans in Hong Kong experienced social isolation, anxiety, and economic hardship resulting from fears of their association with Ebola.

1.5   CONCLUDING REMARKS

This chapter is concluded by considering some of the lessons that have, or should have, been learned from past pandemics. Colvin and McLaughlin (2020) draw three lessons from the Spanish flu pandemic of 1918. The first of these lessons is that the public health response to the spread of the disease must focus on containment – after all, deaths are linked closely to infections. The second lesson is that good information is essential for disease control, in which case they warn of a media blackout or an active disinformation campaign. They argue that the truth always comes out eventually, in which case nothing is to be gained from hiding it. The third lesson is that we must prepare for the economic and human consequences of the virus and act to minimise its impact.

These are words of wisdom but have we really learned these lessons? As far as containment is concerned, some countries have done rather well, but others have not. Some of the countries that have not done well cannot do well because of constrained resources. Other countries that can do well did not do well because of political and other considerations (the UK and US). The second lesson has not been learned, again because of political considerations. At one time, the President of Brazil wanted to impose an information blackout by refraining from the publication of daily reports on new cases and deaths. He actually did that until he was told not to by a judge. The third lesson has not been learned, as indicated by improper and discriminatory economic policy and healthcare systems.

2. Measures and determinants of the severity of COVID-19

2.1 INTRODUCTION

The word 'severity' as used in this chapter refers to the extent to which the virus is infecting and killing people, which depends on the timeliness and nature of the response of the public health authorities (performance) and factors beyond their control, such as the geographical location of the country, its demographics, and the availability of resources, financial and otherwise. Also important is the public attitude towards the implementation of measures taken to control the spread of the disease. It follows that severity, as used here, is a reflection of the spread of the virus and how deadly it has been. In this sense, severity is determined by government actions, country preparedness and socio-economic factors.

Divergence in the performance of countries in their endeavours to contain the coronavirus has been quite conspicuous. Countries differ with respect to their responses to the pandemic, as some acted quickly, while others responded slowly. Some countries paid close attention to the guidance provided by, and the scientific findings of, the World Health Organization while others did so to a lesser extent. Some countries ramped up the production and deployment of test kits and personal protection equipment, while others assigned lower priority to this endeavour. Some countries adopted tough measures while others took a more relaxed attitude. Some countries have populations that accept and abide by public policy measures while others do not. Some countries have leaders who take the virus seriously, while others have leaders who think that it is nothing to worry about.

Differences in severity are not only determined by response to the pandemic but also by socio-economic differences, even though a rapid and appropriate response proved to be a critical factor. Some countries adopted severe restrictions, others moderate restrictions and some adopted light restrictions. Severe restrictions include lockdowns that restrict all but essential movement outside the family home, with the requirement of permits and the wearing of masks for approved activities (such as essential shopping). Under this regime, bars, restaurants, schools and offices are closed. All sport, religious and other public gatherings are banned, and only workers deemed essential may work outside home. Travel in and out of the country is restricted. Under moderate restrictions, people are allowed to leave their homes as long as they follow social distancing guidelines. Small, socially distanced gatherings are also permitted. Some commercial outlets may open under restricted conditions. Schools are typically closed or operating on a shift system, and workers are encouraged to work from home if they can. Masks are encouraged but they are not mandatory. Under light restrictions, most businesses are allowed to operate, while offices and schools stay open (sometimes at reduced capacity). Large events are restricted. Extra cleaning and record-keeping requirements may be in place for those operating businesses and other venues that attract crowds.

Differences in the response to the pandemic may not fully explain differences in severity and performance with respect to the containment of the virus. Other factors have been identified, including, among others, the political system, the level of economic development, the quality of the healthcare system, the prevalence of obesity, age structure, population density, income inequality, the role of testing and international tourist arrivals. Severity and performance have been measured in different ways, using infection and mortality rates (Chaudhry et al., 2020; Moosa, 2020b; Moosa and Khatatbeh, 2020, 2021a, 2021b, 2021c; Lowy Institute, 2021), doubling time of the total number of cases and deaths (Jamison et al., 2020), and the reproduction rate (Haug et al., 2020).

As expected, the studies dealing with this issue have produced varying results. In this chapter we examine the measures and determinants of the severity of COVID-19, which reflects country performance with respect to the containment of the virus. Three sections describe measures of severity, including the reproduction rate, infection and mortality rates, and a statistical measure of severity. This is followed by a discussion of the determinants of severity as identified in the literature.

2.2 THE REPRODUCTION RATE (*R*) AS A MEASURE OF SEVERITY

The origin of *R*, the rate at which the virus spreads, can be traced back to demography, where it is used to measure the reproduction of people. In epidemiology, *R* is a measure of the spread of infection in a population, not the speed at which the infection grows (even though spread and speed are related, just like distance and speed). Unless the entire population is tested, *R* cannot be measured directly. Rather, it is estimated ex post from current and previous numbers of cases and deaths. Figure 2.1 shows how the infection moves from patient zero (the first to be infected) to the population at different values of *R*, ranging between 1.5 and 3.0. It is clear that a small change in the value of R makes a significant difference to the spread of the virus.

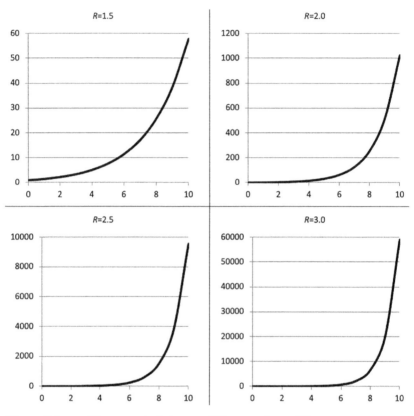

Figure 2.1   The spread of virus at different values of R

Distinction is made between R_0, which is the basic reproduction rate calculated at the beginning of the outbreak, on the assumption that everyone is susceptible to infection, and R_t (or R_e or effective R) which is calculated over time as the pandemic progresses by considering people who might have gained immunity, either because they have survived infection or because they have been vaccinated. R_0 can be thought of as the expected number of cases generated directly by one case in a population where all individuals are susceptible to infection (Milligan and Barrett, 2015). According to Fraser et al. (2009), the definition describes the state where no other individuals are infected or immunised (naturally or through vaccination). Haug et al. (2020) use R_t to assess the effectiveness of non-pharmaceutical interventions (NPIs) to mitigate the spread of the coronavirus. Their results indicate that a suitable combination of NPIs is necessary to curb the spread of the virus and that less disruptive and costly NPIs can be as effective as more intrusive and drastic ones (for example, a national lockdown). They demonstrate how the effectiveness of NPIs depends on the local context such as timing of their adoption.

The relation between R_t and R_0 can be illustrated by introducing the role of social distancing, which is intended to reduce the basic reproduction rate, with the objective of reaching the condition $R_t < 1$, indicating containment of the virus. In a basic model of social distancing, a proportion, f, of the population follow the rules to reduce interpersonal contacts to a fraction, α, of the normal level. It follows that

$$R_t = [1 - (1 - \alpha^2) f] R_0 \qquad (2.1)$$

For example, if $f = 0.5$ (that is, 50% of the population reduce social contacts) and $\alpha = 0.4$ (that is, they reduce social contacts to 40% of the normal level), the reproduction rate will be reduced by 58% (that is, $R_t = 0.42 R_0$). It is important to bear in mind that even a small reduction in the reproduction rate can be effective in delaying the exponential growth and spread of a disease. If the condition $R_t < 1$ is maintained for a sufficiently long time, containment is achieved, as the number of cases starts to decline. However, the number of cases may still be high, which means that this situation does not represent containment.

Mathematically, R_t depends on two parameters, f and α, such that $0 < f < 1$ and $0 < \alpha < 1$. If $\alpha = 1$ and $f = 0$, then $R_t = R_0$, which is the case of no social distancing whatsoever. If $\alpha < 1$ and $f > 0$, it follows that $R_t < R_0$. The rate of change of R over time is given by

$$\frac{dR_t}{dt} = \frac{\partial R_t}{\partial f} \cdot \frac{df}{dt} + \frac{\partial R_t}{\partial \alpha} \cdot \frac{d\alpha}{dt} \qquad (2.2)$$

which means that for R to decline over time, $df / dt > 0$ and/or $d\alpha / dt < 0$. This also means that more and more people practise social distancing and/or reduce their contacts by an increasing fraction. Naturally, new cases will continue to emerge during periods of social distancing for two reasons. The first is that people need to go shopping as and when they need food and other essential household goods, while essential workers continue to go to work. The second is that the benefits of social distancing will not be felt until these policies have been in place for a period of time that is equal to the incubation period. Many individuals who contracted COVID-19 in the weeks before the start of social distancing will not be diagnosed until they begin to show symptoms, which can take up to 14 days.

The number of infections (cases) can be related to the reproduction rate as shown by Barr and Tassier (2020b):

$$I_t = a_0 R_t^t \tag{2.3}$$

where a_0 is the initial number of cases. The reproduction rate can be viewed as the product of the contact rate, C, transmission rate, T, susceptibility rate, S, and duration, D (the time taken from infection to recovery or death). Hence

$$R = C \times T \times S \times D \tag{2.4}$$

On the assumption that T, S and D are constant, it follows that

$$I_t = a_0 (\alpha_0)^t \tag{2.5}$$

where $\alpha_0 = T \times S \times D$. Equation (2.5) shows that the number of cases depends on two factors: the contact rate and time (assuming that the starting point is patient zero, which gives $\alpha_0 = 1$).

Over-reliance on the reproduction rate to trace the progress, or otherwise, of the pandemic has been criticised. According to Adam (2020) 'R has leapt from the pages of academic journals into regular discussions by politicians and newspapers, framed as a number that will shape everyone's lives' and 'fascination might have turned into unhealthy political and media fixation'. He quotes Jeremy Rossman, a virologist at the University of Kent, as saying that 'R is an imprecise estimate that rests on assumptions'. Rossman adds:

> It doesn't capture the current status of an epidemic and can spike up and down when case numbers are low. It is also an average for a population and therefore can hide local variation. Too much attention to it could obscure the importance of other measures, such as trends in numbers of new infections, deaths and hospital admissions, and cohort surveys to see how many people in a population currently have the disease, or have already had it.

Another expert is quoted by Adam (2020) as saying that 'epidemiologists are quite keen on downplaying R, but the politicians seem to have embraced it with enthusiasm', and that 'we're concerned that we've created a monster' because 'R does not tell us what we need to know to manage this'.

R is problematical because it is a lagging indicator and an average. It is a lagging indicator of the status quo because confirmed cases and mortality figures can be used to infer the total number of infections, which come with a significant lag, ranging between one week and three weeks or more. The drawback of an average across a region is that it can miss clusters of infection whereas high incidences of infection among a spatially distinct smaller subsection of a population can sway a larger region's R value. For example, Adam (2020) argues that 'the R_t for the United Kingdom is kept artificially high by the very large numbers of infections and deaths in care homes for older people, and does not reliably represent the risk to the general population'.

Yet another problem with the reproduction rate is that it does not account for superspreaders, those few who pass on the disease many more times than average, perhaps because they mingle with susceptible people in crowded indoor events and venues, and this is why the best way to catch the coronavirus is to be in a crowded bar late at night. A superspreader is an individual who infects a disproportionate number of others. Johnson and Lyons (2020) describe superspreaders in a simple language as follows:

> While it's easy to imagine people infected with COVID-19 have equal chance of transmitting the virus to others, it turns out that's not what happens most of the time. In fact, the pandemic sweeping the globe seems to follow a pattern seen in many other infectious diseases, where it's been observed that only a small proportion of those infected control the bulk of transmission events. This has sometimes been dubbed the 80/20 rule because around 20 per cent of people control around 80 per cent of the infection spread.

The 80–20 rule is also stressed by Adam (2020) who suggests that 'as few as 10–20% of infected people seem to cause 80% of new COVID-19 cases'. Johnson and Lyons (2020) present examples of a superspreader in Australia, China and the US. The first is a Melbourne man who visited a busy pub in south-west Sydney on 3 July 2020, producing 34 pub-linked infections 12 days later. The second is a woman with no symptoms who returned to China from the US and was self-quarantining at home, but after using the lift in her building, 71 cases were recorded. The third story is that of a choir practice in the US that led to 52 infections and two deaths. Depending on R in situations like this may lead to the wrong decision of blanket restrictions as opposed to bans on certain crowded indoor activities. Correa-Martínez et al. (2020) describe the case of 'superspreading and exportation of COVID-19 cases from a ski area in Austria'. Their study is about the transmission of COVID-19 in Germany, Iceland, Norway and Denmark from Ischgl, a popular ski town in the Austrian Alps. For example, of 90 COVID-19 patients in University Hospital Münster (Germany), 36 had visited Ischgl. They also suggest that an unknown number of infected travellers from Ischgl could have entered the US in the nine days between the epidemiological warning of Ischgl issued by Iceland and the 14 March ban on European travellers to the US. The superspreader worked at the après-ski bar.

Figures 2.2 and 2.3 illustrate the difference superspreaders make for the spread of the virus. In Figure 2.2, it is assumed that a superspreader infects ten people as opposed to two for non-superspreaders. As the percentage of super-spreaders changes from 1% to 5% to 8% and then to 10%, the spread of the virus becomes much more extensive. In Figure 2.3, it is assumed that the percentage of superspreaders is 5% while changing the number of people infected by superspreaders from five to ten to 15 and then to 20. We can see that the spread of the virus becomes more extensive as the power of superspreaders to infect people rises.

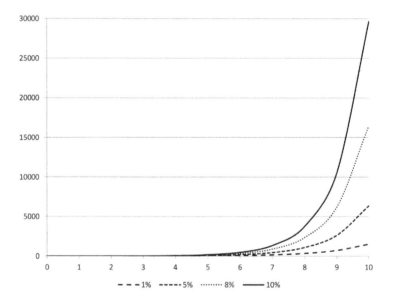

Figure 2.2   The spread of virus at different ratios of superspreaders

Adam (2020) argues that as countries consider when to reopen schools and offices, a key question is not only R_t, but also the actual number of infected people walking around. As an example, he compares between Denmark and the UK when they had similar R_t values, arguing that because the number of infected people walking around Denmark is ten times smaller, it was safer for Denmark than the UK to reopen schools. Adam quotes Sebastian Funk, a disease modeller at the London School of Hygiene and Tropical Medicine (who was advising the British government on the pandemic) as saying that 'when infection numbers are low, maybe you don't care so much about what

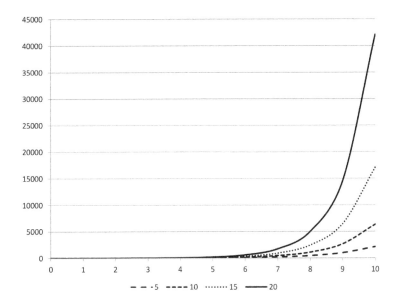

Figure 2.3   The spread of virus and the power of superspreaders

the reproduction number is, or at least don't care if there's some uncertainty in it' and that 'it's far more important to watch for clusters of cases and to set up comprehensive systems to test people, trace their contacts and isolate those infected, than to watch the needle swinging on a colourful dial'.

2.3   INFECTION AND MORTALITY RATES AS MEASURES OF SEVERITY

The Lowy Institute (2021) tracks the performance, in relation to the spread of COVID-19, of 98 countries using six measures that reflect the severity of the pandemic: confirmed cases, confirmed deaths, confirmed cases per million people, confirmed deaths per million people, confirmed cases as a proportion of tests, and tests per thousand people. The period examined spans the 36 weeks that followed every country's hundredth confirmed case of COVID-19, using data available up to 9 January 2021. An equally weighted average of the rankings across those indicators is then calculated for individual countries in each period and normalised to produce a score ranging from 0 (worst perform-ing) to 100 (best performing). On average, countries in the Asia-Pacific region proved the most successful at containing the pandemic. The spread accelerated in much of the Americas (North and South), making it the worst affected region globally. In terms of individual countries, the top five are New Zealand, Vietnam, Taiwan, Thailand and Cyprus, whereas the bottom five are Brazil, Mexico, Colombia, Iran and the US.

The reason why more than one indicator is used is explained by Thompson (2020a) who argues that 'in the fog of pandemic, every statistic tells a story, but no one statistic tells the whole truth'. Here we use 12 different indicators of the severity of COVID-19, calculated according to the following compartmentalisation framework. Every individual in the population, N, is either tested, T^1, or untested, T^0. The tested turn out to be either infected, T^+, or uninfected, T^-. The untested are either uninfected, U^- or infected, U^+. It follows that $T^1=T^++T^-$ and $T^0=U^-+U^+$. The total uninfected are those tested and untested, which gives $U=T^-+U^-$ while the total infected $I=T^++U^+$. The total infected may represent an active case or they could recover or die. Hence, $I=A+D+R$. Any active case can be either critical, CC, or uncritical, UC, which gives $A=CC+UC$. The infection, mortality and testing rates are listed in Table 2.1. By definition, the following identities must hold:

$$N = T^1 + T^0 = I + U \tag{2.6}$$

$$I = A + D + R \tag{2.7}$$

$$\frac{D}{N} + \frac{R}{N} + \frac{A}{N} = \frac{I}{N} \tag{2.8}$$

$$\frac{A}{N} = \frac{CC}{N} + \frac{UC}{N} \tag{2.9}$$

$$\frac{D}{I} + \frac{R}{I} + \frac{A}{I} = 1 \tag{2.10}$$

$$\frac{D}{(I-A)} + \frac{R}{(I-A)} = 1 \tag{2.11}$$

In Figure 2.4 we can see some infection and mortality rates, calculated from raw data obtained from the Worldometers data base for selected countries, covering the period until the end of February 2021. The US has recorded the highest population infection rate, followed by Spain and the UK. In terms of the population mortality rate, the UK is the worst performer, followed by Italy and the US. The US is also the worst performer in terms of active population

Table 2.1   *Infection, mortality and testing rates*

Measure	Meaning	Calculation
Total Infection Rate	Total cases per million of population	I/N
Population Mortality Rate	Deaths per million of population	D/N
Active Population Infection Rate	Active cases per million of population	A/N
Population Recovery Rate	Recoveries per million of population	R/N
Case Mortality Rate	Deaths per case (%)	D/I
Case Recovery Rate	Recoveries per case (%)	R/I
Active Case Infection Rate	Ratio of active to total cases (%)	A/I
Critical Case Rate	Ratio of critical to active cases (%)	CC/A
Realised Case Mortality Rate	Ratio of deaths to net of active cases (%)	$D/(I-A)$
Realised Case Recovery Rate	Ratio of recoveries to net of active cases (%)	$R/(I-A)$
Infection Testing Rate	Total cases per test	I/T
Population Testing Rate	Tests per capita	T/N

infection rate and the second worst performer in terms of active case infection rate (the UK is the worst performer). However, it is interesting to note that the US and UK have done more testing per capita than other countries and that testing per capita is positively correlated with the total infection rate, population mortality rate, active population infection rate and active case infection rate. China is the worst performer in terms of case mortality rate whereas India is the worst performer in terms of critical case rate. At that point in time (end of February 2021) the global number of infections was 113,040,671 divided into the following categories: dead (2.2%), recovered (78.4%) and active cases (19.4%).

These indicators can be calculated over time to observe the progress or otherwise in controlling the virus. Figures 2.5–2.7 display respectively the population infection rate (per million), the population mortality rate (per million) and the case mortality rate (%) over days extending between the first case and the end of February 2021 (the numbers on the horizontal axis represent days since the first reported case). The figures are plotted on a daily basis for six countries (good performers and bad performers) using data provided by Our World in Data (https://ourworldindata.org/). In Figure 2.5 we observe the stabilisation of the population infection rate in Australia, New Zealand and China, but not in the US, UK and Brazil (it looks particularly alarming in the case of Brazil). Almost the same pattern can be observed in Figure 2.6, which displays the population mortality rate (per million). The case mortality rate is shown in Figure 2.7 where we observe a big drop in the UK and Brazil but only because the rate came down from a very high level in both countries.

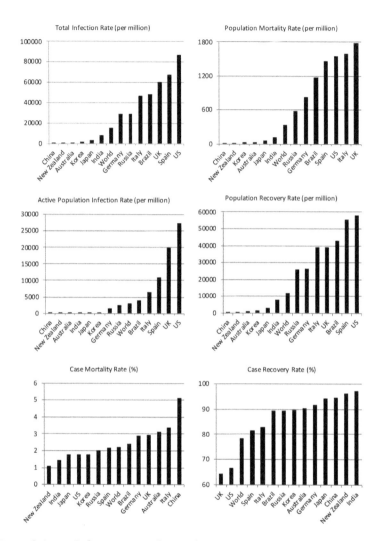

Figure 2.4   Infection, mortality and testing rates

2.4   A STATISTICAL MEASURE OF SEVERITY

The problem with the epidemiological measure of severity is that the condition $R_t < 1$ does not represent containment if the number of cases is still high. As we can see from Figure 2.8, the reproduction rate tells us that the UK and US are in a better shape than Australia and New Zealand, which could not be further

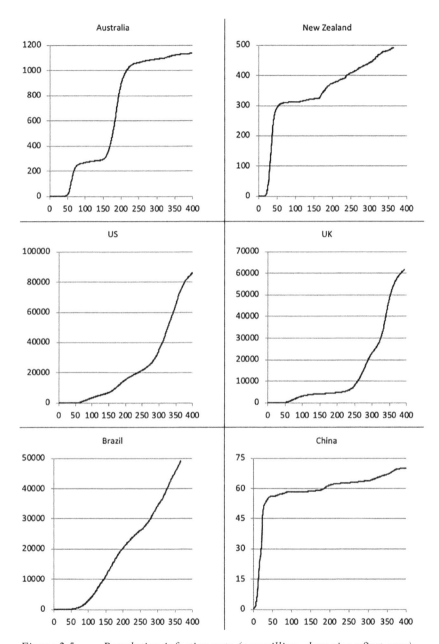

Figure 2.5   *Population infection rate (per million, days since first case)*

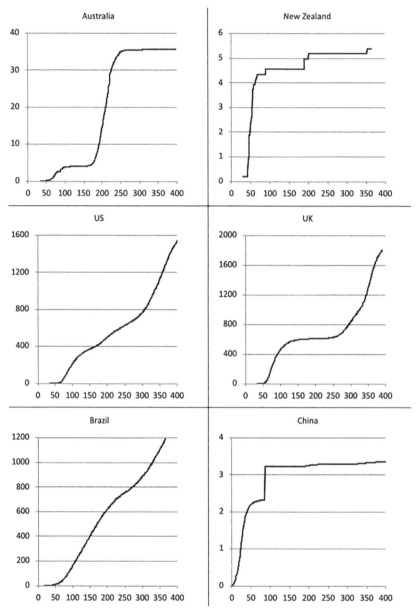

Figure 2.6   *Population mortality rate (per million, days since first case)*

away from the truth. Furthermore, while it is important whether the rates are

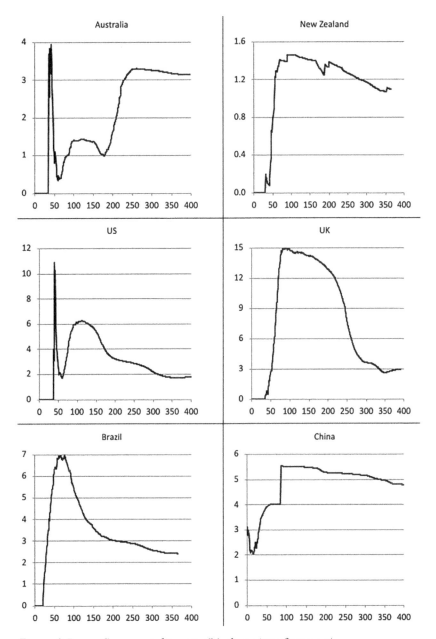

Figure 2.7   Case mortality rate (%, days since first case)

high or low, perhaps it is more important whether the rates are going up or down. The statistical measure suggested here depends on the level and direction of change of new cases, which can also be applied to new deaths.

The statistical measure, which has been proposed by Moosa (2020b), is based on a structural time series model estimated in a time-varying parametric framework. Containment is defined by an insignificant (in a statistical sense) time-varying trend in the number of new cases. The time path of COVID-19 cases (infections) can be represented by a simple version of the structural time series model of Harvey (1989). In its simplest form, the model is written as

$$I_t = \mu_t + \varepsilon_t \tag{2.12}$$

where I is the number of new infection cases, μ_t and ε_t are the unobserved time series components, respectively the trend and the random component. The trend, which represents the long-term movement of I, is specified as

$$\mu_t = \mu_{t-1} + \beta_{t-1} + \eta_t \tag{2.13}$$

$$\beta_t = \beta_{t-1} + \zeta_t \tag{2.14}$$

where $\eta_t \sim NID(0, \sigma_\eta^2)$ and $\zeta_t \sim NID(0, \sigma_\zeta^2)$. μ_t is a random walk with a drift factor, β_t, which follows a first order autoregressive process as represented by equation (2.14). This process collapses to a simple random walk with drift if $\sigma_\zeta^2 = 0$, and to a deterministic linear trend if $\sigma_\eta^2 = 0$ as well. If, on the other hand, $\sigma_\eta^2 = 0$ while $\sigma_\zeta^2 \neq 0$, the process will have a trend that changes relatively smoothly. Harvey (1989) lists all of the possibilities whereas Koopman et al. (2006) identify several models, including a constant term model, local level model, random walk with and without drift, local level with fixed slope, a smooth trend model, etc.

The model is estimated in a time-varying parametric framework using maximum likelihood and the Kalman filter to update the state vector. Estimates are obtained for the level and slope of the series, which are respectively equivalent to the intercept term and the coefficient on a deterministic time trend in a conventional regression equation. For the purpose of this analysis, the virus is considered to be under control if both of these components are statistically insignificant and kept so for some time.

The condition that R is less than one does not imply containment if the number of new cases is high (statistically significant). This is why this statistical measure is more representative of containment. In Table 2.2 we can see seven possible outcomes for the degree of severity as determined by the

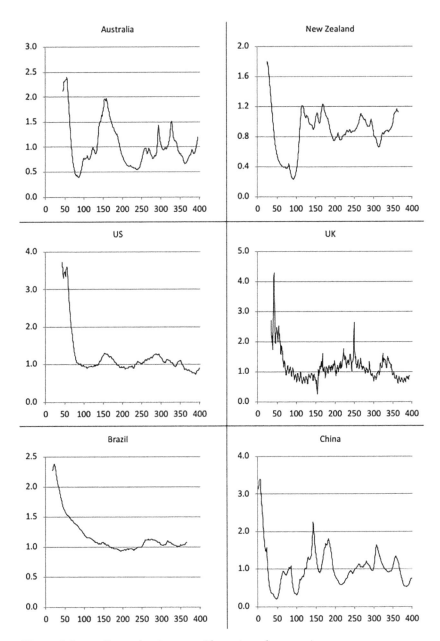

Figure 2.8　　*Reproduction rate (days since first case)*

Table 2.2   Possible outcomes for the degree of severity

β	μ	
	Significant	Insignificant
Significant and Positive	Outbreak is beyond control (6)	Low level of infection – rising rapidly (2)
Insignificant and Positive	High level of infection – stabilising slowly (5)	Under control – slow progress towards zero infections (1)
Insignificant and Negative	High level of infection – on the way to stabilising quickly (4)	Under control – rapid progress towards zero infections (0)
Significant and Negative	High level of infection – stabilising quickly (3)	–

significance of μ and β. The degree of severity takes numerical values ranging between 0 (rapid progress towards zero infections) and 6 (beyond control).

This methodology is applied to data on the six countries depicted in Figures 2.5–2.8. In Figure 2.9 we can see the number of new cases in the six countries, which gives an idea about the number of waves a country has been through. Roughly, Australia has been through two waves, the US and the UK through three waves while New Zealand, China and Brazil have been through one wave, except that the one in Brazil never came to an end. Figure 2.10 displays the trends in the numbers of new cases, which confirm the number of waves and shows that the trend in Brazil is deterministic with no change in the situation for the better.

Table 2.3 reports the estimation results of the model at various points in time to demonstrate changes in the situation, as well as the statistical measure of severity, which assumes values ranging between 0 and 6 (with corresponding shading such that the light shading represents low severity, and vice versa). We can see, for example, that Australia got the virus under control in April 2020, but by August 2020 the virus was beyond control again. New Zealand had a high level of infection that was stabilising slowly in April 2020, but by mid-May, the virus was under control. At the end of February 2021, New Zealand recorded a severity of zero. The UK did very well in containing the first wave in April 2020, but by July 2020 the virus was beyond control. Brazil is a different story altogether, as the virus has been beyond control since March 2020. It is noteworthy that a wave comes to an end by moving from 6 or 5 to 1 or 0, and a new wave emerges by moving to 5 or 6 again.

2.5   DETERMINANTS OF SEVERITY

It has become clear that the severity of COVID-19 varies drastically from one country to another, but it is not clear what explains cross-country differences.

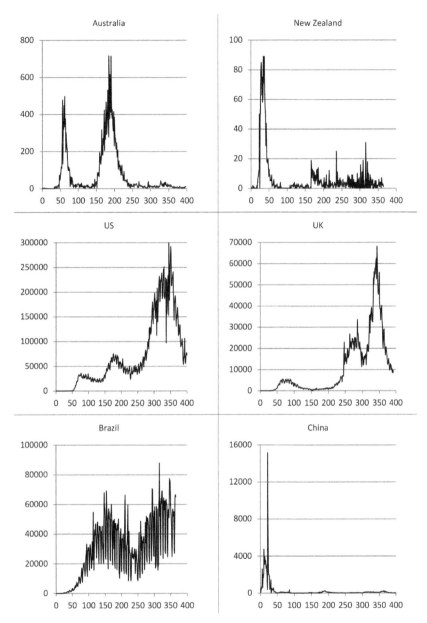

Figure 2.9   New cases (days since first case)

One can only wonder why China and Iran have fewer cases per million (pop-

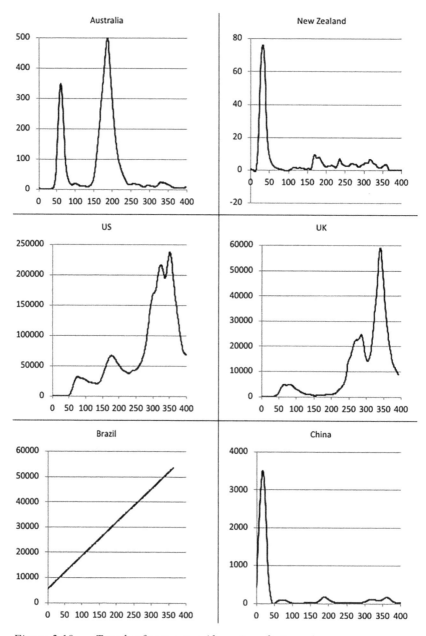

Figure 2.10   Trends of new cases (days since first case)

Table 2.3   *A statistical measure of severity*

Country	Days since First Case	Date	μ	β	Severity
Australia	62	28/03/2020	17.76	4.14	6
	86	21/04/2020	0.81	−0.27	0
	191	04/08/2020	18.81	1.65	5
	264	16/10/2020	0.57	−0.12	0
	397	26/02/2021	0.34	0.08	1
New Zealand	34	02/04/2020	10.23	0.44	5
	81	19/05/2020	0.35	0.17	1
	364	26/02/2021	0.70	−0.24	0
US	69	01/04/2020	54.89	8.22	6
	138	09/06/2020	14.37	−0.97	4
	175	16/07/2020	43.88	3.51	6
	228	07/09/2020	15.98	−1.82	3
	345	02/02/2021	33.15	1.74	5
	400	26/02/2021	8.97	−0.02	4
UK	76	16/04/2020	33.42	1.41	5
	155	04/07/2020	1.38	−0.32	0
	286	12/11/2020	39.33	2.26	6
	298	24/11/2020	19.84	−5.17	3
	343	08/01/2021	60.99	5.67	6
	392	26/02/2021	6.76	−0.52	4
Brazil	114	19/06/2020	21.27	3.57	6
	154	29/07/2020	32.42	22.94	6
	194	07/09/2020	11.32	−1.65	4
	211	24/09/2020	30.21	18.80	6
	229	12/10/2020	26.64	15.56	6
	294	16/12/2020	25.97	13.08	6
	316	07/01/2021	27.16	13.65	6
	366	26/02/2021	34.27	17.93	6
China	11	02/02/2020	6.16	1.94	5
	41	03/03/2020	0.21	−0.51	0
	401	26/02/2021	0.06	0.01	1

ulation infection rate) than the US and UK, given that the latter experienced the first cases at a later stage, and even though they rank one and two in terms of the global health security index, which measures preparedness for and the ability to deal with public health crises. One may also wonder why densely populated Asian countries (such as South Korea, Japan, Taiwan and Singapore) have successfully controlled the virus while it is still rampant in low-density countries such as the US and Brazil. Numerous factors affect the spread of the virus and the ability of countries to contain it, to the extent that it is rather difficult to come up with an exhaustive list of these factors. It has also become apparent that a high infection rate does not necessarily go with a high mortality rate and that they are not necessarily determined equally by the same factors. For example, it is plausible to suggest that the mortality rate is more dependent on the age structure and the quality of the healthcare system than the infection rate. Moosa and Khatatbeh (2021a) show that the infection and mortality rates depend on different factors, except for the number of tests, which is a robust determinant of both.

2.5.1   Population Density

Starting with population density, one would imagine that densely populated countries find it more difficult to contain the virus than otherwise. On 23 March 2020, the journalist Matt Yglesias, known to be sardonic and facetious, tweeted the following: 'The moral of corona virus is that we should adopt the kind of low-density living patterns associated with Asian countries like South Korea, Japan, Taiwan, and Singapore that have successfully controlled its spread' (Barr and Tassier, 2020a). This tweet was meant to be sarcastic, perhaps directed at those blaming population density for making New York City the epicentre of the pandemic in the US. Barr and Tassier argue that even though Asian cities are known for their 'hyper-density', they have figured out ways to slow its spread without destroying the very essence of what makes cities so successful.

Barr and Tassier (2020a) come up with the concept of the 'density paradox', as they wonder about the role of population density in spreading the virus and whether big cities are more vulnerable than smaller ones. Based on a formula that defines the reproduction rate and the assumption that no preventive measures (such as social distancing and self-isolation) are taken, they specify a regression equation whereby the number of cases is determined by several explanatory variables, including population density. By using county-level US data, they obtain results showing that 'population density does matter but is not as large as the popular media would have you believe'. More specifically, they find that (on average) an increase in a county's population density by 20% leads to a rise in the number of cases by about 11–12%. They reach the conclusion that 'more populous counties are likely to have fewer cases on a per capita basis than their sparser counterparts', and go on to argue that epicentres around the world are not located in the largest cities.

The effect of population density works via the contact rate, which is a determinant of the reproduction rate (for example, Hu et al., 2013). Tarwater and Martin (2001) examine the effect of population density on the epidemic outbreak of measles or measles-like infectious diseases and find that a decline in a susceptible contact rate, from four to three, results in a 'dramatic effect on the distribution of contacts over time, the magnitude of the outbreak, and, ultimately, the spread of disease'. A mathematical model is used by Sumdani et al. (2014) to study MERS-CoV (Middle East Respiratory Syndrome-Coronavirus) and identify possible patterns of the spread. They split the population into two groups, with contact rates that are independent of and dependent on population density. By analysing the conditions under which the disease spreads, they observe how population density affects the transmission characteristics predicted by the model. Barr and Tassier (2020b) model the effect of population density by starting with the determinants of the reproduction rate, which include the contact rate. They suggest that density affects the contact rate, which boosts the reproduction rate, leading to more infections in dense areas.

Likewise, Tarwater (1999) examines the relationship between population density and the initial stages of the spread of disease, producing results that support the proposition that the number of new infections is strongly related to the distribution of susceptible contacts. Li et al. (2018) examine possible links between population density and the propagation and magnitude of epidemics, arguing that it is inconclusive for three reasons: (i) a lack of focus on appropriate density intervals; (ii) for density to be a meaningful variable, the population must be distributed as uniformly as possible; and (iii) in propagation of an epidemic the initial proportion of susceptibles is an essential, yet usually unknown factor.

2.5.2 Population Structure

Population structure can be represented by the age structure (for example, population over 65) and urban population (both measured in percentage terms). The age structure is more relevant to the mortality rate than the infection rate. Dowda et al. (2020) highlight the important role of demography and demonstrate how the age structure of a population may help explain differences in mortality rates across countries and how transmission unfolds. They examine the role of age structure in deaths in Italy and South Korea and illustrate how the pandemic could unfold in populations with similar sizes but different age structures, showing a dramatically higher burden of mortality in countries with older populations.

The other population-related factor, urban population, pertains to population density, the concentration of population in crowded cities and urban centres. It is taken to be a separate variable that is distinct from population density because while the population density of a particular country is low, concentration in urban centres leads to a higher contact rate and hence infection rate. Florida (2020) refers to 'the very same clustering of people that makes our great cities more innovative and productive also makes them, and us, vulnerable to infectious disease'. However, some observers disagree, arguing that while New York has done badly, other crowded cities like Singapore, Seoul and Shanghai have done rather well. Fang and Wahba (2020) even argue that, in some cases, urban population density can be a blessing because economies of scale make it necessary for cities to meet a certain threshold of population density to offer higher-grade facilities and services to their residents. Furthermore, it is easier for the residents of dense urban areas (where the coverage of high-speed internet and door-to-door delivery services are conveniently available at competitive prices) to stay at home and avoid unnecessary contact with others.

Conversely, Desai (2020) emphasises the role of urban density, arguing that while high-density urban agglomerations may be sustainable in terms of the economies of scale provided by their populations, these same urban spaces are nearly defenceless in times of unprecedented disease outbreaks. A pandemic poses many risks to the millions who live in dense megacities, both in developed and developing countries. The sheer density of the populations of these cities provides an ideal environment for infections to erupt. He examines the cases of New York and London, both megacities, and how COVID-19 has virtually crippled their public healthcare systems. Acuto (2020) highlights the importance of urban density by arguing that the COVID-19 crisis has 'changed the face of many of our cities and questioned how we should manage urban life in the wake of a pandemic'. Moosa and Khatatbeh (2021a) show that the infection rate depends on urban population rather than the overall population density. Another interesting result is that the mortality rate depends on the age structure of the population and population density but not on the percentage of urban population. Moosa and Khatatbeh (2021b) present empirical evidence on the role played by population density in spreading the coronavirus, based on cross-sectional data covering 172 countries. The results show that population density has a significantly positive effect on the number of cases but not the number of deaths, as the latter is better explained by measures of preparedness. They conclude that the 'density paradox' is not really a paradox. Moosa and Khatatbeh (2021c) find that while different factors determine the infection and mortality rates in developed and developing countries, common factors include population over 65.

2.5.3   Preparedness and Related Factors

An important set of determinants of severity and performance are measures of preparedness and related factors, such as the quality of the healthcare system. These factors include prevention, detection and reporting, speed of response, quality of the healthcare system, compliance with international norms and the risk environment. They are the constituent components of the global health security (GHS) index, which is prepared jointly by the Nuclear Threat Initiative (NTI) and the Johns Hopkins Center for Health Security (in co-operation with the Economist Intelligence Unit, EIU). These factors are measured as indices ranging between zero (the worst) and 100 (the best).

Prevention pertains to the emergence or release of pathogens (including those constituting an extraordinary public health risk) in keeping with the internationally recognised definition of a public health emergency of international concern (which is the expression used by the WHO to describe COVID-19 in a statement released on 31 January 2020). The index representing prevention is constructed from indicators that are used to measure antimicrobial resistance, zoonotic disease, biosecurity, biosafety, dual-use research and culture of responsible science, and immunisation. Detection and reporting pertain to epidemics of potential international concern – those that can spread beyond national or regional borders. The index is constructed from indicators of laboratory systems, real-time surveillance and reporting, epidemiology workforce, and data integration between the human, animal, and environmental health sectors.

The concept of 'rapid response' pertains to the mitigation of the spread of an epidemic. The index used to measure the speed of response is constructed from indicators of emergency preparedness and response planning, exercising response plans, emergency response operation, linking public health and security authorities, risk communication, access to communication infrastructure, and trade and travel restrictions. The quality of the healthcare system is measured by the adequacy and robustness of the system to treat the sick and protect health workers. The index is calculated from indicators of health capacity in clinics, hospitals and community care centres; medical counter-measures and personnel deployment; access to healthcare; communications with healthcare workers during a public health emergency; infection control practices and availability of equipment; and capacity to test and approve new counter-measures.

Compliance with international norms implies commitment to improving national capacity, financing plans to address gaps, and adhering to global norms. The index is constructed from indicators of reporting compliance and disaster risk reduction, cross-border agreements on public health emergency response, international commitments, completion and publication of pathway assessments, financing, and commitment to the sharing of genetic and biological data and specimens. The risk environment pertains to a country's vulnerability to biological threats. The index is constructed from indicators of political and security risk, socio-economic resilience, infrastructure adequacy, environmental risk, and public health vulnerabilities that may affect the ability of a country to prevent, detect, or respond to epidemics and pandemics.

Some observers are sceptical about the accuracy and soundness of these indices – for example, the US comes in top position in terms of the overall index, yet it has the highest COVID-19 infection and mortality rates. Bell (2020) tries to dispel misconceptions regarding the overall score of 83.5 (out of a possible 100) received by the US. She argues that the score and rank assigned to the US do not indicate that the country is adequately prepared to respond to potentially catastrophic outbreaks of infectious disease. She also argues that significant preparedness gaps remain in the US and that some of those gaps are playing out in the current crisis. The response of the US to the COVID-19 outbreak to date shows that capacity alone is insufficient if that capacity is not fully leveraged. The problem in the US, however, is lack of access to healthcare, on which it is ranked as 175 out of 195 countries. A lack of guaranteed access to healthcare for all citizens leaves them vulnerable in times of emergency, including health workers, as there is no federal commitment to prioritising healthcare services for workers who become sick.

These factors have been used rarely in the empirical studies of the determinants of the severity of COVID-19. For example, Moosa and Khatatbeh (2021c) find that the risk environment is a robust determinant of the severity of COVID-19 in both developed and developing countries. Chaudhry et al. (2020) reveal the role played by full lockdowns and reduced country vulnerability to biological threats. Moosa and Khatatbeh (2020) find that the risk environment is a robust determinant of the population mortality rate and that prevention is a robust determinant of the case mortality rate.

2.5.4   The Role of Time

Time has three dimensions: time since first case, time since lockdown, and the number of cases at the start of lockdown. Time since first case is used as a determinant by Barr and Tassier (2020b) and by Moosa and Khatatbeh (2020). Time since the start of lockdown is also used by Moosa and Khatatbeh (2020) on the grounds that infections and deaths can be reduced by taking action sooner rather than later. The number of cases at the start of lockdown is important because the timing of lockdown matters more in relation to the infection rate. If lockdown is imposed when the infection rate is low, it is easier to contain the virus than when the infection rate is already high.

Chaudhry et al. (2020) find that increasing COVID-19 cases are associated with longer time to border closures from the first reported case. Barr and

Tassier (2020b) illustrate the importance of time since first case on the basis that $I_t = a_0 R_t$, where I is the number of cases, R is the reproduction rate and a_0 is the initial number of cases. It is intuitive to suggest that, *ceteris paribus*, the longer the time it has been since the discovery of the first case, the larger will be the number of cases.

2.5.5   The Role of Testing

The role of testing is ambiguous. Massive testing, followed by the isolation of infected people, should reduce the infection and consequently the mortality rate. On the other hand, more testing reveals more (hidden) cases. By using panel data, Razzak (2020) finds 'reasonable evidence' indicating that testing reduces death. Moosa and Khatatbeh (2020) find the number of tests per million to be a robust determinant of the case mortality rate. Based on data on the 13 countries (and the world) appearing in Figure 2.4, Figure 2.11 shows positive correlation between testing per capita and the infection and mortality rates. Moosa and Khatatbeh (2020) find that testing per million of the population is a robust determinant of the case mortality rate.

2.5.6   International Tourist Arrivals

A major determinant of the severity of COVID-19 is international tourist arrivals, which is why countries tend to close borders during a pandemic. In response to the announcement by the WHO on 30 January 2020 that the Coronavirus was a 'public health emergency of international concern', more than 70 countries imposed travel restrictions against China. Following the 11 March announcement that COVID-19 was a pandemic, almost every country in the world shut down its borders and closed international airports, except for certain classes of passengers, such as returning citizens. This action, which received public support at least initially, was motivated by a combination of common sense and fear. After all, the virus travels in people, which means (at least in theory) that reducing the movement of people should slow down the spread of the virus. More specifically, the imposition of international travel restrictions stems from belief in the transmission of the virus by arriving visitors and returning citizens from infected locations.

The imposition of travel restrictions to prevent the spread of a virus is not a new phenomenon that is specific to COVID-19 because travel restrictions have been used repeatedly to combat pandemics. In the 14th century, European kingdoms quarantined ships to prevent the spread of the Bubonic Plague. The word 'quarantine' comes from 'quarantena', meaning 'forty days', used in 14th–15th-century Venetian and designating the period that all ships were required to be isolated before passengers and crew could go ashore during

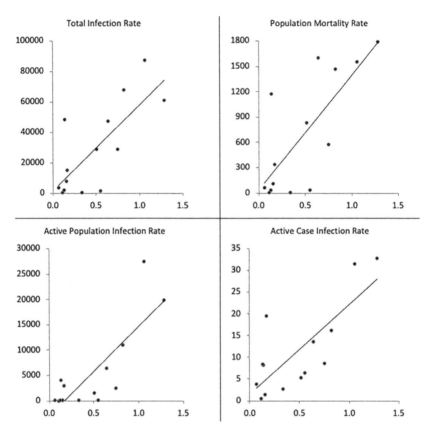

Figure 2.11   Infection and mortality rates as functions of testing per capita

the Black Death pandemic (see, for example, Mayer, 2018). In the 1800s, standardised rules around travel and disease were developed, and international health co-operation began with the first International Sanitary Conference in Paris, which opened on 23 July 1851. In the 1900s international sanitary conventions were established, leading to the emergence of international health regulations.

It has been observed that the worst-hit countries (such as the US and UK) are homes to some of the world's busiest international airports, handling hundreds of millions of passengers every year. Barr and Tassier (2020b) use the proximity of a major airport as one of the explanatory variables on the grounds that passenger arrivals represent one of the determinants of the contact rate, which consequently determines the infection and mortality rates.

If international arrivals are a determinant of the severity of COVID-19, then quarantine and border closure are justifiable. A widely held view on international travel restrictions is that they may be unnecessary, unjustifiable and motivated by non-scientific considerations. Chinazzi et al. (2020) argue that the travel restrictions imposed to combat COVID-19 have only modestly delayed the spread of the virus outside of Wuhan and that reduction of the cases imported from China only lasted about two to three weeks, after which the number of international cases ticked upwards. Yu and Keralis (2020) suggest that travel restrictions are ineffective as an infection control measure and that they may do more harm than good. Wells et al. (2020) produce results showing that travel restrictions are insufficient to contain the global spread of COVID-19. Brumfiel and Wilburn (2020) argue that border closures have done little to stop COVID-19 and that, going forward, travel restrictions will play only a small role in containing the virus. The WHO has repeatedly declared that bans on international travel cannot stay in place indefinitely and that countries should do more to reduce the spread of the novel Coronavirus within their borders (Aljazeera, 2020). Pillinger (2020) argues that travel restrictions represent a 'bad policy' and 'irresponsible violations of international law', suggesting that travel restrictions may be ineffective because they are imposed too late or because travellers circumvent them.

On the other hand, some observers think that international travel bans are effective. For example, Jerving (2020) refers to 'many in the international community' who credit travel restrictions, quarantines and border closures with limiting the cases in countries outside of China. Stanhope and Weinstein (2020) refer to the 'apparent efficacy' of 'this proactive approach' and wonder why travel restrictions have been criticised as unscientific and in breach of international health regulations. Instead, they suggest that travel restrictions may be used to delay and attenuate the peak in case numbers to reduce the burden on the healthcare system, allowing for preparations to be made to manage the outbreak more effectively. They conclude that Australia's rapid introduction of travel restrictions is consistent with an evidence-based approach that prioritises the precautionary principle and saving lives.

Moosa and Khatatbeh (2020), who describe the imposition of international travel restrictions to prevent the spread of the Coronavirus as a 'controversial issue', examine the effect of international tourist arrivals on the population and case mortality rates, using a cross-sectional sample covering 146 countries. In addition to international tourist arrivals, 12 other explanatory variables are examined. The results of the empirical analysis show that international tourist arrivals have a greater effect on the severity of COVID-19 than any of the other 12 factors, including the components of the global health security index, demographic factors, two time variables (time since first reported case and time since the start of lockdown), and the number of tests. This means that the imposition of international travel bans is justifiable by the objective of containing the virus.

2.5.7   Other Determinants of Severity

Other determinants of the severity of COVID-19 include, but are not limited to, the political system, population, economic development, obesity, income inequality and climate. The Lowy Institute (2021) suggests that the political system is relevant because it reflects how governments convince or compel their citizens to adhere to preventive measures such as stay-at-home orders, lockdowns, and border closures. The results show that, on average, countries with authoritarian governments had no prolonged advantage in suppressing the virus. The Institute also shows that smaller countries with populations of fewer than 10 million people consistently outperform their larger counterparts.

Economic development (or whether the underlying country is rich or poor) is yet another factor, in the sense that countries with higher per capita incomes have more resources available to fight the COVID-19 pandemic. The results of the Lowy Institute show that developed countries have performed better on average than developing countries for most of the crisis to date. Moosa and Khatatbeh (2021c) show that the determinants of severity differ for developing and developed countries.

Chaudhry et al. (2020) find that increasing COVID-19 cases are associated with higher levels of obesity. They also find that the mortality rate is significantly associated with higher obesity prevalence and per capita GDP. The evidence on climate (temperature and humidity) seems to be inconclusive. O'Reilly et al. (2020) argue that the finding that high temperature and humidity hinder the transmission of the virus (for example, Araujo and Naimi, 2020; Sajadi et al., 2020; Wang et al., 2020) are prone to confounding, including the delay in spread to warmer regions of the world due to travel patterns. Thus, they note, it is essential to contextualise these findings, considering the current global spread of COVID-19.

2.6   CONCLUSION

This chapter is about the measures and determinants of the severity of COVID-19. The word 'severity' is not used to categorise patients as having moderate, severe and very severe cases of the disease, which is important for the allocation of hospital beds as the healthcare system is overwhelmed by the arrival of new cases. Rather, the word is used to indicate the overall situation in a country and whether or not the virus is under control. In other words, severity is an indication of the extent of the containment of the virus, in which case high severity implies failure to contain the virus (and therefore poor performance in this sense).

Cross-country differences in the severity of COVID-19 can be attributed to differences in the timeliness and adequacy of the response to the pandemic and to some uncontrollable factors such as population density and age structure. In this chapter, three different measures of severity are considered: the epidemiological measure, represented by the reproduction rate; infection and mortality rates; and a statistical measure based on structural time series modelling. It is suggested that the statistical measure, which is calculated from an analysis of the trend of new cases, is more accurate because what matters is not only how high or low the cases (or deaths) are but also where they are heading. Thus the situation may be as bad as 'outbreak is beyond control' or as good as 'under control with rapid progress towards zero infections'.

Assessing the severity of COVID-19 is crucial for determining the appropriateness of mitigation strategies and to enable planning for healthcare needs as the pandemic unfolds. However, crude case mortality rates obtained by dividing the number of deaths by the number of cases can be misleading. This is because there can be a period of 2–3 weeks between a person developing symptoms, the case subsequently being detected and reported, and observation of the final clinical outcome. During a growing epidemic, the final clinical outcome of most of the reported cases is typically unknown. Simply dividing the cumulative reported number of deaths by the cumulative number of reported cases will therefore underestimate the true case mortality rate early in a pandemic or an epidemic. Furthermore, during the exponential growth phase of the pandemic, the observed time lags between the onset of symptoms and the materialisation of outcome (recovery or death) are censored, and naive estimates of the observed times from symptom onset to outcome provide biased estimates of the actual distributions. Ignoring this effect leads to downward bias in the estimated case mortality rate during the early growth phase of the pandemic. The reproduction rate is a lagging indicator, which can be rather misleading. This is why a statistical measure of severity is described and applied to data on six countries with various degrees of success or failure to control the virus.

3. The effects and consequences of COVID-19

3.1 INTRODUCTION

The COVID-19 pandemic has impacted the world in ways that have not been experienced in generations. It is unquestionably one of the most significant global events in recent history, affecting every aspect of daily life. On 19 May 2020, Federal Reserve Chairman, Jerome Powell, said the following (Powell, 2020):

> Since the pandemic arrived in force just two months ago, more than 20 million people have lost their jobs, reversing nearly 10 years of job gains. This precipitous drop in economic activity has caused a level of pain that is hard to capture in words, as lives are upended amid great uncertainty about the future.

In October 2020, a joint statement by four international organisations (ILO, FAO, IFAD and WHO) described the situation as follows (World Health Organization, 2020c):

> The COVID-19 pandemic has led to a dramatic loss of human life worldwide and presents an unprecedented challenge to public health, food systems and the world of work. The economic and social disruption caused by the pandemic is devastating: tens of millions of people are at risk of falling into extreme poverty, while the number of undernourished people, currently estimated at nearly 690 million, could increase by up to 132 million by the end of the year.

The pandemic is a rare type of shock (a 'black swan') to the world economy. Its sudden and massive impact on economic activity came at a time when the legacy of the global financial crisis, and the subsequent great recession, were still weighing on the balance sheets of the public and private sectors and when people were still suffering the consequences of the austerity measures adopted by most countries. COVID-19 is not only a public health crisis; it has also severely affected the global economy and financial markets. Among the consequences of the disease mitigation measures that have been implemented in many countries are significant reductions in income, higher unemployment rates, and disruptions in the transportation, service and manufacturing industries.

This chapter is devoted to an examination of the economic and social effects of COVID-19. We start with the macroeconomic effects, which are explained with the help of theoretical models. The financial effects examined in this chapter include the effects on corporate debt, stock markets, oil prices, banks and financial institutions, and foreign exchange markets. The sectoral effects cover GDP by sector, arts and cultural heritage, aviation, sporting events, international tourism and higher education. The socio-economic effects include the effects on crime, domestic violence and poverty. A comparison between the COVID-19 crisis and the global financial crisis is presented in the concluding section.

3.2   MACROECONOMIC EFFECTS

A new term has been added to the list of household macroeconomic terms, which already contains 'great recession' and 'great depression'. The new term is 'coronavirus recession' or 'COVID-19 recession'. By any measure, the COVID-19 recession is at least greater than the great recession and comparable to the Great Depression. According to Wolf (2020) 'it is much the biggest crisis the world has confronted since World War II and the biggest economic disaster since the Depression of the 1930s'.

While some observers believe that the COVID-19 recession is less destructive than the great recession induced by the global financial crisis, the numbers show otherwise. One of those observers who think that the COVID-19 recession is not as alarming as it is portrayed to be is Sheiner (2020), who calls it a 'slowdown' and 'possible recession', arguing that 'it is possible that this downturn will be a lot shorter and shallower than the Great Recession'. The difference between the two recessions, according to her, lie in the 'the fundamental imbalances that had to be worked off following the great recession'. On the other hand, Hansen (2020) compares between the two recessions on the basis of numbers. During the height of the great recession (in March 2009) 800,000 jobs were eliminated and about 8.6 million jobs were lost in total during the entire recession. On this occasion, more than 20 million jobs were eliminated in April 2020 alone, and more than 33 million jobs have been lost since the advent of the pandemic. If the fiscal response is proportional to the severity of the recession, then the great recession pales into insignificance compared to the COVID-19 recession. In 2008 and 2009, US lawmakers passed two stimulus packages worth $700 billion and nearly $800 billion (under Presidents Bush and Obama, respectively), which paved the way for controversial bank bailouts. In two months alone in 2020, the US Congress authorised some $3 trillion in rescue spending to cushion the blow of the virus.

Kiersz and Reinicke (2020) present five charts showing how the coronavirus crisis has dwarfed the great recession in just two months. These charts cover initial unemployment claims, cumulative initial unemployment claims, unemployment rate, retail and food services sales and GDP.

In order to assess the possible impact of COVID-19 on the economy, it is important to focus not only on the epidemiological profile of the virus but also on the ways in which consumers, businesses and governments responded to it. The pandemic shapes economic losses through supply chains, demand and financial markets, affecting business investment, household consumption and international trade. The process works both in the traditional supply–demand framework and through the introduction of potentially large levels of uncertainty. This uncertainty in turn undermines the monetary stimulus, as central banks cut interest rates to zero, hoping that people and companies will borrow to consume and invest. However, uncertainty discourages borrowing and spending even at zero interest rate. Those who have savings spend less because of uncertainty with respect to future income and employment. This is why interest rate cuts to the bone represent an impotent policy.

A classic recession involves a shortfall of demand relative to supply. This is an ordinary situation where policy-makers know how to fill the gap in the supply–demand balance, typically via fiscal expansion. The COVID recession, however, is more complicated because it involves both supply and demand shocks. Hence, the macroeconomic effects of COVID-19 can be examined by distinguishing between the supply-side and demand-side effects of the pandemic. A supply shock is anything that reduces the economy's capacity to produce goods and services at given prices. Lockdown measures preventing workers from going to work represent a supply shock, and so does absenteeism and interruption to international trade. A demand shock, on the other hand, reduces the ability or willingness of consumers to purchase goods and services at given prices. For example, a demand shock (to the hospitality sector) occurs when people avoid restaurants for fear of contagion.

A question remains as to whether the macroeconomic effect of the pandemic has been caused predominantly by a supply or demand shock. Brinca et al. (2020) use data on US hours worked and real wages to estimate labour demand and supply shocks for the aggregate economy and for different sectors. They assume that if hours and wages (prices and quantities) move in the same direction, they assign a higher probability to those movements being caused by a demand shock. On the other hand, if hours and wages move in opposite directions, they assign a higher probability to a supply shock. Their results suggest that labour supply shocks accounted for most of the fall in hours in March and April 2020, but demand shocks were also important. In terms of total private employment (hours worked), their calculations indicate that the demand shock was about 36% of the total shock in March and 29% in April 2020.

The supply-side effect is represented by shrinking output when the supply shock is produced by the spread of the disease and the measures taken to slow it down. When workers stay at home (either because they are already infected or because they fear being infected by other workers) output drops significantly. Subsequently and consequently, the global interconnectedness of supply chains produces knock-on effects, even in countries or regions that are not affected, or affected to a small extent, by the virus. This means that producers worldwide are affected by the lack of availability of parts, giving rise to supply bottlenecks. As a matter of fact, disruptions to global supply chains represent one of the clearest effects of COVID-19 as manufacturers outside China were forced to reduce production. This happened because China shut down factories in regions affected by the virus as a preventive measure.

The supply-side effect does not arise only because of declining output in affected countries (regions) and the interconnectedness of supply chains, but also because of diminishing confidence. The virus creates uncertainty, forcing firms to cut back on investment and adopt a wait-and-see attitude before expanding production. If uncertainty prevails for a prolonged period of time, investment projects will be put on the back burner or taken off the to-do list. Another contributor to the supply shock is lost productivity due to sickness and mortality. On this occasion, the supply shock came first as workers were quarantined to reduce the spread of the virus through social interaction. The drop in economic activity, initially in China, has had international repercussions as firms experienced delays in the supplies of intermediate and finished goods through supply chains.

The demand-side effect is represented by shrinking demand for non-essential goods and services. Travel restrictions reduce demand for tourism and hospitality. Waiters and chefs who are sent home by the owners of empty restaurants see their income vanish, which curbs their spending on the goods and services they would otherwise consume. In general, shrinking demand is caused by loss of jobs or hours worked, temporary or otherwise. Furthermore, lack of confidence and rampant uncertainty makes people reluctant to buy consumer durables, at least until the dust settles. No matter how low interest rates are, workers who are uncertain about the future will not borrow and buy consumer durables.

The fall in demand, however, does not hit all sectors as panic buying sets in. Demand rises for the goods used to fight the pandemic such as pharmaceuticals, and essential food and other grocery items. Panic buying of toilet paper became an international phenomenon. In the 17 February 2020 issue of the *New York Times*, it was reported that a delivery person in Hong Kong was robbed of his toilet paper at knifepoint. However, increased spending on essential items and hoarding leaves less of the disposable income available for spending on other goods and services, particularly in the presence of price gouging. Dick (2020) reports that an Australian online retailer revealed that the company was planning to award millions of dollars' worth of incentives to its top two executives as coronavirus-driven sales soared and that the generous bonus came following 'alleged price gouging of products during the pandemic'. A further contributory factor is soaring levels of household debt, which had been accumulated in the run-up to the crisis.

The current crisis began as a supply shock. As the global economy has become more interdependent in recent decades, most products are produced as part of a global value chain where an item, such as a car or mobile device, consists of parts manufactured all over the world, and involving multiple border crossings before final assembly at a specific location. For example, the production of iPhone 5S, 6 and 6S requires parts produced in various countries: the accelerometer in Germany, audio chips in Japan, battery in China, camera in Brazil, compass in Taiwan, glass screen in India, gyroscope in Switzerland, flash memory in Japan, and so on. Likewise, an aeroplane consists of parts that are sourced from different countries: wings from Germany, electronics from Japan (with chips made in China) and seats assembled in Mexico (with textiles and thread from India). The earliest implications of the COVID crisis came in January 2020 as plant closures in China and other parts of Asia led to interruptions in the supply chain and concerns about dwindling inventories. As the virus spread from Asia to Europe, the crisis switched from supply concerns to a broader demand crisis as the measures introduced to contain the spread of the virus (social distancing, travel restrictions, cancellation of sporting events, closure of shops and restaurants, and mandatory quarantine measures) impeded or brought to a halt most forms of economic activity.

To illustrate the macroeconomic effect of COVID-19, Fornaro and Wolf (2020b) use what they call a 'stripped-down version of the standard New Keynesian model' as suggested by Gali (2009). In this model, employment and output are determined by aggregate demand, which in turn depends positively on productivity growth. The positive relation between aggregate demand and productivity growth is that the latter leads to expectations of a higher level of income in the future, which induces people to spend more (Lorenzoni, 2009). In Figure 3.1, the positive relationship between productivity growth (G) and employment (L) is represented by the upward-sloping AD curve.

The economy is initially at full employment at L_0. If the pandemic causes a persistent drop in productivity growth, from G_0 to G_1, aggregate demand declines and involuntary unemployment $L_0 - L_1$ appears. This is a demand-driven recession, to which the policy response would be to reduce interest rates to boost aggregate demand. In Figure 3.2 an upward-sloping GG curve represents a situation where aggregate demand affects productivity growth when firms invest in capital formation. A persistent negative supply shock caused by COVID-19 can be represented by a downward shift in the GG

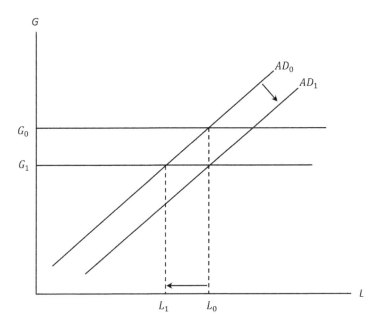

Figure 3.1   A COVID-19 demand shock in the new Keynesian model

curve to GG_1. In this case a supply–demand doom loop develops whereby the initial negative supply shock depresses aggregate demand, which forces firms to cut back on investment, generating an endogenous drop in productivity growth. In turn, the slowdown in productivity growth causes a further cut in demand, which again reduces productivity growth. This vicious spiral, or supply–demand doom loop, amplifies the impact of the initial supply shock on employment and productivity growth. The result is a persistent decline in employment from L_0 to L_1, L_2 and L_3.

Supply and demand shocks can be illustrated by using the aggregate demand–aggregate supply model. In Figure 3.3, *AD* is the aggregate demand curve, *SAS* is the short-run aggregate supply curve and *LAS* is the long-run aggregate supply curve, which defines the full-employment level of output. Initially, the economy is at full employment equilibrium where output is y_0. The supply shock, which is represented by a leftward shift in the *SAS* curve to SAS_1, reduces the level of output to y_1. The demand shock, which is represented by a leftward shift in the *AD* curve to AD_1, reduces the level of output further to y_2. As a result, employment shrinks.

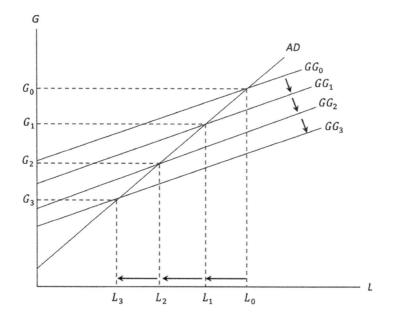

Figure 3.2   Supply–demand doom loop

The effect of COVID-19 can also be seen in terms of disruptions to the circular flow of income, as represented by the circular flow diagram. The diagram displays flows of money, goods and services between various sectors of the economy. In this representation, households own capital and labour, which they sell to businesses to be used in the production of goods and services. Subsequently, households buy the goods and services with the money they receive from businesses, thereby completing the circuit and keeping the economy ticking. The key point is that the economy continues running only when the money keeps flowing around, such that a flow-disruption anywhere causes a slowdown everywhere. In Figure 3.4, a version of the circular flow of income shows interaction amongst households, firms, the financial sector, the government and the rest of the world where the arrows indicate the directions of the flows of money, goods and services. Table 3.1 displays possible disruptions caused by COVID-19, showing how each flow can be disrupted and what causes the disruption.

What happened on the ground is alarming, to say the least. As a result, the IMF, OECD and the World Bank revised their forecasts downwards between

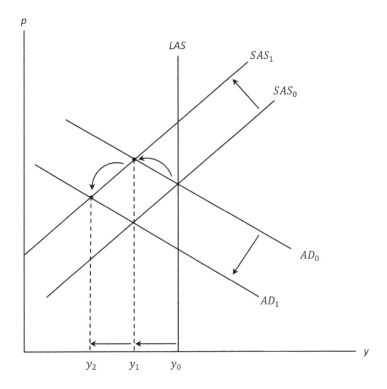

Figure 3.3   Supply and demand shocks in the AD–AS model

late 2019 and mid-2020, reflecting the rapidly deteriorating state of the global economy and the marked decline in the projected growth rate. In the January 2021 issue of the *World Economic Outlook*, the IMF published its forecasts for a rebound in growth in 2021 following the collapse of output in 2020, as shown in Figure 3.5. Out of the major economies, the hardest hit were the UK, France and Italy, with output losses in excess of 9%. Only China registered a positive growth rate of 2.3%, presumably because of its prompt control of the virus. The slowdown in the US economy can be seen in monthly figures on industrial production and capacity utilisation as reported by the Federal Reserve System. In Figure 3.6, we can see the total industrial production index and various components, which reached the lowest point in April 2020, then recovered (with the exception of utilities that reached its lowest point in May 2020). Figure 3.7 displays capacity utilisation, which hit the lowest point in April or May 2020.

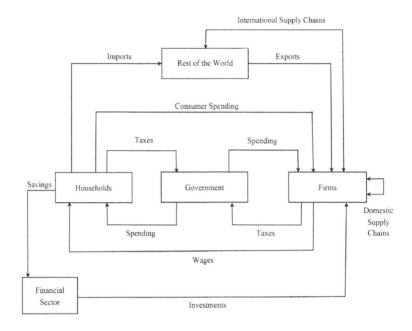

Figure 3.4   The effect of COVID-19 in the circular flow of income

3.3   FINANCIAL EFFECTS

The financial effects of COVID-19 include the effects on corporate debt, stock and commodity markets and the financial sector in general. Economic turmoil associated with the pandemic has had wide-ranging and severe impacts upon financial markets, including stock, bond, and oil (futures) markets.

3.3.1   Effect on Corporate Debt

Any economic crisis is likely to be more serious in the presence of huge amounts of corporate debt. COVID-19 hit the world economy while a corporate debt bubble was becoming more 'bubbly' as non-financial firms continued to accumulate large amounts of corporate bonds. Global corporate debt rose from 84% of gross world product in 2009 to 92% in 2019 – this is a 'modest' amount of about $72 trillion. Referring to COVID-19 as 'the scare', *The Economist* (2020a) puts it as follows:

> The scare has four elements: a queasy long-term rise in borrowing; a looming cash crunch at firms as offices and factories are shut and quarantines imposed; the

Table 3.1   *Possible disruptions to flows of money, goods and services*

From	To	Disruption Caused by
Households	Financial Sector	Household bankruptcies and financial distress caused by loss of income and redundancies
Financial Sector	Firms	The financial sector is less willing to lend and firms are less willing to borrow because of uncertainty and diminished demand
Firms	Households	Temporary or permanent lay-offs
Households	Firms	Diminished consumption and postponement of spending on consumer durables
Households	Rest of the World	Diminished spending on imports
Rest of the World	Firms	Diminished exports and payments for supply chain transactions
Firms	Rest of the World	Diminished imports and payments for supply chain transactions
Firms	Firms	Diminished payments for supply chain transactions
Government	Firms	Re-prioritisation of government spending and increased transfer payments
Firms	Government	Diminished tax revenue
Households	Government	Diminished tax revenue
Government	Households	Increased transfer payments

gumming-up of some credit markets; and doubts about the resilience of banks and debt funds that would bear any losses.

The concern is that the economic instability caused by COVID-19 may initiate the bursting of the corporate debt bubble, and when that happens bankruptcies will soar, with further adverse consequences for output and employment.

Even before the advent of COVID-19, regulators and investors appeared to be concerned about the large amounts of risky corporate debt, which would make financial markets vulnerable, hitting in particular mutual funds. A decade of historically low interest rates and addiction to debt has allowed corporate entities to sell record amounts of bonds to investors seeking a better return than what could be earned on a bank deposit. Lynch (2019) warns of the hazard of a new debt surge by major corporations that would 'unleash fresh turmoil'. Kolakowski (2019) notes that record high corporate debt threatens the bond market, the stock market and the broader economy. Lund (2018) wonders if growing corporate debt is a bubble that is waiting to burst as the average quality of borrowers has declined. In the US, 22% of non-financial corporate debt outstanding comprises 'junk' issued by speculative-grade entities, and another 40% are rated BBB, just one notch above junk. This accumulation of

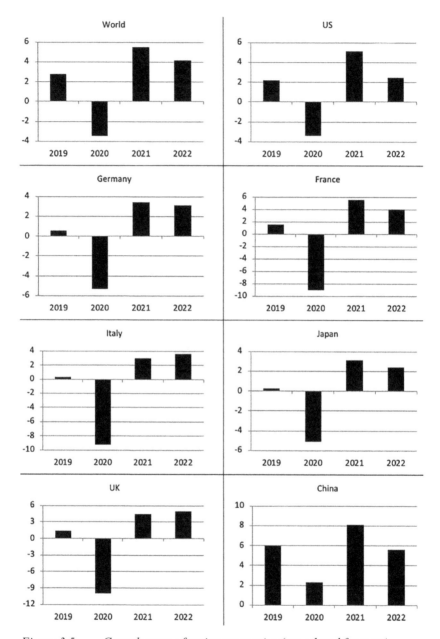

Figure 3.5   Growth rates of major economies (actual and forecast)

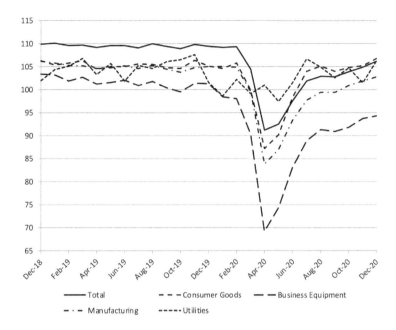

Figure 3.6   US industrial production (2012=100)

corporate bonds, which coincides with soaring corporate debt in developing countries, is made worse by the fragile finances of bond-issuing companies.

This phenomenon is not to be blamed on borrowing firms but rather on the twisted thinking of those in charge of monetary policy. For over a decade, artificially low interest rates and bond yields have caused a mispricing of risk as investors look eagerly for higher yields. Companies that do not make enough operating profit to pay off their debts (the so-called 'zombie firms') are only able to survive by refinancing their loans repeatedly, which they have been able to do because low interest rates make lenders more willing to acquire higher yield corporate debt. In a 2018 study of 14 high-income countries, the Bank for International Settlements found that zombie firms increased from 2% of all firms in the 1980s to 12% in 2016. By March 2020, one-sixth of all publicly traded companies in the US did not make enough profit to cover the interest on their debt (Lynch, 2019).

Miller and Boston (2020) warn that the slowdown in consumer and business spending triggered by COVID-19 could unleash a wave of defaults among heavily leveraged firms. They suggest that 'coronavirus is threatening to expose the Achilles heel of the U.S. economy: heavily leveraged companies' and that

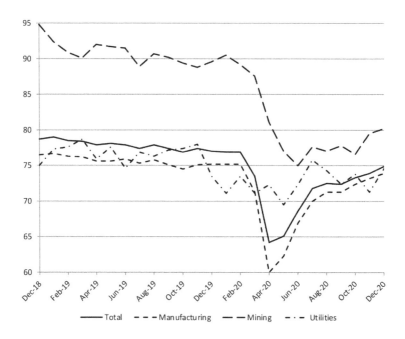

Figure 3.7   US capacity utilisation (2012=100)

'a wave of defaults would intensify the economic impact of COVID-19'. In February 2020 the OECD noted that 'today's stock of outstanding corporate bonds has lower overall credit quality, higher payback requirements, longer maturities and inferior covenant protection', which 'may amplify the negative effects that an economic downturn would have on the non-financial corporate sector and the overall economy' (Çelik et al., 2020). If the corporate debt bubble bursts, bonds would be repriced, resulting in massive losses by mutual funds, high-yield funds, pension funds, and endowments with corporate bond assets. Similar to what happened during the global financial crisis, this may make lenders more cautious, leading to a shrinking of the entire bond market and higher rates for mortgages, car loans, and small-business loans.

In short, COVID-19 comes at a time when the level of corporate indebtedness is very high as a result of a very unwise policy of maintaining ultra-low interest rates for a long time. The loss of business caused by COVID-19 will put firms in a position where they are unable to service their debt. As a result, they will go bankrupt. The bright side of it is that COVID-19 will kill zombie firms that should have ceased to exist a long time ago – this is good for the economy. Another bright side is that COVID-19 will (hopefully) lead to higher levels of interest rates, which is the normal state of affairs. Low nominal interest rates and high but undeclared inflation has wiped out the middle class and demolished responsible investors and pensioners. A higher level of interest rates will rectify a very unhealthy situation.

3.3.2   Effect on Stock Markets

The advent of COVID-19 created uncertainty, coupled with rising fears and global economic shutdown. Stock markets collapsed but a quick recovery followed. The Dow Jones Industrial Average (DJIA) lost about one-third of its value between 14 February and 23 March 2020. On 12 February, the DJIA, NASDAQ Composite, and the S&P 500 index finished at record highs (actually, the NASDAQ and S&P 500 reached subsequent record highs on 19 February). From 24 to 28 February 2020, stock markets worldwide reported their largest one-week declines since the global financial crisis. In early March 2020, markets became extremely volatile, with large swings.

On 9 March 2020, most markets reported severe contractions, mainly in response to the pandemic and an oil price war between Russia and OPEC countries led by Saudi Arabia. However, fiscal and monetary interventions propelled markets, which were later aided by the anticipation that a vaccine would at least reduce the severity of the pandemic. In Figure 3.8 we observe the S&P500 index over the period 31 December 2019–1 March 2021. The index recorded a high of 3386 on 19 February 2020, declining to its lowest value of 2237 on 23 March 2020. By 18 August 2020, the index regained all of the losses caused by the pandemic and on 1 March 2021, the index was up 74.4% on the March 2020 trough.

Explaining market recovery in the midst of a COVID-19-triggered economic collapse is not straightforward. After all, the market is supposed to be a reflection of what happens in the real economy, or at least it is a leading economic indicator of economic activity. Based on a quote from Matt King, global head of credit strategy at Citigroup, Stewart (2020) suggests that 'the stock market isn't the economy, but right now, it seems particularly divorced from what's happening on the ground' and that 'the gap between markets and economic data has never been larger'. He further writes the following:

> Earlier in the coronavirus crisis, Wall Street had a meltdown. Stocks plunged amid fears of the disease's spread and its potential impact on the global economy, sometimes to the point that trading was halted altogether to rein in the chaos. But in recent weeks, the market has been doing okay. It's not at the record highs it was in mid-February, but it's not bad – the S&P 500 is hovering around where it was last fall. And given the state of the world – a deadly global pandemic with no end

Figure 3.8   *S&P 500 index (0=31 December 2019)*

in sight, 30 million Americans recently out of jobs, an economy that's fallen off of a cliff – a relatively rosy stock market is particularly perplexing.

Several explanations can be put forward for this 'head-scratching' observation. The first explanation is expansionary monetary and fiscal policies. On the monetary policy side, quantitative easing has been resumed with vengeance, leading to massive monetary expansion. Since March 2020, the Fed has committed to lend or buy trillions of dollars' worth of financial assets. The Bank of Japan is doing much the same as the Fed for the world's third largest economy, and the European Central Bank is not far behind. Stewart (2020) argues that 'the Federal Reserve and, to a perhaps lesser but still significant extent, Congress have taken extraordinary measures to pump money into the economy and prop up markets'. When amounts of about one-third of GDP are pumped in a very short period of time, he argues, investors' nerves are calmed and the fundamentals do not matter. The propelling force is 'that kind of liquidity deluge'.

How does the availability of liquidity help the market? One possibility is that the availability of cheap loans is keeping zombie companies artificially alive. Otherwise, sound firms going through temporary difficulties can borrow and stay afloat until the health crisis is over. The other possibility is stock buy-backs, which were rampant in the run-up to COVID-19. However, the facts on the ground show otherwise, as COVID-19 has discouraged stock buy-backs because firms are hoarding cash (James Tobin's notion of 'liquidity preference as behaviour towards risk'). According to Constable (2020) 'the COVID-19 pandemic may have torpedoed one of corporate America's favorite activities: Buying back their own shares'. In the first three quarters of 2020, stock buy-backs were down 41%, to $266 billion, over the same period of 2019, according to data from Wells Fargo strategists (Sonenshine, 2020). The sharpest drop came in the second quarter of 2020, when lockdowns and corporate confidence were at their worst and when companies were doing whatever they could to conserve cash. However, it is expected that stock buy-backs will resume as confidence in economic recovery goes up. The stock market is set to record new highs.

A rising stock price index hides winners and losers. When the index falls, some stocks do well and some do not. During the 2020 decline, companies like Amazon, Costco, Clorox, Microsoft, Apple, Facebook, Walmart and Zoom were doing well. However, companies in the hospitality and tourism sector saw their stock prices plunge. According to Karabell (2020) this is what happened:

> While markets are not moving on real-time economic fundamentals, they are moving on reasonable judgements of fundamentals going forward and distinguishing between industries that look to be hardest hit from those that might even benefit from the dramatic economic dislocations that COVID-19 responses are creating. If everything were going up indiscriminately, that would indicate markets were fully detached. They are not.

One has to remember also that small businesses and companies that are not publicly traded have been hit hard, but that does not show up in stock price indices.

Another possibility is that the recovery is temporary. Karabell (2020) quotes Jeffrey Gundlach, one of the most influential bond managers, as warning that markets will soon head south fast and urging people to be more 'wary of panaceas' and that 'the recovery could be like a "dead-cat bounce"', similar to what happened in 2008. Some market watchers believe that all the liquidity in the world cannot compensate for the collapse of real-world economic activity and that flooding markets with liquidity provides temporary relief. It is like a situation where flooding a drought stricken area with water is no substitute for rain. Likewise, Stewart (2020) refers to 'plenty of voices out there warning that just because the market is up now doesn't mean it will stay that way'. He quotes high-profile investor Jeffrey Gundlach as saying that he was shorting the market, meaning that he was betting it would go back down. These views, which were expressed in April and May 2020, have so far proven to be wrong by vibrant stock markets.

Support for the market comes from the lack of alternative investment opportunities in a world of ultra-low interest rates. Investors do not have much choice in investment outlets, given that deposits and bonds provide super-low (if not negative) returns. There is also the fear of missing out, and it appears that retail investors have been playing the markets while under lockdown. Overall, it just seems that markets may be feeling a bit more optimistic than science about the future. The stock market is sometimes considered to be a leading indicator of the economy. At the onset of the pandemic, it sounded the alarm before the economic data did, giving up 30% of its value in the course of a month. If stock prices are indeed a leading indicator of economic activity, this means that investors think that conditions will be better, particularly with the rolling out of vaccines worldwide. This seems to be what the IMF believes.

It would be interesting to compare the effect of COVID-19 on stock markets relative to previous crises according to data provided by Sauter and Stebbins (2020). This is shown in Table 3.2, where we can see what happened to the Dow Jones in a number of crises going back to the panic of 1901. Two indicators are reported, a period decline and the largest one-day decline in each episode. In terms of the period decline, the global financial crisis recorded the biggest decline of 53.7%. The COVID-19 crisis caused a decline of 35%, more than what happened in the Dot-com bubble, the German invasion of France, the collapse of LTCM and the invasion of Kuwait. In terms of the largest one-day decline, COVID-19 is second only to Black Monday of 1987. It is more than the crash of 1929 and the panic of 1907.

A stock market-related scandal surfaced in the early stages of the pandemic as some US politicians traded on the basis of insider information. This is what is known as the 2020 Congressional insider trading scandal, which involved some senators who sold their stock holdings before the stock market crash on 20 February 2020, using information given to them at a closed Senate meeting. On 24 January 2020, the Senate Committees on Health and Foreign Relations held a closed meeting, with only senators present, to brief them about the COVID-19 outbreak and how it would affect the US (see, for example, Kelly, 2020).

3.3.3   Effect on Oil Prices

The COVID-19 pandemic and consequent confinement measures led to an unprecedented contraction in economic activity and consequently a collapse in the demand for oil, both crude and products. The result is one of the biggest price shocks the energy market has experienced since the first oil shock of 1973. Figure 3.9 shows the daily price of Brent (in dollars per barrel) over the

Table 3.2   *A list of stock market crashes (DJIA)*

Event	Period Decline			Largest One-Day Decline	
	From	To	Change (%)	Date	Change (%)
Panic of 1901	6 May 1901	9 May 1901	−10.8	9 May 1901	−6.1
Panic of 1907	7 Jan 1907	15 Nov 1907	−45.0	14 Mar 1907	−8.3
Crash of 1929	16 Sep 1929	13 Nov 1929	−46.6	28 Oct 1929	−12.8
Recession of 1937–38	4 Sep 1937	31 Mar 1938	−42.6	19 Nov 1937	−5.9
German invasion of France	10 May 1940	10 Jun 1940	−24.5	14 May 1940	−6.8
End of World War II	29 May 1946	9 Oct 1946	−23.2	3 Sep 1946	−5.6
Slide of 1962	28 Dec 1961	26 Jun 1962	−26.8	28 May 1962	−5.7
Tech Stock Crash of 1970	20 Apr 1970	26 May 1970	−18.7	25 May 1970	−3.1
1973–74 Stock Market Crash	11 Jan 1973	6 Dec 1974	−45.1	18 Nov 1974	−3.5
Black Monday	19 Oct 1987	19 Oct 1987	−22.6	19 Oct 1987	−22.6
Invasion of Kuwait	2 Aug 1990	10 Aug 1990	−18.4	6 Aug 1990	−3.3
Collapse of LTCM	19 Jul 1998	31 Aug 1998	−19.2	31 Aug 1998	−6.4
Dot-com Bubble	19 May 2002	9 Oct 2002	−31.4	19 Jul 2002	−4.6
Global Financial Crisis	10 Sep 2007	9 Mar 2009	−53.7	15 Oct 2008	−4.6
US Debt Downgrade	1 Aug 2011	10 Aug 2011	−11.7	8 Aug 2011	−5.5
Chinese Market Turbulence	24 Jun 2015	25 Aug 2015	−13.6	24 Aug 2015	−3.6
COVID-19 Outbreak	12 Feb 2020	20 Mar 2020	−35.0	16 Mar 2020	−12.9

period 31 December 2019–22 February 2021. During this period, the price was at its highest level on 6 January ($70.25). The COVID-triggered decline took the price down to $9.12 on 21 April 2020, but then the price started rising to reach the level of $64.73 on 22 February 2021. On 20 April 2020, the futures price of West Texas Intermediate crude to be delivered in May became negative, which is an unprecedented event (Figure 3.10). This was a result of uninterrupted supply and a much reduced demand, as oil storage facilities reached maximum capacity. Analysts characterised the event as an anomaly of the closing of the May futures market coupled with the lack of available storage in that time frame.

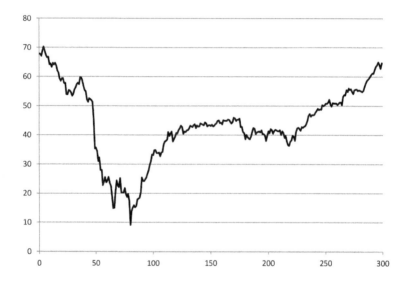

Figure 3.9   Price of Brent crude oil ($/barrel, 0=31/12/2019)

The price decline was mainly demand-driven, resulting from shrinking demand for travel and weakness in manufacturing activity. The Organization of the Petroleum Exporting Countries (OPEC) met in Vienna on 5 March 2020 to discuss a potential cut in production to balance the loss in demand, reaching a tentative agreement to cut oil production by 1.5 million barrels per day, which would bring it to the lowest level since the invasion of Iraq in 2003. Russia refused to co-operate with OPEC, effectively ending the agreement that it had maintained with OPEC since 2016, on the belief that the growth of shale oil extraction in the US (which was not party to any agreement with OPEC) would require continued cuts for the foreseeable future.

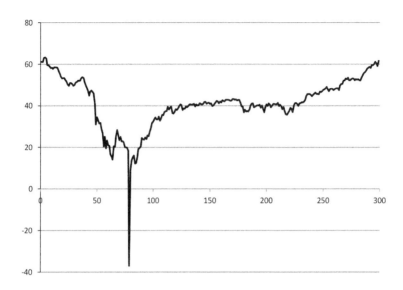

Figure 3.10   Futures price of West Texas Intermediate crude ($/barrel, 0=31/12/2019)

Oil prices recovered on expectation of a rebound in energy demand. China's exit from lockdown measures saw Chinese demand almost back to normal levels in April 2020. Oil prices have been propelled by the advent of positive news on the COVID front, particularly news on the roll-out of vaccines and the promise that comes with it to put an end to the spread of the virus. The upward trend in crude prices was also boosted by the gradual decline in US shale production and inventories. The move in early January 2021, by OPEC+ to restrain output into mid-2021, and an extra 'gift' from Saudi Arabia to remove another one million barrels from the market, provided the impetus for WTI to rise firmly (see, for example, Messler, 2021).

3.3.4   Effect on Banks and Financial Institutions

As we saw in the circular flow of income diagram (Figure 3.4), banks are affected by the decline in the flow of deposits and loan defaults, both from the household and corporate sectors. Aldasoro et al. (2020) examine the effect of COVID-19 on banks in terms of stock prices and reach three conclusions. The first is that banks' performance on equity and debt markets since the COVID-19 outbreak has been on par with that experienced after the collapse of Lehman Brothers in 2008. The second is that during the initial phase, the market sell-off swept over all banks, which underperformed significantly relative to other sectors. The third is that the subsequent stabilisation, brought about by policy response, has favoured banks with higher profitability and healthier balance sheets. Less profitable banks saw their long-term rating outlooks revised to negative.

However, with unemployment numbers rising rapidly, job losses could result in defaults on mortgages and delinquencies on rent payments, unless financial institutions provide loan forbearance or a mechanism evolves to provide financial assistance. In turn, mortgage defaults have an adverse effect on the market for mortgage-backed securities and consequently the availability of funds for mortgages. On the other hand, banks will benefit greatly from negative interest rates as they charge customers for the privilege (that is, customers' privilege) of looking after their money while still charging 20% on credit card bills. At the crunch, banks typically claim (and obtain) the too big to fail status. Their balance sheets may be unhealthy but they know how to pull the strings. Furthermore, banks are protected from failure (even if it is self-inflicted) by the bail-in legislation adopted by many countries, which allows them to confiscate deposits if and when they need to do that. Banks, as usual and unlike the household sector, do not need to worry (but bank customers have a lot to worry about).

3.3.5   Effect on the Foreign Exchange Market

Similar to conditions during the 2008–2009 financial crisis, the dollar emerged as the preferred currency by investors at the early stages of the pandemic. Figure 3.11 displays the dollar's trade-weighted effective exchange rate over the period 31 December 2019–26 February 2021. The dollar appreciated by 8.5% during the period between 3 March and 23 March 2020 to reach its peak of 126.5. Thereafter, it started to depreciate, losing 16.6% of its value between 23 March 2020 and 26 February 2021.

The rise and fall of the dollar during the pandemic can be explained easily. The dollar benefits from uncertainty and bad economic conditions. At the early stages of the pandemic in 2020, investors found the dollar attractive as a safe-haven currency. The whole of the US economy is considered as a safe haven by investors, which means that they tend to switch to dollar-denominated assets when the world economy is going down. The dollar is still the dominant global currency, as shown by the BIS triennial survey of the global foreign exchange market which was conducted in 2019 (Bank for International Settlements, 2019). The subsequent depreciation has been due improvement in economic conditions and perhaps the realisation that quantitative easing may bring about hyperinflation. Roach (2021) presents three reasons why the dollar

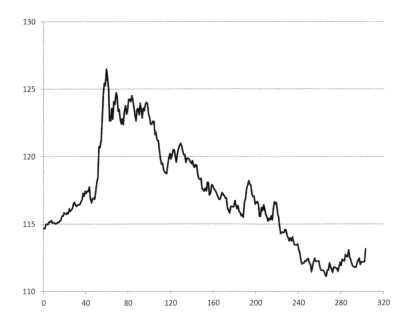

*Figure 3.11   The dollar's trade-weighted effective exchange rate
                 (0=31/12/2019)*

would continue to depreciate: (i) a sharp widening in the US current-account deficit, (ii) the rise of the euro, and (iii) reluctance of the Federal Reserve to do something about the weakness of the currency. This is why in June 2020 he predicted that the dollar would decline by 35% by the end of 2021, which remains to be seen. The feeling that the dollar has been overvalued is another reason why it is felt that a correction is necessary.

3.4   EFFECTS BY SECTOR/INDUSTRY

In this section we examine the sectoral effects of the pandemic, starting with the sectors identified in the process of calculating GDP as aggregate output. This is followed by looking at arts and cultural heritage, aviation, sport, tourism, and higher education.

3.4.1   GDP by Sector

The effects of the pandemic on the sectors of the US economy can be seen in Figures 3.12–3.14. Figure 3.12 displays percentage changes in GDP and its components in the first quarter of 2020 compared to the fourth quarter of 2019. We can see that the overall GDP declined by 4.8%, while the output of car manufacturers declined by 33.2%. Only the output of the food and beverages sector rose, which is not surprising. Figure 3.13 displays net changes in US jobs (in millions) in April 2020, showing that the hardest-hit hospitality sector recorded a loss of 7.5 million jobs. Figure 3.14 shows changes in the hours worked in April 2020 due to supply and demand shocks, according to the figures provided by Brinca et al. (2020). We can see that supply shocks were more damaging than demand shocks for all sectors.

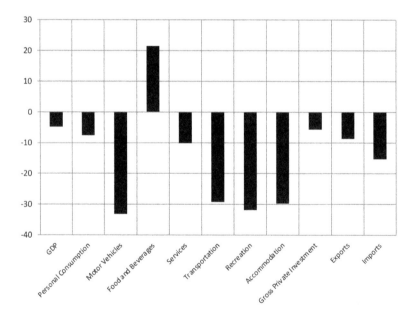

Figure 3.12   Changes in US GDP and its components (first quarter 2020, %)

3.4.2   Arts and Cultural Heritage

The COVID-19 pandemic has had a substantial impact on the arts and cultural heritage sector. The uncertainty created by the crisis affected adversely the

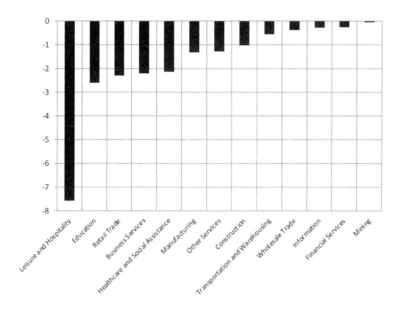

Figure 3.13   Net changes in US employment (April 2020, in millions)

operations of organisations and individuals (employed and independent) across the sector. By March 2020, most cultural organisations across the world had been closed indefinitely or had their services curtailed significantly. Exhibitions, events and concerts were cancelled or postponed. On 10 March 2021 French protesters occupied three of the country's four national theatres to demand an end to the closure of cultural venues, as frustration grew with the months-long halt to performances.

The film industry was also hit hard as cinemas were closed, festivals cancelled or postponed, and film releases moved to future dates or delayed indefinitely. For example, the latest James Bond movie, *No Time to Die*, was originally scheduled for release in April 2020, but it has been postponed, originally to November 2020, then to October 2021. Other blockbusters originally scheduled to be released between March and November 2020 were postponed or cancelled around the world, with film productions also being put on halt. Examples are *Locked Down*, *Outside the Wire*, *Coming 2 America*, *Chaos Walking*, *The King's Man* and *The Many Saints of Newark*.

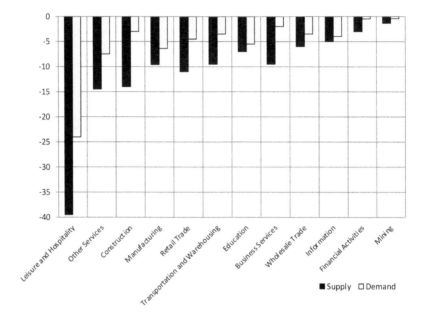

Figure 3.14   Changes in hours worked due to supply and demand shocks
(April 2020, %)

3.4.3   Aviation

The aviation sector (including airlines, airports and aircraft manufacturers) has been dealt a big blow due to travel restrictions. Significant reductions in passenger numbers have resulted in flight cancellation or empty flights, which led to a massive reduction in airline revenues and forced many of them to lay off employees or declare bankruptcy. Some have attempted to avoid refunding cancelled trips in order to reduce their losses. Aircraft manufacturers and airport operators have also laid off employees. The effect on airlines can be envisaged through the state of British Airways as described by Calder (2020):

> Three months ago, British Airways and its staff were beginning what was expected to be their most successful year ever. Today, in common with the rest of the airline industry, BA is on life support as scheduled flying reaches a near standstill. A combination of international flight bans, national lockdowns and passenger concerns about the coronavirus have created the biggest crisis in modern aviation history. In response, British Airways is to suspend 36,000 employees.

Every airline has a story to tell about their response to the pandemic. Norwegian Air cancelled 85% of its flights and temporarily laid off 90% of its employees. Philippine Airlines cancelled 69 weekly flights to China and 17 weekly flights to South Korea. Qantas initially reduced capacity on its international routes by around 25% and grounded eight of its ten Airbus A380 aircraft. On 19 March 2020, Qantas confirmed that it would suspend about 60% of domestic flights, put two-thirds of its employees on leave, suspend all international flights, and ground more than 150 of its aircraft. Qatar Airways reduced fleet operations to 75% and announced that the Airbus A380 fleet might get retired by the end of 2020 instead of 2028. The airline also delayed deliveries of other upcoming aircraft on order until at least 2022. In 2021, Qatar Airways confirmed that it would retire half of its Airbus A380 fleet by the end of 2021 and the remaining half of the fleet will be retired by 2028 (CNN, 2021).

3.4.4   Sporting Events

The COVID-19 pandemic has caused the most significant disruption to the worldwide sporting calendar since World War II. Sport events have been cancelled or postponed across the world. The 2020 Summer Olympics and Paralympics were scheduled to take place in Tokyo starting on 24 July 2020, but instead the events were held during the period 23 July to 8 August 2021 without spectators. Although the next Winter Olympics are scheduled to take place in 2022 (to be hosted by China), the pandemic has already impacted qualifying events in specific sports. Even after the resumption of national football leagues, the matches have been played without fans, costing football associations and clubs huge amounts of money.

3.4.5   International Tourism

In 2019 international arrivals worldwide surpassed 1.5 billion for the first time, but the spectacular growth of tourism since the global financial crisis was brought to an abrupt end by COVID-19. The pandemic has had a significant impact on the tourism industry due to travel restrictions and shrinking demand for travel. The United Nations World Tourism Organization (UNWTO) has raised alarm about the state of tourism, suggesting that 'tourism suffered the greatest crisis on record in 2020 following an unprecedented health, social and economic emergency amid the outbreak of the COVID-19 pandemic' (UNWTO, 2021). The estimates provided by the UNWTO indicate that inter-national tourist arrivals plunged by 74% in 2020 over the previous year, which translates into an estimated loss of $1.3 trillion in revenues, more than 11 times the loss recorded in 2009 as a result of the global financial crisis. The massive drop in the number of arrivals and tourism revenue can be seen in Figure 3.15 according to data provided by the UNWTO.

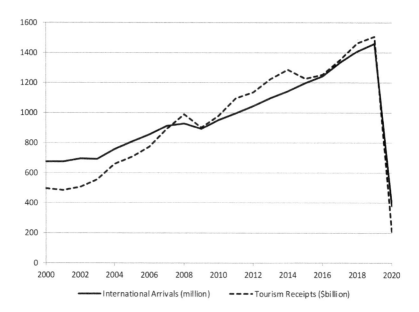

Figure 3.15   *International tourist arrivals (million) and tourism revenue ($ billion)*

Academic research has dealt with the effect of COVID-19 on tourism, identifying as a silver lining the potential environmental implications. Gössling et al. (2020) assert that tourism is particularly susceptible to actions taken to counteract pandemics because of restricted mobility and social distancing. They compare the impact of COVID-19 to previous epidemic/pandemics and other types of global crises and explore how the pandemic may change society, the economy, and tourism. They argue that COVID-19 is an analogue to the ongoing climate crisis, and that there is a need to question the volume growth tourism model advocated by tourism organisations.

Brouder (2020) notes that 'COVID-19 presents a once in a generation opportunity where the institutional pump is primed for transformation'. Whether that leads to a radical transformation of the tourism sector remains to be seen but, the argument goes, 'the imprint it will leave on both the demand and supply of tourism will have long-term, incremental impacts for years to come and ultimately move us closer towards the transformation of tourism'. Niewiadomski (2020) argues that the pandemic offers the tourism industry 'an unprecedented opportunity for a re-boot – an unrepeatable chance to re-develop in line with the tenets of sustainability and to do away with various "dark sides" of tourism's growth such as environmental degradation, economic exploitation or overcrowding'. Lapointe (2020) suggests that one of the transformations induced by the pandemic has been a 'turning of the tourism sectors to a greater orientation towards their host communities'. He contemplates a 'relinking of tourism to the needs of the host communities as part of a survival strategy in a time when there are no tourists, and could become, in the long run, a resilience strategy'.

3.4.6 Higher Education

Higher education is yet another sector that has been affected badly by the pandemic, particularly in the Anglo-American world where universities are profit-maximising firms with highly paid CEOs (otherwise known as vice-chancellors or presidents) and a clientele of fee-paying overseas students. Universities have been thrown into disarray as the pandemic forced them to convert to online-only courses while struggling against financial difficulties. In the US in particular, new domestic applications are likely to go down as many students and their parents may no longer be in a position to afford exorbitant tuition fees (paid to acquire degrees that do not boost employability) as a result of being laid off, furloughed, unable to pay off loans, or needing to dip into their savings. On the other hand, it has been observed that the number of students tends to go up in a recession as they try to 'wait it out', hoping that once the recession is over, the chance of getting a job is greater. In this sense, only time will truly tell what kind of a long-term impact COVID-19 will have on universities.

Like businesses, universities are feeling significant pressure on their finances, which is why they have been reassessing their financial positions by maintaining essential expenditures only and implementing severe cost-cutting and saving measures, including reduction in the numbers of academic and non-academic employees and/or cutting salaries and benefits (not the bonus of the CEO, of course). For example, Australian universities, which are heavily dependent on Chinese students, claim that they will lose up to $16 billion by 2023 due to the impact of COVID-19 (Karp, 2020). Universities may even resort to lowering standards of admission to generate more revenue from student fees. As long as fee-paying overseas students are not allowed to enter the country, financial difficulties will persist, which is particularly because universities are reluctant to get rid of unnecessary inflated bureaucratic apparatuses. At the same time, students will go through financial hardship. According to a survey of 1,020 students at the University of Sydney, three-quarters of respondents anticipate financial hardship and 45% expect to be forced to suspend or withdraw from their studies in the next six months owing to lack of funds (Woolston, 2020).

Profit-maximising universities are making students and (mostly academic) staff pay for the crisis in higher education, while the people on top and their entourages still receive bonuses and congratulate each other on a job well-done. In this sense, they behave like bankers but unlike banks, which receive government assistance when they are in trouble, universities were denied financial assistance during the current crisis. This is because institutions of higher education are expected to get out of trouble by competing for customers of increasingly inferior quality. This is the spirit of the free market.

3.5   SOCIO-ECONOMIC EFFECTS

In this section we consider the socio-economic effects of the pandemic. Specifically, we consider the effects on crime, domestic violence and poverty. Inequality will be discussed in Chapter 9 whereas food insecurity and homelessness will be addressed in Chapter 8.

3.5.1   Crime

The non-pharmaceutical interventions pursued by governments to tackle COVID-19 have led to a drastic fall in crime (or at least certain kinds of crime) in many communities around the world. The main reason for the change is stay-at-home orders, which impact the routine activities of entire populations. In the midst of the pandemic, the crime rate dropped even among regions that have the highest levels of violence. As a result of movement restrictions, fewer people can be found on the streets, lowering the incidence of violent encounters. Thefts and residential burglaries have declined as more and more people stay at home. According to Fattah (2020), 'the "stay-at-home" mandates brought about a "positive byproduct" – that of declining crime across the US'.

In Chicago, one of America's most violent cities, drug arrests plummeted 42% in the weeks following the city's shutdown, compared with the same period in 2019 (Lederer, 2020). Overall, Chicago's crime declined 10% following the advent of the pandemic, a phenomenon that can be observed in other major cities. Jacoby et al. (2020) report that crime rates plunged in cities and counties across the US over the second half of March 2020 as the pandemic drove millions of residents to stay at home. They attribute the trend to 'both a purposeful reduction in police activity and officer-initiated stops and the effect of stay-at-home orders that have closed huge swaths of Main Street and pushed people into their homes and out of traditional crime hot spots, such as bars, clubs and social events'.

Several studies have been conducted to examine the early evidence on the effect of COVID-19 on crime. One of the earliest studies, with perhaps the most striking results, was conducted by Shayegh and Malpede (2020), which identified an overall drop in crime by 43% in San Francisco and by 50% in Oakland following the implementation of stay-at-home orders. Pietrawska et al. (2020) identified a five-week change in crimes occurring at restaurants in Chicago (a 74% reduction) while city-wide crime declined by 35%. Felson et al. (2020) examined burglary in Detroit during three periods, one before putting in place stay-at-home orders and two periods under orders. Their findings indicate an overall 32% decline in burglary, with the most substantial change occurring in the third period.

Stickle and Felson (2020) argue that the single most salient aspect of the steep fall in crime rates during the pandemic are the legal stay-at-home orders implemented to slow the spread of the virus by promoting social distancing. They also suggest that crime rates have indeed changed but unequally across crime type. As more people spend more time online, cybercrime has increased (for example, Warrell and Fildes, 2020). Work from home means that more and more corporate data is accessed from homes where the level of security may not be as good as what is found in office systems. Online criminals are also setting up fake coronavirus-related websites, offering at very low prices natural and pharmaceutical cures, vaccines, testing kits, masks and other items in short supply. The fake websites steal credit card information and put individuals' health at risk with fake and low-quality medical products.

A new form of criminal activity is conducted by making phone calls to tell people on the receiving end that their bank accounts will be closed because of criminal activity (terrorism is a favourite word here as well) or that they will be arrested because of tax fraud. This criminal activity (intended, it seems, to extract information) may not be related to the pandemic directly, but it exploits the increasing vulnerability of people. It may even be perpetrated by people who are in a dire financial situation because of the pandemic. It seems, therefore, that this is an ingenious market-based solution to the economic hardship inflicted by the pandemic.

3.5.2   Domestic Violence

Amid the COVID-19 pandemic, an increase in domestic violence has been reported across the world. Referring to the 'horrifying global surge [in domestic violence]', United Nations Secretary-General António Guterres has called for a domestic violence 'ceasefire'. Having appealed repeatedly for a ceasefire in conflicts around the world, to focus on the shared struggle to overcome the virus, the Secretary-General pointed out that violence is not confined to the battlefield, and that 'for many women and girls, the threat looms largest where they should be safest: in their own homes' (UN News, 2020).

Domestic violence, which is common across the world, spikes when households are exposed to strains caused by worries about security, health and money, and cramped in confined living conditions. Pandemics, financial insecurity, stress and uncertainty have led to increased aggression at home, which was seen previously during the global financial crisis and natural disasters such as the 2011 Christchurch earthquake. Under these conditions, abusers are able to control their victims' daily lives.

3.5.3   Poverty

A consensus view has emerged that COVID-19 will aggravate poverty worldwide. Sumner et al. (2020) provide estimates of the potential short-term economic impact of COVID-19 on global poverty through contractions in per capita household income or consumption. They demonstrate that the pandemic poses a real challenge to the UN Sustainable Development Goal of eradicating poverty by 2030 because global poverty could be on the rise for the first time since 1990, which represents a reversal of the progress in this respect. They find that in some regions, the adverse impacts could result in poverty levels similar to those recorded 30 years ago.

Other estimates have been prepared by the International Labour Organization (ILO) and the International Food Policy Research Institute (IFPRI). The ILO (2020) estimates, which are focused on the working population, suggest that between 9 and 35 million new working poor would appear in developing countries in 2020 (at the higher World Bank poverty line of $3.20 per day). The IFPRI estimates, prepared by Vos et al. (2020a, 2020b) on the basis of the IFPRI's own global CGE model, show that a one percentage point slowdown in global GDP growth would lead to rising poverty (at the lower World Bank poverty line of $1.90 per day) by between 14 and 22 million people.

Poverty will be augmented by the fall in remittances caused by COVID-19. For many low-income countries, the economic shock will be magnified by the loss of remittances, the money sent home by the migrant and guest workers employed in foreign countries. Remittance flows into low-income countries represent a lifeline that supports households and provides much needed tax revenue. Sayeh and Chami (2020) compare COVID-19 with previous economic crises, arguing that the pandemic poses an even greater threat to countries that rely heavily on remittance income. The global nature of this crisis means that recipient countries will see remittance flows dry up, and that they will simultaneously experience outflows of private capital, as well as a likely reduction in aid from struggling donors.

A related issue is that of hunger. COVID-19 has arrived at a time of unprecedented global need, with a record 168 million people already requiring humanitarian assistance at the beginning of 2020 (UNOCHA, 2020). World hunger levels have been rising since 2015 with over 820 million people going hungry on a daily basis (FAO, 2019) and 135 million experiencing acute food insecurity in 2019 (Food Security Information Network, 2020).

3.6   CONCLUDING REMARKS: COVID-19 VS GFC ONCE MORE

Comparing the COVID-19 crisis, which is a health and economic crisis, with the global financial crisis, which is a financial and economic crisis, has become a common topic of conversation. Naturally, financial crises lead to economic crises, and vice versa, which means that the COVID-19 crisis is a health–economic–financial crisis. We have seen that while some observers believe that the COVID-19 recession is less destructive than the great recession induced by the global financial crisis, the numbers show otherwise. If the response to the crisis provides any indication to its severity, then the COVID crisis has been much more destructive than the global financial crisis. Some countries (such as Australia) managed to escape the recession caused by the GFC but not the recession caused by the virus.

There are, of course, aspects of similarity and difference between the two crises. The common features include sharp declines in stock prices, financial sector turbulence, interest rate cuts and large-scale fiscal stimulus packages. Unlike the response to the 2008 crisis, which involved liquidity and solvency-related policy measures to get people spending again, the COVID-19 crisis did not start as a financial crisis, but could evolve into one if a recovery in economic activity is delayed. While larger firms may have sufficient financial reserves to wait out the crisis, many economic activities (such as restaurants and retail operations) work on very tight margins, which puts them in a position where they are unable to pay employees after closures lasting more than a few days. Many people will also need to balance childcare and work during quarantine or social distancing measures.

One key difference between the global financial crisis and the COVID-19 crisis is that the GFC was the result of an endogenous shock while the coronavirus crisis was produced by an exogenous shock. As an endogenous shock, the GFC originated from within the system. The troubles started in the US mortgage market as credit standards declined, and when those risks began to unwind, a massive credit crisis materialised. As a result, financial markets froze, liquidity dried up, and a painful recession ensued. An exogenous shock, on the other hand, originates from outside the system, like an asteroid hitting the planet and eliminating the dinosaurs. The coronavirus strike, like an asteroid strike, is an exogenous shock, leading to a public health crisis and consequently an economic crisis. Another difference is that the COVID crisis arose at a time when banks were in a better shape than they were in 2007 – or at least this is what we are led to believe, given that banks have been back in business as usual in the aftermath of the GFC.

The most important similarity is that the global financial crisis provided an opportunity to take drastic actions to correct the status quo, but that opportunity was wasted. The COVID-19 crisis is providing yet another opportunity to change the status quo. Whether or not this opportunity is taken is another question. Following a consideration of the response to the crisis in Chapter 4, four chapters are devoted to what can be done to change the status quo by taking the opportunity provided by the COVID-19 crisis. In Chapter 10, we will re-examine the proposition that the COVID-19 crisis was caused by an exogenous shock.

4. Public policy response to the pandemic

4.1 INTRODUCTION

COVID-19 has evolved into a global public health and economic crisis that has affected the $90 trillion world economy beyond anything experienced for a very long time. The public policy response requires the balancing of competing objectives involving public health and the economy. These objectives include, *inter alia*: (i) financing huge budget deficits caused by increasing spending to support unemployed workers and social safety nets; (ii) providing financial support for strained national healthcare systems; and (iii) implementing fiscal and monetary policies that support economic activity, while also assisting businesses experiencing financial distress. As the economic effects of the pandemic become increasingly conspicuous, policy-makers are giving more weight to policies that address the immediate economic effects at the expense of long-term considerations such as debt accumulation. The response covers public health, macroeconomic and financial market issues that are addressed through a combination of monetary, fiscal and other policies, including border closures, quarantines and restrictions on social interaction.

In response to growing concerns over the global economic impact of the pandemic, the G-7 finance ministers and central bankers released a statement on 3 March 2020, indicating that they would 'use all appropriate policy tools' to sustain economic growth (Long, 2020). The finance ministers also pledged fiscal support to ensure that healthcare systems can sustain efforts to fight the outbreak (Giles et al., 2020). In most cases, however, countries have pursued their own specific strategies, in some cases including banning the exports of medical equipment.

This chapter is about the response to the pandemic, starting with the public health response, which (in the absence of effective pharmaceutical treatments) takes the form of non-pharmaceutical intervention. It will be demonstrated that when interest rates are already low or negative, the macroeconomic response mostly takes the form of a fiscal response. Another important issue covered in this chapter is that of the policy dilemma represented by the choice between human and economic fatality.

4.2   THE PUBLIC HEALTH RESPONSE

In the absence of effective pharmaceutical treatments and vaccines, the public health authorities resort to the use of non-pharmaceutical intervention (NPI), which helps in two ways. The first is that reducing the transmission rate leads to lower levels of infections and deaths. The second is that NPI shifts the peak of the epidemiological curve further out in time, hoping that drugs and vaccines may be available. Ferguson et al. (2020) distinguish between a suppression policy and a mitigation policy. A suppression policy 'aims to reverse epidemic growth, reducing case numbers to low levels and maintaining that situation indefinitely' by restricting travel, closing schools, prohibiting gatherings, and so on. A mitigation policy, on the other hand, 'focuses on slowing but not necessarily stopping epidemic spread' – it is less intrusive on the freedom of movement and less costly to the economy. They present a cost–benefit analysis of extending a suppression policy to multiple weeks before eventually replacing it with a mitigation policy until pharmaceutical treatments become available.

As a result of the pandemic, the terms 'lockdown' and 'social distancing' have become household expressions. A lockdown is a requirement for people to stay where they are, usually due to specific risks to themselves or others if they can move freely. In a lockdown, only essential businesses are allowed to remain open. While a lockdown enforces social distancing, the latter can be followed by people voluntarily. Social distancing (also called physical distancing) is a set of non-pharmaceutical interventions or measures intended to prevent the spread of a contagious disease by maintaining a physical distance between people and reducing the number of times people come into close contact with each other. The Center for Disease Control and Prevention (CDC) describes social distancing as 'methods for reducing frequency and closeness of contact between people in order to decrease the risk of transmission of disease' (Kinlaw and Levine, 2007). During the COVID-19 pandemic, the CDC revised the definition of social distancing to the following: 'remaining out of congregate settings, avoiding mass gatherings, and maintaining distance (approximately six feet or two meters) from others when possible' (Pearce, 2020).

Social distancing requires people to keep a certain distance from others (the distance may differ from time to time and country to country) and avoiding large-group gatherings. It also means no hugs, no kisses and no handshakes. By reducing the probability that a given uninfected person will come into physical contact with an infected person, the transmission of the disease can be suppressed. Social distancing is used for the purpose of 'flattening the curve' – that is, preventing surges in illness that could overwhelm the healthcare system. Sometimes, distinction is made between 'physical distancing' and 'social distancing' on the grounds that while a physical distance is needed to reduce transmission, people can remain socially connected via technology (hence the rise of Zoom).

Social distancing, a public health practice that aims to prevent sick people from coming into close contact with healthy people in order to reduce opportunities for disease transmission, is most effective when the infectious disease spreads via droplet contact (coughing or sneezing), direct physical contact (including sexual contact), and indirect physical contact (for example, by touching a contaminated surface). In the case of airborne transmission, the use of masks is more effective than social distancing. The effectiveness of social distancing is compromised if the virus is transmitted primarily via contaminated water, food or insects.

Social distancing is implemented by taking actions including the following: (i) suspension of in-person classes and converting to remote online instruction; (ii) cancelling events, including sporting events, festivals and parades; (iii) encouraging or mandating flexible work options, such as working from home; (iv) cancelling large gatherings, including conferences; and (v) suspending religious services. These measures have 'side effects', including loneliness, reduced productivity and the loss of other benefits associated with human interaction. UNESCO (2020) identifies a large number of adverse consequences of school closure, including interrupted learning, poor nutrition, confusion and stress, gaps in childcare, high economic costs, unintended strain on healthcare systems, increased pressure on schools and school systems that remain open, rise in dropout rates, increased exposure to violence and exploitation, and social isolation.

The effectiveness of social distancing has been examined repeatedly. Islam et al. (2020) use a natural experiment to evaluate the association between physical distancing and the incidence of COVID-19 globally. They use the experiment to measure the incidence rate ratios (IRRs) of the pandemic before and after the implementation of physical distancing measures, including the closure of public transport, schools and workplaces, as well as restrictions on mass gatherings. The IRR is calculated by dividing the incidence rate among the exposed portion of the population by the incidence rate in the unexposed portion of the population. Their results show that social distancing is associated with reductions in the incidence of COVID-19 globally but no evidence is found for an additional effect of public transport closure when other distancing measures are in place. They also find that earlier implementation of lockdown is associated with a larger reduction in the incidence of COVID-19. Yang et al. (2020) present a model that is used to examine the effectiveness of social distancing in New York City. Their results show that social distancing reduced the number of infections by 72% and the number of deaths by 76% by the end of 2020. They conclude that social distancing for the entire population and the protection of the elderly in public facilities is the most effective control measure in reducing severe infections and mortality. The effectiveness of social distancing can be justified theoretically in that it reduces the reproduction rate (as shown in Chapter 3) and empirically (Moosa, 2020b).

Several terms are associated with social distancing and NPI in general. Isolation, which may be voluntary or compelled by the authorities, refers to the separation of a person or people known or reasonably believed to be infected or contagious from those who are not infected in order to prevent spread of the disease. Quarantine is intended to separate a person who is believed to have been exposed to a communicable disease but not yet symptomatic from others who have not been so exposed. A stay-at-home order (also known as a safer-at-home order or a movement control order) is intended to restrict movements of people by ordering them to stay at home except for essential workers. A curfew is an order specifying the time when people are required to return to and stay at home. A *cordon sanitaire* (French for 'sanitary cordon') is the restriction of movement of people into or out of a specific area, such as a community, region or country. Protective sequestration is a measure taken to protect a small, defined, and still-healthy population from a contagious disease, which is why it is sometimes referred to as 'reverse *cordon sanitaire*'.

4.3   THE FISCAL RESPONSE

In the US, several fiscal measures were adopted in response to the pandemic. On 5 March 2020, Congress appropriated $8.3 billion in emergency funding to support efforts to fight COVID-19. On 18 March 2020, President Trump signed the Families First COVID-19 Response Act to provide paid sick leave and free testing and expand food assistance and unemployment benefits. On 25 March 2020, the Senate adopted the COVID-19 Aid, Relief, and Economic Security (CARES) Act to provide direct payments to taxpayers, loans and guarantees to airlines and other industries, as well as assistance for small businesses. On 23 April 2020, the House passed the Paycheck Protection Program (PPP) and Health Care Enhancement Act, to provide $484 billion for small businesses, healthcare providers, and COVID-19 testing. Towards the end of 2020, a $900-billion stimulus package was approved. And on 11 March 2021, President Biden signed into law a $1.9 trillion Coronavirus Relief Bill.

Similar actions were taken in other countries. On 12 March 2020, the Australian government announced a $11.4 billion stimulus package that includes support for business investment, cash flow assistance for small and medium-sized business and employees, and household stimulus payments. On 30 March, the government announced a package of $79.85 billion to subsidise the wages of an estimated 6 million people. In Brazil, the government announced on 16 March a fiscal stimulus package of $28.6 billion to mitigate the impact of the pandemic and boost the economy. On 25 March the Canadian government doubled the value of an aid package previously announced to help people and businesses, whereby people affected by the pandemic would receive a monthly allowance. Other measures were taken, including delayed student loan repayments.

Similar steps were taken by European countries. On 17 March 2020, the French government announced that it would spend $50 billion to help small businesses and employees struggling with the outbreak, through an expanded partial-unemployment package in which the state pays the salaries of employees who are not needed during the crisis. In the UK, the government announced on 11 March 2020 a stimulus package of $39 billion to support the labour market, help the healthcare system and support the economy. Among the specific measures were a tax cut for retailers, cash grants to small businesses, a mandate to provide sick pay for people who need to self-isolate, subsidies to cover the costs of sick pay for small businesses, and expanded access to government benefits for the self-employed and unemployed. On 17 March the British government unveiled a package of $424 billion to provide guaranteed loans for businesses that need cash to pay rent or suppliers and to cover tax cuts and grants for businesses, a three-month mortgage payment holiday for borrowers affected by the virus, and a one-year 'business rates' holiday for businesses in the retail, leisure and hospitality industry.

While these measures are appropriate and commendable, a question remains on financing, bearing in mind that a government can finance spending by borrowing, taxation and 'printing' money. It seems that most governments chose the most dangerous means of financing, which is 'printing' money, a policy that is bound to have inflationary consequences. In Figure 4.1 we can see that the growth of the US monetary base accelerated during the pandemic, which resembles what happened during the global financial crisis. Between February and December 2020, the monetary base rose by 51%. The same pattern can be seen in other countries.

If money printing is not the ideal means of financing the fiscal stimulus, what is the alternative? Well, there are at least three other alternatives, but they are politically unacceptable in countries run by governments holding neoliberalism as an ideology and looking after the oligarchy as opposed to the majority of the people. The first is redirection of public spending away from financing military adventures to where it is needed by the majority of people. The US spends one trillion dollars a year on the military (the majority of discretionary spending) when defence of the nation can be achieved effectively with one-fifth of this amount. Australia does not need submarines to send to the South China Sea and warplanes to bomb villages in Iraq and Afghanistan – the money can be used for more useful and socially desirable purposes. The

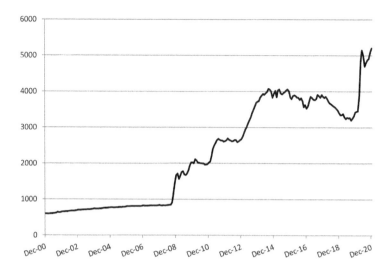

Figure 4.1   US monetary base ($ billion)

UK does not need new aircraft carriers, now that Britannia is no longer ruling the waves. European countries do not need to finance the operations of NATO near the Russian border.

The second means of financing is taxation, more specifically taxing the income and wealth of the super-rich. Following the Port Arthur massacre of April 1996, the Australian government initiated the 'National Firearms Buyback Program', which ran from October 1996 to September 1997, and led to the retrieval of 650,000 guns. The program, which cost $304 million in compensation and $63 million in administration, was financed through taxation, by raising the Medicare levy from 1.5% to 1.7%. Why can't governments do the same now by taxing the super-rich? Most of the billionaires will be as well off as they were before the advent of the pandemic even if they pay a one-off wealth tax of 30%. Dealing more firmly with tax evasion by the rich will bring about billions of dollars in tax revenue.

This is why the proposal put forward by Senator Elizabeth Warren to impose a wealth tax on those with net worths of more than $50 million is both timely and sensible (for example, Stankiewicz, 2021). According to this proposal, an annual tax of 2% (or 2 cents) will be levied on every dollar above $50 million and 3% (or 3 cents) on every dollar above $1 billion. This means that the first $50 million is tax exempt, implying that this tax will only affect marginally 0.1% of the US population. This is not as outrageous as it is portrayed to be by the 0.1% and their lobbyists and advocates who believe (or pretend to believe) in the trickle-down effect. The tax will generate revenue that can be used to finance the budget deficit without causing any financial pain for the 0.1%. This is more sensible than the already existing wealth tax imposed on the family homes of the middle class and those who own homes but live on pay-cheque-by-pay-cheque budgets. Senator Warren is right in saying that 'most Americans won't mind being rich enough to pay it' and that 'most people would rather be rich and pay 2 or 3 cents' (Stankiewicz, 2021).

The third alternative is to take land and natural resources under public ownership – that is, by nationalising the mining sector. This idea can be traced back to Thomas Paine who in 1780 published a pamphlet entitled *Public Good* in which he made the case that territories west of the 13 colonies that had been part of the British Empire belonged after the Declaration of Independence to the American government, and did not belong to any of the 13 states or to any individual speculators (Paine, 2018). A royal charter of 1609 had granted the Virginia Company land stretching to the Pacific Ocean. A small group of wealthy Virginia land speculators had taken advantage of this royal charter to claim title to huge swathes of land, including much land west of the 13 colonies. Paine argued that these lands belonged to the American government as represented by the Continental Congress, which made his wealthy Virginia friends rather angry (including George Washington, Thomas Jefferson and James Madison, all of whom had claimed huge wild tracts that, according to Paine, should have been government-owned).

Like Paine, it is beyond me why natural resources, which are supposed to be owned by the people of their country of citizenship, are given to individuals and corporate interests for them to extract and sell the resources for private profit without paying taxes. This means of financing will be suitable for a resource-rich country like Australia, but this is unlikely to happen. When a particular prime minister came up with the idea of imposing a mining tax (let alone nationalising the mining sector), he was promptly deposed and replaced with his deputy in effectively a *coup d'état* (just imagine the outcry if something like this happens in Africa). The power of the oligarchy will prevent something like this from happening, while free marketeers and right-wing politicians will call this 'socialism', which is a dirty word for them.

Another important point to make here is that public support programmes may involve corruption, favouritism and cronyism, which is why some money goes to people and companies that do not need it. In an article published in the *American Conservative* in July 2020, the author says 'you wouldn't believe who got a small business loan' (Bufalino, 2020). The author claims that 'the swamp in Washington is funneling PPP (Paycheck Protection Program) funds to billionaires, country clubs, lobbyists, political allies, Wall Street, and big business'. The PPP was intended to provide relief to small businesses (with 500 or fewer employees) hurt by COVID-19 in order for them to retain and pay their employees. Yet, the beneficiaries include Wall Street firms, elite law firms (45 law firms received at least $210 million in PPP loans), members of Congress (through firms owned by them), allies to President Trump (including a Kushner family real estate project and conservative media organisations), the Church of Scientology (worth more than $1.2 billion), foreign firms (such as Korea Air), and billionaires (including the owner of a shoe and fashion company that is valued at over $3 billion).

4.4   THE MONETARY RESPONSE

The monetary response to the pandemic has taken the form of reducing interest rates and the provision of liquidity via quantitative easing. In the US, the Fed resumed the so-called 'forward guidance', which refers to public communications on future plans for short-term interest rates, a practice that was initiated following the 2008 financial crisis. As monetary policy returned to normal in recent years (with the abandonment of QE) forward guidance was phased out, but the pandemic brought it back. When the Fed reduced short-term interest rates to zero on 15 March 2000, it announced that it 'expects to maintain this target range until it is confident that the economy has weathered recent events and is on track to achieve its maximum employment and price stability goals' (Congressional Research Service, 2021). Figure 4.2 displays the US discount rate, which was brought down by the monetary response to the pandemic, thus halting progress towards the return to normal monetary policy whereby the discount rate was raised gradually.

The return to QE was signalled on 23 March 2020, when the Fed announced that it would boost its purchases of Treasury securities and mortgage-backed securities issued by government agencies or government-sponsored enterprises to 'the amounts needed to support smooth market functioning and effective transmission of monetary policy' (Congressional Research Service, 2021). During the week of 23 March, QE was undertaken at the unprecedented rate of up to $125 billion daily. As a result, the value of the Fed's balance sheet is projected to exceed its post-financial crisis peak of $4.5 trillion. The operation is simply buying assets using money created out of thin air. One notable difference from previous rounds of QE is that the Fed is purchasing securities of different maturities, so that the effect likely would not be concentrated on long-term rates.

Reducing interest rates towards zero, and perhaps negative territory, has become a hobby of central banks around the world on the grounds that low interest rates boost the economy, which is nonsense. In the UK, similar actions were taken. On 11 March 2020, the Bank of England cut its benchmark interest rate by half a percentage point to 0.25%, and on 19 March, the benchmark rate was cut by 15 basis points to 0.1%. On the same day, the Bank of England

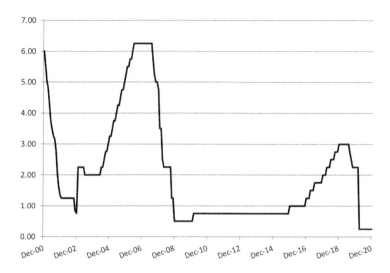

Figure 4.2   US discount rate (%)

added 200 billion pounds to its asset purchase programme (including sovereign and private debt). On 2 April, the size of the corporate bond purchase
programme was doubled. In New Zealand, the Reserve Bank cut the official
cash rate by 75 basis points on 16 March to a record low of 0.25%, and pledged
to keep it at this level for at least 12 months. On 22 March, the Reserve Bank
announced that it would purchase up to $17 billion of government bonds in the
secondary market over the following 12 months. On 12 March, the European
Central Bank announced that it would provide banks with loans at −0.75%,
below the −0.5% deposit rate, and that it would increase bond purchases by
120 billion euros (with a focus on corporate debt). On 3 March, the Reserve
Bank of Australia cut the cash rate by 25 basis points to 0.5% and on 19 March
the cash rate was cut again by 25 basis points to 0.25%. Simultaneously, the
Bank targeted the 3-year government bond yield at 0.25% via purchases in the
secondary market.

One would think that these central banks have high calibre economists
who design sound policy, but what kind of economist believes that in the
midst of a recession households and firms borrow and buy consumer durables
and invest in production facilities, only because interest rates are low? No
low interest rate will convince a potential entrepreneur to borrow and open
a restaurant when tens of thousands of restaurants are closing down. No low
interest rate will convince a person to borrow and buy a new car when this

person has already lost their job or they anticipate a job loss. No low interest rate will convince an airline to borrow and buy new planes when their fleets are grounded. No low interest rate will make the virus go away. No interest rate cut will correct supply-side disruptions. And no interest rate cut will persuade local officials not to close schools, businesses not to cancel conferences, and manufacturers to reopen their plants when they are unable to source parts from suppliers.

The fact of the matter is that investment in real capital formation is not interest rate-sensitive but rather expected return-sensitive. The decision to invest depends on the expected rate of return, not the cost of borrowing. It is either that central banks do not realise this simple fact or that something more sinister motivates the low interest rate policy, which was initiated before the advent of the pandemic, in the process punishing pensioners and risk-averse investors while fuelling asset price bubbles. It seems that the pandemic has been used as an excuse to reduce interest rates even further for the benefits of banks, the oligarchy and corporate interests.

4.5   THE POLICY DILEMMA: HUMAN VERSUS ECONOMIC FATALITY

The public health response to COVID-19 entails huge economic cost in terms of output and employment. The longer the duration of the lockdown, the greater will be the resulting economic cost. On the other hand, relaxing lockdown measures too soon could produce an escalation of infection and death and perhaps a second full-fledged wave and another period of lockdown. This has actually happened in Europe and is likely to happen in Texas as the governor announced that the state will reopen full throttle in early March 2021. Two questions arise here: (i) how do we value human against economic fatality, given that the two are not independent; and (ii) what is the optimal duration of a lockdown? Additional questions are the following: how much of the economic downturn will be driven by shutdowns as opposed to the virus-induced changes in consumer and producer behaviour? What is the net consequence of a lockdown for economic welfare? What factors determine the optimal length of a lockdown? What are the alternatives (if any) to lockdowns that could achieve equivalent or higher benefits at a lower total cost?

Divergent views have emerged on the choice between the resumption of economic activity and continuing a lockdown. On 2 March 2021, the Governor of Texas, Greg Abbott, announced that all businesses would be allowed to reopen at full capacity and that he was rescinding the state-wide mask mandate as of 10 March. The governor said that 'it is now time to open Texas 100%', that 'everybody that wants to work should have that opportunity' and that 'every business that wants to open, should be open' (Homer and Benito,

2021). In response, Harris County Judge Lina Hidalgo said that the decision puts Texans at the risk of another surge. Fort Bend County Judge K.P. George joined the critics and urged residents to continue wearing masks and practising social distancing. The strongest criticism came from former Democratic presidential candidate Beto O'Rourke, who described the decision as a 'death warrant for Texas' and accused Abbott of 'killing the people of Texas' (Homer and Rouege, 2021). Likewise, President Biden criticised the governor of Texas (and the governor of Mississippi) for putting an end to the mask mandates and dropping restrictions on businesses, arguing that 'it's a big mistake' (Woodward, 2021). It remains to say that at the time of the controversy, Texas had the third-highest COVID death toll after California and New York, as more than 44,000 Texans had died from the disease.

This kind of disagreement is understandable because a lockdown brings health benefits for the society by containing the spread of the virus, reducing the number of infections and allowing the healthcare system to treat those infected (as well as those who require healthcare services that are unrelated to the epidemic). On the other hand, a lockdown hurts the economy, because it disrupts economic activity. Unfortunately, disagreement is sometimes based on ideology rather than science and sound economics, and no better example can be presented than that of the dispute between the Brazilian president, Bolsonaro, and state governors (for example, D. Phillips, 2020).

Several studies have been conducted to determine the optimal duration of a lockdown. Scherbina (2020) investigates the optimal duration of what she calls a 'suppression policy' and finds that it depends on the effectiveness of the policy in reducing the rate of transmission, which is measured by the reproduction rate it can achieve. For example, if the reproduction rate is one, the policy should be in place between 30 and 34 weeks. Alvarez et al. (2020) examine the optimal lockdown policy for a planner who wants to control the mortality rate of a pandemic while minimising the output cost of the lockdown by using the SIR epidemiological model and a linear economy to formalise the planner's dynamic control problem. They find that the intensity of the lockdown depends on the gradient of the mortality rate as a function of the infection rate and on the assumed value of a statistical life. Rawson et al. (2020) apply an optimal control framework to a SEIR model to investigate the efficacy of two potential lockdown release strategies. They find that the optimal strategy is to release approximately half the population 2–4 weeks from the end of an initial infection peak, then wait another 3–4 months to allow for a second peak before releasing everyone else. Gonzalez-Eiras and Niepelt (2020) embed a lockdown choice in a simplified epidemiological model and derive formulae for the optimal lockdown intensity and duration. In this formulation, the optimal policy reflects the rate of time preference, epidemiological factors, the hazard rate of vaccine discovery, learning effects in the healthcare sector, and the severity of output losses due to lockdown.

Some authors dismiss the perception of a trade-off between public health and the economy, between saving lives and saving the economy. Smithson (2020) argues that 'no one should be misled into believing there is zero-sum choice between saving lives and saving the economy', which he describes as a 'false dichotomy'. This conclusion is reached by examining, on a bilateral basis, the relation between infection and mortality rates and economic indicators, including GDP per capita (which he wrongly describes as an 'index of national wealth'), exports, imports and private consumption. The analysis looks more like casual empiricism, with some confusion over the direction of causation. For example, Vlandas (2020) argues that causation is bidirectional because health issues undermine growth whereas economic decline generates health problems. This principle is well established in health economics.

Likewise, Hasell (2020) questions the 'assumption' that countries face a trade-off between public health and the economy. By comparing mortality rates with GDP growth rates, he finds the opposite: countries that have managed to protect public health in the pandemic have generally also protected the economy. He concludes as follows:

> Contrary to the idea of a trade-off, we see that countries which suffered the most severe economic downturns – like Peru, Spain and the UK – are generally among the countries with the highest COVID-19 death rate. And the reverse is also true: countries where the economic impact has been modest – like Taiwan, South Korea, and Lithuania – have also managed to keep the death rate low.

The underlying idea is that lockdown causes economic losses but saves lives, which means that high growth should be associated with high mortality rate. Thus, low growth resulting from lockdown should be associated with low mortality rate. However, and as we have seen before, mortality and infection rates are caused by a variety of factors, in which case trying to relate these rates to one factor only, the duration of lockdown, is not a true reflection of reality and casual empiricism at its worst.

Some politicians seem to believe in the trade-off proposition while others do not. There are those who believe that the economic cost of an ongoing lockdown outweighs the risk to lives that a resurgent epidemic might pose. For example, Donald Trump once cautioned that 'we can't have the cure be worse than the disease'. On the other hand, when the British government extended its lockdown in late April 2020, that action was justified on the grounds of saving lives and livelihoods, in the sense that extending the lockdown would reduce the probability of a second wave that would prove even more economically devastating (J. Khan, 2020). While most economists believe that an extended lockdown saves lives, and that it is better for the economy in the long run, this belief is based on the assumptions built into the underlying models. Some of these assumptions may be unrealistic, such as the ability of the government to monitor infection rates accurately and the rules governing the behaviour of workers and consumers.

On the other extreme, a minority of economists believe that any lockdown is a mistake because it devastates the economy in exchange for very little long-run benefit in terms of lives saved. Instead, they suggest that a more limited set of social distancing policies, such as those pursued in Sweden, is closer to the ideal policy. These economists believe that lockdowns only suppress an epidemic but the virus is likely to come back once they are lifted, which is why they wonder whether severe restrictions are actually worth the economic damage they cause. For example, Alexis Toda, an economist at the University of California San Diego, is quoted by J. Khan (2020) as saying: 'People might think I'm crazy, but I am thinking through models and playing with these models and I always come to the same conclusion: that the current lockdown policies in most countries are probably wrong'.

The fact of the matter is that there is no definite answer to the question of how long a lockdown should be because economists are still learning about this situation. J. Khan (2020) quotes Emanuel Ornelas, a professor at the Sao Paolo School of Economics, as saying that 'most economists have only in the past six weeks started to learn about epidemiological models and how to incorporate them into their own economic forecasts'. However, a lesson that we have learned is that countries that lift restrictions prematurely almost always face a second wave of infections, because the restrictions do not reduce the infection rate to levels where it dies out completely. Eichenbaum et al. (2020) conclude that an early end to containment policies initially brings about a big economic boost, but this boost results in a jump in infections that soon plunges the economy into 'a second, persistent recession'. They also conclude that 'prematurely abandoning containment brings about a temporary rise in consumption but no long-lasting economic benefits' and that 'tragically, abandonment leads to a substantial rise in the total number of deaths caused by the epidemic'. Furthermore, if infections come surging back, requiring the reimposition of social distancing, a recessionary effect will arise because the public refuses to trust the government that it is actually safe to go back to work. Gros et al. (2020) describe as a 'non-trivial outcome of [their] study' the proposition that 'strong suppression strategies lead to lower total costs … when containment efforts are not relaxed with falling infection rates'. They also note that 'a short-term control approach of softening containment with falling numbers of new cases is likely to lead to a prolonged endemic period', which means that illness, and its attendant economic pain, will continue.

Like anything else in public policy, the optimal duration of lockdown should be considered in terms of costs and benefits, which tend to be time-varying. At the peak of an epidemic, stopping human interaction brings about a very large health benefit, as it halts contagion (completely, in the case of a perfect enforcement) and prevents additional pressure on an overloaded healthcare system. After the lockdown has been put in place for a while, however, these benefits fall as the health situation becomes more manageable. This means that the marginal health benefit (*MHB*) of lockdown is a negative function of the duration of the lockdown. On the other hand, the economic cost of lockdown rises over time, which means that a lengthy lockdown imposes increasing costs on the society, as firms go bankrupt, workers are laid off and, ultimately, consumption levels (and welfare) drop sharply. This means that the marginal economic cost (*MEC*) of lockdown increases with its duration. The duration of lockdown should be determined by the intersection of the *MHB* and *MEC* curves as shown in Figure 4.3. In this case, the optimal duration that satisfies the condition *MHB* = *MEC* is 11 time periods.

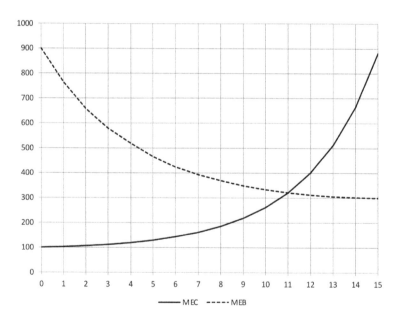

Figure 4.3   Determination of optimal lockdown duration

Ornelas (2020) uses this approach to arrive at three conclusions. The first is that a full (or near-full) lockdown is better at the peak of an epidemic than nothing in countries that were unprepared for it. The second conclusion is that the activities to be suspended should be ordered from those that yield higher health benefits and impose lower economic costs to those that have the opposite effects. The third is that the optimal duration of lockdown changes over time and eventually declines, but it does not drop to zero quickly. Unlike those who do not believe in a trade-off, Ornelas talks about managing the health–economics trade-off over time. It is a matter of costs and benefits.

4.6   CONCLUDING REMARKS

The containment of a pandemic requires a swift response from the government. A pandemic arising from a new virus is unknown territory for policy-makers, giving rise to considerable uncertainty that surrounds the appropriateness of responses and outcomes. Since a pandemic has negative effects on public health, the capacity of the healthcare system and economic prosperity, the response should cover public health and the economy. Thus a response encompasses non-pharmaceutical intervention, a fiscal expansion and a monetary expansion. Given that interest rates are at a record low, any monetary action is impotent, even though it creates asset price bubbles or maintains already existing bubbles. While the fiscal response is effective, concern is warranted about the mode of financing, as governments go for modes that are more politically acceptable but more damaging in the long run, including borrowing and (even worse) monetising the deficit by creating money out of thin air.

The response to the health crisis requires a delicate balancing act to manage a serious public health crisis without causing economic and social devastation. Dealing with COVID-19 is as much an economic challenge as a health challenge. This is why the authorities have to make some difficult choices. For example, should the public health response take the form of suppression or elimination? An elimination strategy involves maximum action intended to exclude the disease and eliminate community transmission – that was the choice in China, Taiwan and New Zealand. A suppression strategy, on the other hand, is intended to reduce case numbers substantially, as in most European countries. These are, however, not the only choices: the alternatives include an exclusion strategy, a mitigation strategy and no strategy. An exclusion strategy involves maximum action to exclude the disease. A mitigation strategy involves action taken to flatten the curve (and lower the peak) to avoid overwhelming the healthcare system. Naturally, when no strategy is chosen, the pandemic will be beyond control. These strategies have varying economic costs, in which case the choice must involve value judgement and a consideration of costs and benefits. Denying the trade-off between public health and the economy does not serve any meaningful purpose and can be very dangerous.

In March 2021, the producer price index in the US rose 1%, higher than the 0.5% rise expected by the *Wall Street Journal*, which means that the PPI rose by 4.2% year over year (Robb, 2021). This may be an indication that the inflationary effect of quantitative easing is emerging at last, particularly in the presence of supply bottlenecks and resurging demand. If inflationary pressure persists, the Fed can follow one of two courses of action: putting an end to the lunacy of zero and negative interest rates or refraining from telling the truth about inflation, which governments do all the time. I hope that the Fed will take the right decision of reversing the direction of interest rates and that the rest of the world will follow. We will have to wait and see.

5. Implications for democracy, militarism and international relations

5.1 DEMOCRACY AND HUMAN RIGHTS

The COVID-19 pandemic has not only affected public health and the economy, but also democracy. As the world took emergency measures to address the crisis, concerns began to emerge that some governments might take advantage of the situation to roll back civil liberties and human rights, moving towards authoritarianism, and using the health crisis as an excuse to do that. Governments tend to use crises to pass laws that would not pass otherwise. The best example is the notorious Patriot Act, which curtailed human rights and civil liberties in the US under the pretext of the 'war on terror'. In any case, democracy has long been under stress, with the rise of home-grown populist and nationalist movements. The pandemic has led to the closure and transformation of parliaments and enabled governments to rule by decree. We have repeatedly seen examples of the curtailment of the fundamental democratic rights to assemble and protest while granting the police more powers to crack down on dissent (look no further than the democracies of the UK and France).

Democracy and human rights have deteriorated in 80 countries as governments responded to the pandemic by engaging in abuse of power, silencing critics, and weakening or shuttering important institutions, often undermining the very systems of accountability needed to protect public health. This assertion is made by Repucci and Slipowitz (2020) on the basis of a survey of 398 journalists, civil society workers, activists and other experts, as well as research on 192 countries conducted by Freedom House's global network of analysts. The results strongly support the proposition that the COVID-19 pandemic is exacerbating the 14 years of consecutive decline in freedom. The problem is particularly acute in struggling democracies and highly repressive states – in other words, settings that already had weak safeguards against abuse of power are suffering the most. The findings, they suggest, 'illustrate the breadth and depth of the assault on democracy'.

As countries around the world went into lockdown, 32 leading scholars working on different aspects of democracy were asked by Afsahi et al. (2020) what they thought of how the pandemic had impacted democracy. The scholars present five insights about the prospects and challenges of enacting democracy, both during and after the pandemic: (i) COVID-19 has had corrosive effects on already endangered democratic institutions, (ii) the pandemic has revealed alternative possibilities for democratic politics in the state of emergency, (iii) it has amplified inequalities and injustices within democracies, (iv) it has demonstrated the need for institutional infrastructure for prolonged solidarity, and (v) it has highlighted the predominance of the nation-state and its limitations. Collectively, these insights open up important normative and practical questions about what democracy should look like in the face of an emergency. On 16 March 2020, the UN Office of the High Commissioner on Human Rights (2020) published a statement advising governments to respond to the pandemic responsibly, voicing concerns regarding possible violations of human rights within the measures undertaken to slow the spread of this virus.

Governments are responsible for protecting their citizens and ensuring their health and safety. In extreme situations, this protection may include a temporary suspension or limiting of civil liberties for the sake of public health. However, these measures must meet a number of criteria in order to be credible and acceptable. They should be limited in scope and duration, have general applicability (that is, not limited to certain segments of the population), be based on legal norms, be proportionate to the situation, respect human dignity, and be subject to review. Unfortunately, a number of countries have taken advantage of the health crisis to implement draconian measures under the pretext of protecting public health. According to Diamond (2020), 'authoritarian regimes in Bangladesh, Belarus, Cambodia, China, Egypt, El Salvador, Syria, Thailand, Turkey, Uganda, Venezuela, and Vietnam have all detained critics, health workers, journalists, and opposition members during the pandemic'. The Philippine President, Rodrigo Duterte, pushed a bill through parliament in March 2020 granting him emergency powers to reallocate the country's budget and direct its hospitals. Even within the European Union, Hungary's Prime Minister, Viktor Orban, succeeded in obtaining the authority to suspend and issue laws and arrest critics of the government's handling of the pandemic. A proposed law in Brazil, intended to counter 'fake news' about the pandemic, threatens to stifle free expression and invade privacy.

Also in Brazil, the Bolsonaro government has, according to Human Rights Watch (2021), 'promoted anti-rights policies on women's rights and disability rights, has lashed out at reporters and civil society groups, and has weakened environmental law enforcement, effectively giving a green light to criminal networks that engage in illegal deforestation in the Amazon and threaten and attack forest defenders'. This came at a time when Bolsonaro was putting the lives and health of Brazilians at great risk by trying to sabotage efforts to halt the spread of COVID-19. The Director of Human Rights Watch, Kenneth Roth, argues that the Biden administration should 'embed respect for human rights in its domestic and foreign policy, in a way that is more likely to survive future US administrations that might be less committed to human rights'. In March 2021, as Brazil's death toll from the COVID-19 pandemic was approaching 275,000, it was revealed that the Biden administration pressured Bolsonaro not to buy the Sputnik V vaccine which, according to McEvoy (2021), may have cost 'many thousands of lives' – this in itself is a violation of human rights.

We have to entertain the possibility that the pandemic may lead to a reduction of individual rights after the end of the crisis. This is likely to happen because some exceptional measures taken to deal with an emergency might eventually fall within the scope of ordinary legislation. A good excuse would be that the pandemic may resurface if conditions are relaxed. The Patriot Act, introduced by using terrorism as an excuse, is an example of a piece of legislation that has infringed on civil liberties in the US by allowing security agencies to spy on citizens without due process. In France, after the 2015 Paris terrorist attacks, an anti-terrorism law reduced civil liberties by curtailing judicial oversight of security tools. It seems that the normalisation of emergency measures has become a trend in democracies, reflecting changes in the value assigned to freedom. Under a real or imaginary threat, people become more disposed to give up some of their constitutional rights (freedom versus safety). In Australia, more than 200 community groups have backed a report calling on the Australian government to strengthen its commitment to human rights amid the pandemic. The report, which was prepared ahead of a United Nations Human Rights Council review of Australia, said that the pandemic was likely to exacerbate existing human rights problems across the country (Michael, 2020).

Vardi (2020), who argues that crises have been exploited to introduce dangerous policies, identifies three areas of concern: (i) criminalising dissent, (ii) expanding legislative authorities by declaring states of emergency, and (iii) increasing technological surveillance. Democratic countries are increasingly giving more power to the police and border security personnel. In Australia, the border security personnel are notoriously aggressive and intrusive, but the pandemic has provided an opportunity to give them even more powers, which has been on the wish-list of Peter Dutton, the Minister for Home Affairs, for some time. In France, a controversial law preventing people from taking photos of the police, even if they are committing a criminal act, triggered massive demonstration. In Britain, hundreds gathered at Bristol's College Green on 21 March 2021 to demonstrate against plans to give police more powers to shut down peaceful protests. Some of the demonstrators carried placards saying 'Say no to UK Police State' and 'Freedom to Protest is Fundamental to Democracy' and 'Kill the Bill' (Skopeliti, 2021). As usual, governments always do what they like, even in a democracy. The pandemic has been convenient for this purpose.

5.2   COVID-19 AS A JUSTIFICATION FOR MASS SURVEILLANCE

The pandemic has made mass surveillance justifiable on the grounds of public health. The techniques used for surveillance include phone monitoring, contact tracing apps, and physical surveillance such as CCTV with facial recognition. As usual, these are supposed to be temporary measures that will be dismantled when the virus has gone, but (again) governments are known to introduce abusive measures in exceptional times but exceptional times go on for ever.

Contact tracing is a monitoring process in which an infected individual identifies all other individuals with whom they may have been in contact. Once they have been identified, those contacts are informed, monitored, and sometimes instructed to self-isolate or quarantine. Traditionally, contact tracing relied on skilled workers who interview infected individuals to learn about their activities and the people they encountered after becoming ill, and then monitor those contacts for illness. In the age of the mobile phone, skilled workers are not required. According to Ferretti et al. (2020) COVID-19 spreads too quickly and asymptomatically to be controllable through traditional contact tracing methods. To alleviate the need for long-term mass social distancing, they argue that communities will need to deploy 'instant digital contact tracing'.

Naturally, governments tend to highlight the advantages of the modern version of contact tracing but ignore the disadvantages and side effects. Ram and Gray (2020) argue that 'despite the public health benefits touted by proponents, it is not clear that digital contact tracing can achieve its lavish claims, nor is it evident that it can do so without imposing disproportionate privacy harms'. For example, they suggest that current technological limitations, as well as limitations in testing and support for quarantining identified contacts, undermine the efficacy of digital contact tracing that the proponents take for granted. As for privacy, digital contact tracing efforts already raise a significant cause for concern. These mass surveillance programmes reveal location data indiscriminately. Although they are defended on the grounds of emergency and the urgent need to manage the health crisis, experience reveals the potential for abuse.

The techniques of digital contact tracing differ from one country to another. In China, the government requires residents to download a smartphone app that tracks their movements and assigns them a colour (red, yellow or green) corresponding to their asserted public health risk. These colour codes regulate access to subways, malls and other public venues. No one knows how the colour is assigned, and the app 'appears to share information with the police, setting a template for new forms of automated social control that could persist long after the epidemic subsides' (Mozur et al., 2020). In South

Korea, the government reportedly pushes cell phone alerts about infected individuals, sending detailed information, including 'credit-card history, with a minute-to-minute record of their comings and goings from various local businesses' (Thompson, 2020b). In Singapore, citizens are required to download an app, TraceTogether, which records when it comes into contact with other phones that use the app. Israel has hastily repurposed mass location data secretly collected for counterterrorism purposes to track potentially infected individuals wherever they go (Halbfinger et al., 2020). The US government is already tapping bulk mobile phone location data, including tracking the 'presence and movement of people in certain areas of geographic interest' (Tau, 2020). Google analyses location data from its app users' devices to generate 'COVID-19 Community Mobility Reports' for every county in the US. These reports 'chart movement trends over time by geography, across different categories of places such as retail and recreation, groceries and pharmacies, parks, transit stations, workplaces, and residential' (Google, 2020).

Physical surveillance may be carried out by using CCTV with facial recognition. In Moscow, the government is using the city's CCTV network of 170,000 cameras to monitor people with facial-recognition software and punish those who do not comply with quarantine and self-isolation restrictions. This approach, which has also been used in China, cannot be circumvented by leaving phones at home, and it has been given a public-relations boost by the pandemic. In one week in March 2020, Moscow police claimed to have caught and fined 200 people who violated quarantine and self-isolation using facial recognition. According to a Russian media report, some of the alleged violators who were fined had been outside for less than half a minute before they were picked up by a camera (Ilyushina, 2020). On that occasion, Oleg Baranov, Moscow's police chief, said the following: 'we want there to be even more cameras so that that there is no dark corner or side street left', adding that work is underway to install 9,000 more cameras. This is a big investment that will not be wasted when the virus has gone. Mass surveillance, Moscow style, will continue – otherwise, the installation of all of these cameras would be a waste of money.

A question in search of an answer is the following: what happens once the pandemic is over? Many are concerned that the extraordinary measures taken to fight the pandemic will become permanent and used for other purposes, further aggravating threats to privacy, political and civil rights. The adoption of more surveillance technologies is always risky because, as the expression goes, 'when one door opens, it hardly closes again'. As Edward Snowden argued in his recent interview with *Vice*, once we abdicate certain civil liberties due to an emergency, it might be hard to get them back or at least fully back (Dowd, 2020). While it is difficult to argue against heightened surveillance in the middle of a deadly pandemic, the risk is that once mass surveillance regimes are enabled, they are unlikely to be watered down (let alone removed) because they will have been legitimatised as useful and necessary for public good. History demonstrates vividly that surveillance powers claimed on emergency grounds are likely to remain after the emergency has passed because they are useful tools of social control targeted against individuals and groups listed in the bad books of the authorities.

5.3   THE RISE OF FASCISM

Fascism is a political system based on a very powerful leader, state control of social and economic life, and extreme pride in country and race, with no expression of political disagreement allowed. Tait (2020) describes fascism as a totalitarian government that emphasises ideologically based collective identity ('Western' values as Australian values), dictatorial leadership (ruling by decree) and the mass mobilisation of society for the 'nation's benefit'. This system involves suppression of dissent (underfunding the public broadcaster, arresting journalists to chill criticism and having a one media outlet monopoly as the spokesperson for the government), and an economy that is run for the benefit of corporate interest. Fascists use crises to make their power absolute by exploiting people's anxieties and fears. Following World War I, fascists in Italy exploited the perceived threat of socialism to gain support among the elite and middle class. A Staff Report of the Federal Reserve System found that high death tolls from the 1918 influenza pandemic helped the Nazis gain power in Germany and that the share of votes won by the Nazis was higher in regions with high death tolls (Taylor, 2020).

Right-wing populist governments have taken advantage of the panic generated by the COVID-19 pandemic to grab more power in Hungary and Poland, to give just two examples. The nationalist government in Hungary passed a law granting almost absolute discretionary authority to the prime minister, side-lining all parliamentary due process, and allowing him to rule by decree indefinitely. Under the law, he also has the power to punish anyone who spreads 'false information' (according to the government's own determination) with a sentence of up to five years behind bars. Tait (2020) warns that the slippery slope to a fascist state is gentle and paved with beguiling reassurances that this is only for the duration of the pandemic (like some loss of our democratic freedoms were only for the duration of the 'war of terror'). From an Australian perspective, he identifies, as sources of concern, the exclusion of the federal opposition, parliaments going into recess except for limited sittings, rule through delegated legislation by the federal government, a national COVID-19 coordination commission handpicked from the corporate sector by the Prime Minister to lead Australia's response, bids by the Home Affairs Minister to obtain more surveillance powers, and the failure of many within the media to criticise these developments. In Romania, the 2020 election was characterised by the emergence of the fascist Alliance for the Unity of Romanians (AUR) party, which took 9% of the vote (Tudora and Zamfir, 2020). This is an unknown political entity (founded in 2019) which as late as September 2020 polled less than 1%.

Similar developments have occurred in other countries. In Italy, both the League and Brothers of Italy (right wing parties) repeatedly associate illegal immigration with the spread of COVID-19 and accuse the government of applying a double standard in favour of immigrants that penalised Italian businesses and freedom of movement (De Maio, 2020). In India, the Epidemic Diseases Act of 1897 was invoked by Prime Minister Modi to allow for inspection and segregation to contain the pandemic. The Act implemented multiple medical surveillance measures like plague passports, exemption certificates, and even detentions. In Russia, new rules have been approved against fake news about the virus, which could be reflected in increased persecution of independent media, and similar measures have been taken in Serbia and Turkey. Tant (2020) argues that 'authoritarianism is again on the march in America and around the world today' and puts forward the sarcastic view that 'unless we guard our liberties and exercise our collective responsibilities, "the land of the free and the home of the brave" could become the land of the lockstep and the home of the craven'.

Dixon (2020) refers to what he calls the 'fascist emergency playbook', which describes what a fascist government would do to exert control over a country by using an emergency as an excuse. To start with, the crisis is used to restrict civil liberties and suspend public institutions, consolidate power, reduce institutional checks and balances, and curtail access to elections and other forms of participatory governance. Fear is very important, which is why fascist governments promote a sense of fear and individual helplessness to create a culture where people consent to the power of the state. Democratic institutions are replaced with autocratic institutions using the emergency as an excuse. Last, but not least, scapegoats are created for the emergency, including immigrants, people of colour, disabled people, and ethnic and religious minorities to distract public attention away from the failures of the state and the loss of civil liberties.

The term 'health fascism' is used by Creighton (2021) in reference to the sacrifice of basic individual rights to the 'greater health collective' without the slightest attempt at justification, amid fear-mongering propaganda and censorship. He makes a comparison between a 'selfish' person who 'wants to mind their own business and get on with life' and the 'caring' person who supports a police state and health fascism. The pandemic, according to Creighton, 'witnessed the most extraordinary attack on freedoms by democratic governments in modern history, making a mockery of such human rights acts and conventions'. What is important, however, is that the extraordinary, intrusive measures taken by governments and the extra powers given to the police and law-enforcement agencies do not become permanent, even though this is what governments aspire for.

5.4   NATIONALISM AND MILITARISM

One of the unfortunate consequences of the pandemic is that it has been used to glorify the military (as well as law enforcement and spy agencies) for its role in fighting the pandemic. The same thing happened in the aftermath of the 9/11 attacks, when 'Western' governments opened their wallets to the military and spy agencies to fight terrorists. The need for the army in the struggle against COVID-19 is justified by Kalkman (2020, p. 100) as follows:

> One main motivation for deploying armed forces in response to the COVID-19 outbreak is the fact that armed forces have specific capabilities that civilian health agencies lack (in sufficient quantity). The examples in the opening paragraph show that armed forces have specific expertise and slack resources that can crucially support and complement civilian response endeavours. Medical facilities and services are easily overwhelmed when a pandemic breaks out, while armed forces are capable of rapidly mobilizing significant (medical) resources and are comparatively well-organized to operate under conditions of uncertainty and stress.

Likewise, Chewning et al. (2020) are full of praise of the military:

> Having served in militaries and worked closely with them, we have a keen appreciation of the strengths of their leadership. We also recognize that the military culture is unique, characterized by a shared sense of mission, values, and standards; by unquestioning adherence to authority when required; and by extensive training and procedural practice. Even bearing these differences in mind, however, government and business leaders can learn lessons from the best military practices.

These arguments ring the bell: that the military do things better than civilians sounds similar to the claim that private-sector employees are smarter than public-sector employees. But then the military is a public enterprise, in which case (according to the free market argument) they cannot be better than the civilians working for the private sector. Yes, the military have slack resources because (in the name of 'national security') they are given more than what they can spend. And yes, the military culture is unique, characterised by a shared sense of mission, and this is why war crimes committed by the military in far-away, defenceless countries go largely unnoticed. What about the leadership shown by the military in Myanmar – do they have a unique culture as Chewning et al. claim? What about the military regimes that committed atrocities (by using a unique culture) in Chile and Argentina in the 1970s and 1980s? Perhaps only 'Western' militaries have a culture that makes them 'good guys', but what about the atrocities committed in Iraq and Afghanistan by the American, British and Australian militaries? I would love to find out what 'unique culture' they (those who proudly served in the military) are talking about. Compare what they say with what a decorated major general of the US Marine Corps, Smedley Butler, once said: 'I wouldn't go to war again as I have done to protect some lousy investment of the bankers' (Butler, 1933).

An implication of the pandemic is that this should be a wake-up call to work co-operatively to save humanity from massive global death and economic collapse rather than continue to devote $1.8 trillion a year to waging wars and engaging in vast military build-ups, in the process slaughtering people who cannot defend themselves in a brutal exercise of the 'West versus the Rest'. What is happening is exactly the opposite, even though the public purse is empty. Undeterred by the disastrous situation and mounting death toll, the British government announced in November 2020 the largest rise in the military budget since the Cold War, as the military were promised an additional £16.5 billion of taxpayers' money. On 16 March 2021, the British government announced that it would boost the stockpile of nuclear warheads in response to the 'deteriorating security environment' (Chuter, 2021). When will Boris Johnson realise that there are better ways to kill a virus (the enemy) than nuclear warheads?

It has been suggested by the Edmund Rice Centre (2020) that the Department of Defence (read Department of War or Department of Aggression) should be replaced with the Department of Actual Defence that is focused on human survival by addressing the collapsing ecosystem, poverty, physical and mental health, violence, inadequacy of public facilities, crime and safety. Instead of indoctrinating soldiers to hate the Chinese, Russians, North Koreans and Iranians (let alone the Iraqis, Afghans, Yemenis, Syrians, Libyans and Venezuelans) we should train pro-environment workers, disaster-relief workers and suicide-prevention workers in the tasks of protecting the environment, relieving disasters and preventing suicide, as opposed to preparing people to kill large numbers of the 'enemy'. The Edmund Rice Centre calls for disbanding the military, not redirecting it.

Unfortunately, it seems that there is a push in the US for new aggressive action against Iran, its proxy forces, and countries such as Venezuela, who are distracted by the pandemic. Under the cover of COVID-19, the US has escalated its military threats against other countries, ordering stepped-up action by its forces that risks war with Iran and, possibly, Venezuela. This is what Biden meant when he said 'America is back', and this is why he called Putin a 'killer' and started building coalitions (of the willing, of course) against China. Biden makes Trump look like a harmless dove.

COVID-19 appears to be strengthening authoritarian political tendencies, which go hand-in-hand with militarism. From an Australian perspective, the Edmund Rice Centre (2020) makes the following comment:

> The current pandemic provides the perfect cover in Australia for a covert way of doing things or not doing things that should be done. We could get into a war in the Persian Gulf, with no explanation. We can withdraw from a reliance on allies that have presented our Asian neighbours as threats for decades. We have an opportunity to assert our independence by reorienting our priorities by withdrawing our troops out of the Middle East, the Philippines, and the South China Sea. We could scrap the French submarine contract in lieu of offsetting the debt that will be faced for the COVID-19. We could put our efforts into saving lives, not destroying them. We could build up goodwill with our Asian and Pacific neighbours – something that more armaments cannot achieve.

One positive development under COVID is that military spending is undergoing increasing public scrutiny due to its direct contribution to the lack of financial resources available to governments for dealing with the pandemic. Acheson (2020) recommends the closure of foreign military bases (believed to cost American taxpayers from $25 billion to $150 billion per year) to divert more resources to fighting COVID-19, and he argues that 'bloated military budgets warrant serious critique and massive cuts'. This is why, even in the midst of a pandemic, governments step up the rhetoric about Russian aggression, Chinese military build-up, North Korean threat, Iranian meddling, etc.

A global rise of nationalism came with the pandemic as individuals and entire countries are starting to behave in very selfish ways. Asians faced racist attacks everywhere around the world in January and February 2020 (and these attacks are still going on). Around the same time, a truck filled with medical supplies was stopped at the German–Swiss border, after Chancellor Angela Merkel allegedly banned most exports of protective medical equipment. A diplomatic spat between Germany and its neighbours Austria and Switzerland ensued (Dahinten and Wabl, 2020). A further dispute erupted after President Trump attempted to persuade CureVac (a German biopharmaceutical company with a headquarter in Tübingen) to move from Germany to the US. This led to fears among the German government that the US was trying to get exclusive access to a possible treatment (Bennhold and Sanger, 2020).

The term 'vaccine nationalism' has emerged in reference to actions taken by governments that sign agreements with pharmaceutical manufacturers to supply their own populations with vaccines before they become available for other countries. The World Health Organisation has expressed its concerns about vaccine nationalism, warning that unilateral deals with wealthy countries will make the vaccines inaccessible to those in some of the poorest parts of the world (Khan, 2021). Vaccine nationalism has led to vaccine wars

– for example, in March 2021, the EU threatened to stop sending vaccines to countries (mainly the UK) that were not selling vaccines in return (Colchester and Norman, 2021). As part of the new Cold War, the Biden administration is putting pressure on some countries (particularly in Latin America) not to use the Russian and Chinese vaccines.

5.5   THE WAR ON CASH

The war on cash is defined by Whitehead (2020) as a 'concerted campaign to shift consumers towards a digital mode of commerce that can easily be monitored, tracked, tabulated, mined for data, hacked, hijacked and confiscated when convenient'. Scott (2016) suggests that banks, governments, credit card companies and 'fintech evangelists' want us to believe that a cashless future is inevitable and good. He tells the following story:

> Several months ago I stayed in an offbeat Amsterdam hotel that brewed its own beer but refused to accept cash for it. Instead, they forced me to use the Visa payment card network to get my UK bank to transfer €4 to their Dutch bank via the elaborate international correspondent banking system.

The concern, according to Scott, is 'about a potential future world in which we'd have to report our every economic move to a bank, and the effect this could have on marginalised people'. A cashless society effectively means 'ask-your-banks-for-permission-to-pay society'. The justification is simple: criminals use cash, it fuels the shadow economy, it is unsafe, and it facilitates tax evasion. Scott (2016) debunks these arguments as follows:

> These arguments have notable shortcomings. Criminals use many things that we keep – like cars – and fighting crime doesn't take priority over maintaining other social goods like civil liberties. The 'shadow economy' is a derogatory term used by elites to describe the economic activities of people they neither understand nor care about. As for safety, having your wallet cash stolen pales in comparison to having your savings obliterated in a digital account hack. And if you care about tax justice, start with the mass corporate tax avoidance facilitated by the formal banking sector.

Lepecq (2020) quotes Yves Mersch, Member of the Executive Board of the ECB as saying:

> Advocates of a cashless society tend to fall into three distinct camps. The first camp, the alchemists, wants to overcome the restrictions that the zero lower bound (ZLB) imposes on monetary policy. The second, the law and order camp, wants to cancel the primary means of payment for illicit activities. And the third camp, the fintech (financial technology) alliance, anticipates major business opportunities arising from the elimination of the high storage, issuance, and handling costs of cash that the financial industry currently faces.

The war on cash has sometimes taken the form of outright attacks (such as when the Indian government aggressively degraded the Indian cash system during their so-called 'demonetisation'). More often, however, it has taken the form of consistent propaganda (Visa openly talks about their campaign to make cash seem 'peculiar' to people), amidst a drive to transform the environment in such a way as to make cash increasingly inconvenient to use (such as shutting down ATMs). More aggressively, some governments working for the interest of banks have been trying to introduce legislation against the use of cash. The Australian government, for example, was trying to push in legislation whereby anyone using more than $10,000 to settle a transaction would be put behind bars (yet another facet of fascism).

In reality, the war on cash is a component of an elaborate scheme put in place for the benefit of the banking oligarchy. This scheme involves, in addition to the war on cash, ultra-low or negative interest rates and the bail-in legislation whereby deposits can be confiscated to recapitalise failed banks and pay their CEOs bonuses and golden parachutes. A policy of ultra-low or negative interest rates is justified on the grounds that it is conducive to economic recovery when in fact it is a dangerous policy that encourages the accumulation of debt and maintains asset price bubbles (let alone that it does not work). The bottom line, however, is that such a policy enables banks to pay almost nothing to depositors (even charge them for the privilege) while still charging the most vulnerable 20% on credit cards.

Furthermore, non-cash transactions are convenient for a police state that indulges in mass surveillance. Forbes (2016) suggests that 'the real reason for this war on cash – start with the big bills and then work your way down – is an ugly power grab by Big Government'. Electronic transactions make it easier for Big Brother to see what we are doing, thereby making it simpler to bar activities it does not like. These activities, according to Forbes (2016), include 'purchasing salt, sugar, big bottles of soda and Big Macs'. By making cash transactions illegal, or convincing people not to use cash, the coalition of government and banking oligarchy benefit in different ways: more profit for banks and greater surveillance power for the government.

Dowd (2017) has written a devastating critique of the war on cash, which is pursued in the name of combating the underground economy, tax evasion and the Coronavirus. This is how he describes the situation:

> The abolition of cash threatens to destroy what is left of our privacy and our freedom: we wouldn't be able to buy a stick of gum without the government knowing about it and giving its approval. The cash abolitionists want total control over your money and what you can do with it. Besides making us all entirely dependent on the whim of the state, banning cash also threatens to cause widespread economic damage and have a devastating impact on the most vulnerable in our society. Quite simply, the government's war against cash is the state's war against us.

In what can be taken as an argument against abolishing cash transactions, Dowd lists the benefits of cash as follows: (i) it is a very efficient way of handling small transactions; (ii) it is costless and easy to use; (iii) cash transactions are immediate and flexible; (iv) cash is highly anonymous; (v) cash does not need a password; (vi) unlike a bank account, it cannot be hacked; (vii) it involves the state of the art in anti-counterfeiting technology, which makes it more difficult to replicate or corrupt than digital currency; and (viii) the usefulness of cash is not dependent on sophisticated technology that might break down. I am sure that some credit card lovers have switched to cash following mishaps such as the loss incurred as a result of producing a credit card in a crowded bar late at night, or the other mishap of finding oneself unable to pay a hotel bill in a foreign country because the credit card does not work.

The pandemic has been good for those who do not want to see cash anymore. There has been a trend towards the total exclusion of cash on the basis of hygiene, in part propagated by stories of cash being a dangerous trans-mitter of the virus, even though little evidence supports this claim. According to Grass (2020) 'the corona crisis has introduced a whole new direction for anti-cash rhetoric and fresh arguments in favor of a digital economy'. He goes on to say the following:

> Even in the early stages of the pandemic, when essentially nothing was concretely known about the virus or its transmission, the seeds of new fears were already being planted by sensational media reports and fear-mongering political and institutional figures. The insidious idea that 'you can catch COVID through cash' may have been prematurely spread, but it did stick in most people's minds. This is, of course, understandable given the extremely high levels of uncertainty and anxiety in the general public.

Another factor that concretely helped the shift away from physical cash was an entirely practical one – inability to use cash under lockdown. When physical stores are forced to shut down, they are replaced with online shops offering contactless delivery. Under these conditions, cash gives way to digital means of payment. Because of the pandemic, cash is portrayed not just as a danger to society and to national security, but also as a direct health hazard due to the coronavirus.

The International Currency Association (2020) expressed its concern about the rise of misinformation regarding the use of cash, which is portrayed to be a virus transmitter. To counter misinformation about the risk posed by cash, the ICA published a list of statements that show otherwise. The World Health Organization is neither advising nor discouraging the public to avoid cash payments, while encouraging frequent hand washing and adhering to basic hygiene. Stephanie Brickman, senior communications consultant of WHO, is quoted by Euronews (2020) as saying: 'The virus will not survive for very long on surfaces, particularly on a dry surface like a banknote'. There is no evidence indicating that banknotes transmit the coronavirus or that they are more strongly contaminated than any other surfaces, objects and other payment methods. A study of the Bank for International Settlements quotes scientists as saying that the probability of transmission via banknotes is low when compared with other frequently touched objects (Auer et al., 2020). The authors of the report go on to say the following:

> To date, there are no known cases of COVID-19 transmission via banknotes or coins. Moreover, it is unclear if such transmission is material compared with person-to-person transmission or transmission through other objects or physical proximity. The fact that the virus survives best on non-porous materials, such as plastic or stainless steel, means that debit or credit card terminals or PIN pads could transmit the virus too.

Even central banks have defended the use of cash. For example, the Bank of England has noted that 'the risk posed by handling a polymer note is no greater than touching any other common surfaces such as handrails, doorknobs or credit cards' (Brignall et al., 2020). The South African Reserve Bank (2020a, 2020b) has responded to scams by clarifying that there is no evidence of transmission by cash and that it is not withdrawing cash from circulation.

In July 2020 PayPal executives cited the death of cash as the company posted record earnings. According to CNBC, PayPal CFO (John Rainey) said that 'the death of cash has arrived' (Stankiewicz, 2019). Company executives said that the society has reached an 'inflection point' when it comes to the 'death of cash' and noted that 70% of consumers now fear for their health when it comes to paying in stores (Lepecq, 2020). However, while there has been a decline in the use of cash as a means of payment during the pandemic, the overall demand for cash has experienced an unprecedented growth. In Figure 5.1 we can see that the demand for cash in the US grew rapidly in 2020. The *Sydney Morning Herald* reported on 9 April 2020 that 'Australians did not just hoard loo paper and tinned tomatoes as the coronavirus pandemic spread through the country last month – they started stockpiling cash' (Wright, 2020). During the pandemic, Lepecq (2020) points out, consumers have paid more with digital instruments, but they have stored more in cash. This cannot represent the death of cash.

The pandemic has provided an excuse for governments to move to a cashless society, not because cash is used by criminals or used for tax evasion, but because it is good for the banking oligarchy and for Big Brother. The war on cash is good for the banking industry, which is striving to close branches and remove ATMs to boost the bottom line and the bonus paid to the CEO. For governments (Big Brother), a cashless society is 'easily monitored, controlled, manipulated, weaponised and locked down'. This is why Whitehead (2020)

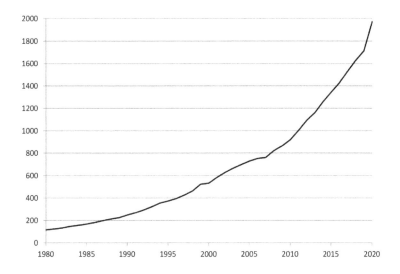

Figure 5.1   Currency in circulation in the US ($ billion)

believes that 'the government and its corporate partners-in-crime have been waging a subtle war on cash for some time now'. The war on cash is being sold to the public as a means of fighting terrorists, drug dealers, tax evaders and now the Coronavirus. In reality, as Dowd (2017) puts it, the war on cash is the 'state's war against us'.

5.6   INTERNATIONAL RELATIONS

The COVID-19 pandemic has affected international relations and caused diplomatic tensions, making it necessary to rethink existing approaches to international relations, with a greater focus on issues such as health diplomacy, the politics of crisis and border politics. Diplomatic relations have been affected due to tensions around trade and transport of medicines, diagnostic tests, hospital equipment and vaccines. Another aspect of international relations is that the leaders of some countries have accused other countries of not containing the disease effectively, resulting in the uncontrolled spread of the virus. This is not new because pandemics have always affected international relations and the geopolitical landscape. Drezner (2020) notes that the historical relationship between pandemics and international relations reveals three insights: (i) diseases have transformed world politics for millennia, (ii) the relationship between pandemics and politics is reciprocal, and (iii) a series of economic and ideational advances over the past two centuries have muted (but did not eliminate) the effects of pandemics on world politics.

Health diplomacy is defined by Fazal (2020) as 'international aid or cooperation meant to promote health or that uses health programming to promote non-health-related foreign aims'. The COVID-19 pandemic has, according to Fazal (2020), provided numerous examples of states putting health in foreign policy, a practice that is likely to continue after the pandemic. Health diplomacy may take several forms, including engagement with global international organisations and bilateral aid intended to support existing foreign investments. While pandemics require international co-operation for the purpose of mitigation and containment, they also create opportunities for states to pursue foreign policy objectives that serve their national interest rather than global health.

The politics of crisis, with reference to COVID-19, is dealt with by Lipscy (2020) who suggests that crises compel leaders to make high-stakes decisions under conditions of threat, uncertainty, and time pressure. This means that the politics of crisis pertains to why some countries are more vulnerable to major crises, such as pandemics, whereas others respond more quickly and aggressively. Drezner (2020) notes that pandemics and politics are intertwined, because initial policy decisions can have pronounced effects on the spread of disease. The mortality rates of the 1918 pandemic differed greatly, depending on the initial decisions of political leaders, and the same is true of COVID-19. Some countries (such as Vietnam, South Korea and New Zealand) have been extremely effective in containing the spread, whereas other countries (such as Brazil, Russia, the US and the UK) have performed poorly.

The issue of border politics, as a response to the COVID-19 pandemic, is dealt with by Kenwick and Simmons (2020) who suggest that prior to the advent of the pandemic, border orientation was already on the rise worldwide. This trend has made it convenient for governments to externalise the virus, rather than taking costly but ultimately more effective domestic mitigation measures. They argue that the pervasive use of external border controls in the face of the virus reflects growing anxieties about border security in the modern international system and express the view that despite the intensification of globalisation and scientific evidence, unilateral border control is a very tempting tool for sovereign states to wield in the face of a pandemic. While 186 countries responded to the pandemic with external border restrictions, only 127 countries have enacted social distancing provisions, and often with much weaker enforcement.

Whether or not COVID-19 will be consequential for international relations is an open question. Drezner (2020) argues that 'COVID-19 will not have transformative effects on world politics'. He refers to the concept of 'critical junctures' in which multiple aspects of international relations change in a short period of time, and suggests that COVID-19 is not going to be judged as a critical juncture. He suggests that despite its pronounced short-term impact, COVID-19 is unlikely to have the transformative effects on international relations that so many are confidently predicting. Instead, he presents reasons for believing that the distribution of power and interest will remain largely unchanged in a post-COVID world. This view is not shared by the majority of international relations scholars.

Those predicting changes in international relations include Campbell and Doshi (2020) who think that the US could face a 'Suez moment' because of its failure to meet the challenge. Kahl and Berengaut (2020) warn that 'even after the virus recedes, the geopolitical wreckage it leaves in its wake could be profound'. Busby (2020) believes that COVID-19 may be 'the most consequential event of the early 21st century, upending modern life, globalization, and relations between countries'. Kaplan (2020) notes that 'Coronavirus is the historical marker between the first phase of globalization and the second'. Summers (2020) believes that the effect will be even more sweeping:

> The COVID-19 crisis is the third major shock to the global system in the 21st century, following the 2001 terror attacks and the 2008 financial crisis. I suspect it is by far the most significant … If the 21st century turns out to be an Asian century as the 20th was an American one, the pandemic may well be remembered as the turning point. We are living through not just dramatic events but what may well be a hinge in history.

The reason why Drezner (2020) believes that COVID-19 will be inconsequential, as far as international relations are concerned, is that previous pandemics caused no changes. For example, the 2003 SARS outbreak did not slow China's rise in the international system, and the 2009 H1N1 pandemic 'caused barely a ripple in international relations'. Drezner (2020) supports his argument by the results of a snap poll conducted in May of 2020 where 54% of IR scholars disagreed with the proposition that the COVID-19 pandemic will fundamentally alter the distribution of power in world politics. However, SARS, Ebola and Zika were not as global as COVID-19, which is why it is different this time. SARS, for example, infected just over 8,000 people and killed less than 800 during the period November 2002–July 2003. It was a minor event compared to COVID-19. As for the results of the snap poll, 54% may not be significantly different (in a statistical sense) from 46% (the percentage of IR scholars who agreed with the proposition).

The COVID-19 pandemic raises the issue of whether or not the US will lose world leadership to China because of its performance with respect to the handling of the health crisis. Even before the advent of COVID-19, scholars were debating how much China had closed the relative power gap with the US (for example, Beckley, 2020; Drezner, 2014; Kirshner, 2014). COVID-19 raises legitimate questions about the acceleration of a hegemonic transition between China and the US. While the disease originated in China, Beijing had mostly contained the virus by March 2020, going so far as to send personal protective equipment (PPE) and other medical supplies to hard-hit European countries. Premier Xi Jinping pledged billions of dollars to the WHO to fund research into a vaccine. Throughout the pandemic, China has been trying to portray itself as a supplier of global public goods. In contrast, the US response was at best haphazard and at worst inept. Walt (2020) describes the US response to the pandemic as follows: 'far from making America great again, this epic policy failure will further tarnish the United States' reputation as a country that knows how to do things effectively'. According to Nye (2011), a key source of soft power is the demonstration of policy competence whereas policy incompetence eviscerates soft power.

Some observers use the response to the pandemic to portray the US as a failed state (Fukuyama, 2020; Packer, 2020). Rapp-Hooper (2020) warns that 'if the United States continues to founder while China offers supplies and coordination, international partners will naturally perceive China's leadership to have strengthened'. Akon and Rahman (2020) argue that the internal policies of the US and its European allies have plunged the whole world into uncertainty, whereas China emerges as a new saviour by providing assistance to affected countries. For example, China provided assistance to Italy to fight the pandemic when Italy could not get assistance from the EU. China also sent much needed medical supplies (masks, protective suits and gloves) to France and Spain. Serbia received significant medical assistance from China after dismissing European solidarity as a 'fairy tale' (Campbell and Doshi, 2020). In the Middle East, China sent a medical team with seven specialists to Iraq and Iran. In Southeast Asia, China showed its solidarity by sending a medical team and necessary equipment (including test kits, masks and personal protective equipment) to the Philippines, Indonesia, Thailand, Cambodia, Laos, Myanmar and Malaysia. Even the Japanese National Institute of Infectious Diseases received donated testing kits from China (Chakraborty, 2020).

The US, on the other hand, has failed to maintain close relations with the vulnerable countries, not even with its close allies, even though one of the features of a global leader is to respond quickly if any country faces any crisis. Akon and Rahman (2020) argue that the failure of the US to provide support to affected countries is considered as the 'fallen star of the old world'. The US, they argue, is losing its supremacy so far as to lead the world in this pandemic crisis. Instead of helping countries in its backyard, the US has been busy putting pressure on Latin American countries to reject the Sputnik V vaccine under the pretext of 'combatting malign influences in the Americas', going as far as putting pressure on Panama not to accept an offer of help from Cuban doctors (McEvoy, 2021).

However, one should take seriously the point raised by Drezner (2020) that 'the hard-power capabilities of the United States remain formidable despite the country's abysmal performance during the pandemic'. What he fails to understand is that a major reason for the 'country's abysmal performance during the pandemic' is the lack of resources caused by the 'formidable hard-power capabilities'. The US is already building anti-Chinese coalitions (of the willing). On 12 March 2021, the first Quad summit was held virtually involving the US, India, Japan and Australia. The declared objective of the meeting was 'to discuss regional and global issues of shared interest and exchange views on practical areas of cooperation towards maintaining a free, open and inclusive Indo-Pacific region'. This is a diplomatic way of saying that the talks were about how to counter the influence of China in the Indo-Pacific region. Biden has already threatened that Putin will pay a price for meddling in US elections and accused Iran of doing the same. The brand new US Secretary of State, no less hawkish than his predecessor, takes every opportunity to give the Chinese lessons in democracy and human rights. We can only hold our fingers crossed that the Thucydides Trap (that war breaks out because a rising power challenges the incumbent power) does not come true.

5.7   CONCLUDING REMARKS

'You never want a serious crisis to go to waste', said Rahm Emanuel shortly after his appointment as chief of staff to President-Elect Barack Obama regarding the global financial crisis. He elaborated by saying: 'What I mean by that is it's an opportunity to do things that you think you could not do before'. It is for this statement and similar ones that Emanuel is considered 'one of our time's most Machiavellian politicians' (Winters, 2020).

Emanuel, however, was right – this is what governments do all the time. They never allow a serious crisis to go to waste, but rather use it to pursue hidden agendas and pass laws that are difficult to pass otherwise. Only 9/11 could have allowed the draconian Patriot Act to pass easily by Congress, with the blessing of ordinary people who would eventually be the victims of this tyrannical legislation. The COVID-19 pandemic is by far a bigger crisis than 9/11 by any metric, particularly the number of dead, which is why it is only natural for governments to use the crisis to pass draconian laws.

Epidemics have altered the course of history in more than one way since they have given rise to certain socio-political and cultural developments. They produce specific vulnerabilities and issues in every society. As a crisis, COVID-19 is helping governments, even in democratic countries, to curtail civil liberties and violate human rights. It has assisted the rise of fascism and given governments a pretext for intensifying the war on cash for the benefit of Big Brother and the banking oligarchy. It has provided justification for mass surveillance. In this respect, governments seem to have become as Machiavellian as the Machiavellian politician referred to by Winters (2020).

6. Rethinking the free market doctrine

6.1 INTRODUCTION

Pandemics and their economic consequences introduce drastic changes. The Spanish flu of 1918, which infected a quarter of the world population, led to the rise of public healthcare systems. In the aftermath of the Spanish flu, a consensus emerged about the need for universal healthcare and that healthcare should not be viewed as an individual responsibility, which is what free marketeers think. The Black Death of the 14th century killed around 60% of the population of Europe. It also killed the then prevailing economic system of feudalism, which depended on a large number of peasants working the land to support the 1% of that time. By killing so many peasants, the Black Death made a major contribution to eroding the foundations of the dominant economic system of the time, which preceded capitalism. Likewise, the COVID-19 pandemic is showing that collective problems require collective solutions and a government that provides for the essential needs of its citizens. The pandemic is forcing a rethinking of the free market doctrine and the role of government in economic activity.

Since the 1980s, belief in the power of the market and the free market doctrine has led to a status quo where governments take a back seat, allowing the private sector to steer the economy for the benefit of the oligarchy. Allegedly, this is how economies should be run because only the private sector creates wealth and jobs, the private sector is more efficient than the public sector, and because people working in the private sector are smarter and more innovative than those working in the public sector. As a result, the governments of countries run by free marketeers have been put in a position where they are not always properly prepared and equipped to deal with crises such as COVID-19. Free markets cannot deal with a crisis of this magnitude, let alone any crisis.

Free marketeers believe that governments are not supposed to participate in or regulate economic activity. However, the private sector demands government intervention and expects it to be delivered to save the economy when a disaster strikes by providing taxpayers' money or money created out of thin air by indulging in quantitative easing. While free marketeers proclaim the imperative of fiscal austerity and the limitations of public policy, the advent of COVID-19 forced the private sector and corporate media to beg for unlimited public spending in order to save the economy (meaning corporate interests). The problem is that the demonising of the public sector by free marketeers and their supporters in government has weakened the ability of the government to manage a massive crisis such as this one as a result of deliberate cutting of funding to institutions providing public goods and services or by outsourcing some public-sector operations to the private sector.

In the UK, one of the bastions of the free market doctrine, and where the doctrine was born (or invented), years of neglect and downsizing of the National Health Service led to a disastrous situation with mounting infections and deaths. The so-called public–private partnerships (PPPs), where taxpayers provide funding while the private sector reaps the profits, have mostly served the interests of the private sector because governments have been unable to ensure that prices are fair, patents are not abused, and that profits are reinvested back into innovation, rather than siphoned out to shareholders.

6.2   THE ADVENT OF COVID-19

Failure to deal adequately with the health and economic ramifications of the pandemic was caused by the deliberate dismantling of state capacities, staggering failures of implementation and a shocking underestimation of the threat (a case of neglected risk). The pandemic hit after four decades of neoliberalism had depleted state capacities in the name of the alleged efficiency of the private sector and the power of the market. Neoliberalism fostered deindustrialisation, through the globalisation of production, and created fragile financial structures secured by state guarantees, with the ultimate objective of boosting short-term profitability. Free marketeers have been promoting the fragmentation and disarticulation of a wide range of systems of provision as individual firms scrambled for short-term profit. The ensuing shortcomings were exacerbated by the destruction of state planning capacity and the disinclination of neoliberal governments to use all necessary means to mobilise industry, labour and private capital for a common purpose during the pandemic.

The production and accumulation of the goods necessary to manage a pandemic are hindered by the manufactured leadership role of the private sector, which is motivated by one thing only (profit). For example, the early stages of COVID-19 witnessed a scramble for personal protective equipment (PPE) and ventilators because they were in short supply. Olsen and Zamora (2020) suggest that the current chaos, which is provoked by the dramatic shortages of basic medical equipment (such as masks, gloves, test kits and ventilators), illustrates the wasteful competition engendered by market-driven solutions. Saad-Filho (2020b) argues that 'the disintegration of the global economy left the wealthiest and most uncompromising neoliberal economies, the USA and the UK, exposed as being unable to produce enough face masks and personal protective equipment for their health staff, not to speak of ventilators to keep their hospitalized population alive'.

It is not that the pandemic was unpredictable, as the idea had been entertained repeatedly, and policy-makers had been aware that it was a matter of when, not if, for a pandemic to strike. Gilding (2020) suggests that COVID-19 was not an unexpected 'black swan' event, but rather 'the first in a herd of stampeding black elephants racing towards us'. By anticipating this scenario, the right action would have been to produce and store goods that are needed to fight the virus. The private sector, which is motivated by the desire to earn a 'quick buck', is not interested in producing and storing goods that it may or may not sell two years down the road. Only a strong public sector could have ordered those goods and stored them for use when the need arose. It would have been even better if the public sector itself had produced those goods by considering social costs and benefits rather than private costs and revenues.

Furthermore, the prevalence of free market thinking has led to the loss of the social safety net for the majority of ordinary people, since social safety nets are found in 'nanny states' only, as postulated by free marketeers. In the US, the loss of one's job also means the loss of health cover, which means that these people are condemned to death or suffering if they are lucky. Under the free market system, where the economy is owned and operated by the private sector, the government is dependent on tax revenue, coming mainly from the middle class in the form of income tax. With limited financial resources, the government resorts to destructive policies, such as excessive borrowing, inflationary money printing (politely known as quantitative easing) and interest rate cuts that hurt pensioners and the middle class.

Dismal failure in fighting the virus is more conspicuous in countries run by free marketeers (such as the US and UK) than countries with strong public sectors. Gilding (2020) argues that countries with a coherent, competent, respected and well-resourced state (everything market fundamentalists have sought to undermine) are likely to have both lower economic and human cost. He also argues that market fundamentalism is no longer even in the interest of the corporate sector or the financial elites because 'it creates unmanageable economic risks and ultimately poses an existential risk to capitalism'. Saad-Filho (2020b) suggests that in early 2020, China bought the world time to prepare for the epidemic, and it offered an example of how to confront it. The governments of other East Asian countries (particularly Singapore, South Korea, Taiwan and Vietnam) came up with more or less intrusive but successful policy alternatives. He goes on to say the following:

> Meanwhile, the West fumbled: faced with a problem that could not be resolved with bribes or by blockading, sanctioning or bombing a distant land, the governments of the wealthiest countries in the world did not know what to do. Unsurprisingly, the

UK and US governments fared especially badly, while the EU, once again, disap-
pointed at an hour of need. (Saad-Filho 2020b, p. 478)

An increasing number of observers think that the COVID-19 pandemic provides an opportunity that was missed in the aftermath of the global financial
crisis: the opportunity to depart from the free market dogma and replace the
objective of profit maximisation with that of welfare maximisation. The free
market ideology was dealt a big blow by the global financial crisis because
deregulation was seen as a major cause of the crisis. Stiglitz (2010) argues for
a restoration of the balance between government and markets, suggesting that
the free market system is broken and that it can be fixed only by 'examining
the underlying theories that have led us into this new bubble capitalism'.

Likewise, Martinez (2009) contends that the proposition that the activities
related to distributing resources and economic growth are better left to the
'invisible hand' seems 'tragically misguided in the wake of the 2008 market
collapse and bailout'. He goes on to describe how 'the flawed myth of the
"invisible hand" distorted our understanding of how modern capitalist markets
developed and actually work'. Harcourt (2011) argues that 'our faith in "free
markets" has severely distorted American politics'. Gray (2009) notes that free
markets have contributed to social breakdown in the US on a scale unknown in
any other developed country. He goes on to say that free markets have generated a long economic boom from which the majority of Americans has hardly
benefited, yet such direct consequences of the free market have not weakened
support for it.

We have already missed an opportunity to kill market fundamentalism in the
aftermath of the global financial crisis and great recession as free marketeers
came back with a vengeance to tell and convince politicians that the road to
salvation goes through a free market – hence the private sector was back in
business as usual. The COVID-19 pandemic is providing another opportunity
to reconsider blind faith in the free market and its invisible hand. For example,
Mazzucato (2020) believes that 'we can use this moment to bring a stakeholder
approach to the centre of capitalism'. Gilding (2020) describes the 'death of
free market fundamentalism and the return of the State' as the most profound
of the 'many long-lasting social and economic impacts of the COVID-19 pandemic'. Even the *Financial Times* (2020) subscribes to this view:

> Radical reforms – reversing the prevailing policy direction of the last four decades –
> will need to be put on the table. Governments will have to accept a more active role
> in the economy. They must see public services as investments rather than liabilities,
> and look for ways to make labour markets less insecure. Redistribution will again
> be on the agenda; the privileges of the elderly and wealthy in question. Policies until
> recently considered eccentric, such as basic income and wealth taxes, will have to
> be in the mix.

Likewise, Isaković (2020) expresses the following view:

> The COVID-19 pandemic has exposed the toxic effects of a system that has for far too long dominated every aspect of our societies. Neoliberalism, as an economic ideology of capitalism, has depleted our public services, turned our education and healthcare into profit-driven businesses, hoarded profits at the expense of underval-ued and underpaid workers, favoured profitability of a militarised world over human security and wellbeing, and aggravated inequalities between people and countries.

The pandemic has created a severe economic crisis that can cause an ideological transformation that further weakens the neoliberal thinking. Kılıç (2020) notes that the neoliberal thinking is inadequate for combating COVID-19 (and the economic problems it has created) and that 'the pandemic further erodes neoliberalism by targeting globalisation and post-Fordism'. He explains why and how COVID-19 prepares for an ideological transformation that has the potential to put an end to the neoliberal thinking. Pope Francis shares the sentiment, suggesting that the pandemic was the latest crisis to prove that market forces alone and 'trickle-down' economic policies had failed to produce the social benefits their proponents claim (Pullella, 2020).

6.3   AVENUES FOR REFORM

Typically, the word 'reform' is used to imply a move towards free markets. This is what the IMF and World Bank preach to developing countries and force neoliberalism down their throats. But 'reform' should mean moving from something bad to something better (such as the move from feudalism to capitalism). The free market ideology has caused significant economic and social damage, which is why it is bad. Reform, therefore, should refer to actions taken to move away from free market thinking, dismantling the control of the private sector over the economy and restoring the dignity of the public sector. The question is: what actions should be taken towards that end?

Gilding (2020) puts forward strong arguments for acting now. He argues that 'there have long been moral, social and environmental risks posed by an unfettered market', which 'present a strong case for action by the State'. He suggests that 'COVID-19 presents a blindingly powerful economic case for change' because 'the dominant political approach in the west is fatally flawed'. He goes on to say:

> It [market fundamentalism] creates a weak and unstable economy, which magnifies risks and is unable to manage shocks. It threatens itself .... The return of the State and a well-regulated market economy will be the only chance we have to do so .... COVID-19 gives us clear evidence that market fundamentalism is a failed economic strategy. Interpreting markets as an ideology or quasi-religious belief system results in unmanageable and systemic economic risks .... Any corporate or financial system

leader who doesn't now become an advocate for a strong, well-resourced and respected State, decent taxes and a strong social safety net, will share responsibility for the decline of capitalism. This has to be a lesson to reshape thinking in the power of the market.

In a post-Corona world, the dignity of the public sector should be restored for the benefit of the 99%, away from the dominance of the private sector that serves the 1% only. This can be done by taking several measures. The response to a crisis (health or otherwise) should not only take the form of injecting funds when a problem arises, but rather governments must invest in, and in some cases create, institutions that help to prevent crises, or put them in a better position to handle crises when they arise. For example, strengthening healthcare systems requires long-term investment as well as the reversal of the trends of recent years involving privatisation, outsourcing and public–private partnerships (PPPs). Governments must take the responsibility of coordinating research and development activities, steering them towards public health goals. Furthermore, governments have a responsibility in shaping the markets by steering innovation to serve public goals. Governments need to structure PPPs for the benefit of social welfare. More drastic, but needed, action would be a bigger role for the public sector, which requires the nationalisation of some private enterprises that were once under public ownership (such as utilities).

Saad-Filho (2020b) suggests that 'neoliberal capitalism has been exposed for its inhumanity and criminality' and that 'COVID-19 has shown that there can be no health policy without solidarity, industrial policy and state capacity'. Accordingly, he puts forward propositions and recommendations to correct the status quo. He sees 'radically neoliberal administrations' as being 'unable to perform the most basic functions of governance: to protect lives and secure livelihoods'. He proposes the nationalisation of the banking system to secure the flow of credit and prevent speculation, arguing that 'if the government can give tens of billions to private-sector firms, taxpayers might as well own them'. In short, he suggests that the economic burden of this crisis will be much higher than that of the global financial crisis, and that there is no way that public services can, or should, bear this burden. The only way out, as he sees it, is through progressive taxation, nationalisation, default where necessary, and a new green growth strategy.

6.4   THE RESPONSE OF FREE MARKETEERS

Free marketeers are likely to bounce back, just like they did in the aftermath of the global financial crisis. In fact, claims are already made that recovery from the pandemic goes through the free market. Take, for example, the free marketeers who argue that the development of a vaccine would not have been possible without the free market principles. In his defence of 'Big Pharma', Ralph (2020) praises the 'global pharmaceuticals sector', which 'has been working for months with academia and governments to develop vaccines at unprecedented speed and financial risk, but also against a backdrop of cynicism from a public weary of controversies from drug price "gouging" to bribery and marketing scandals'. In an editorial, *City A.M.* (2020) suggests that only those who know the principles of free market economics, or those who are observant, realise that 'over the past hundreds of years it has invariably been the private sector, driven by need, who have innovated the world into progress'. The fact of the matter is that the private sector is not driven by need but rather by greed.

As usual, free marketeers do not give the public sector any credit. In truth, the vaccines would not have been developed without government action, even though they were produced by the private sector. Typically, pharmaceutical companies take the risk of innovation in return for a profitable period under patent protection. If the research fails (in the sense that the product has excessive side effects or that it does not provide improvement on existing products) the underlying company will likely fail to recoup the costs of production. This means that the risk of innovation is placed on pharmaceutical companies. However, this time it is different as the risk posed by the pandemic forced governments to accept innovation risk by pre-ordering vaccines without knowing whether or not they were going to be effective. This acceptance provided the incentive for pharmaceutical companies to develop multiple approaches simultaneously in order to find those that work, while letting the government take the risk of those that do not work or are less effective. It has also allowed pharmaceutical companies to progress the vaccines through the necessary regulatory clearance stages more quickly, continuing with testing while seeking regulatory clearance in parallel, rather than sequentially. Big Pharma have also been assured that they would not face law suits if the vaccines produce side effects that can kill or harm people. And they have been receiving billions of dollars of taxpayers' money in the form of research grants and subsidies. Parker (2020) suggests that this can hardly be a triumph for the free market. Rather, he argues, it points to the importance of government policy in setting the right framework for innovation incentives.

For some reason, no one talks about the possibility of a government-run and owned pharmaceutical company producing the vaccine, assuming of course that those working for the government can innovate, which free marketeers do not believe. However, the facts on the ground tell us otherwise. The Soviet Union sent the first satellite, first male cosmonaut, first female cosmonaut and first female dog to space by using technology provided by the public sector. NASA, a US government agency, managed to make moon landing a reality and sent spaceships to Mars and the edge of the solar system by using technology developed in collaboration with the private sector. British Rail was a much better company when it was owned and operated by the public sector than the dozen fragmented companies operating trains in today's Britain. British universities produced much higher quality graduates when they were fully funded by the government than after corporatisation. The US army used to be one of the most self-contained organisations within the government and possibly the world – it has not become more efficient by relying heavily on the private sector (except perhaps in the killing of civilians by employing vicious killers as 'contractors', such as the mercenaries of Blackwater).

There is no technological reason why a government-owned and run company cannot produce vaccines, medical equipment or anything else. Perhaps the employees of a publicly owned company are more innovative because they enjoy a higher level of job security than their counterparts in the private sector. And perhaps they would feel motivated, just by knowing that the CEO earns 10 times the median wage rather than the almost 2,000 times earned by the CEO of McDonald's (mainly because the kids who prepare the burgers and sweep the floor are paid slave wages).

While we are still on the issue of vaccines, let us consider distribution according to the free market principles. The vaccine would be obtained by the highest bidders, while those who cannot pay will be excluded. The People's Vaccine Alliance (a network of organisations including Amnesty International, Oxfam and Global Justice Now) says that there is not enough to go round and that drug companies should share their technology to make sure that more doses are produced (BBC, 2020a). Their analysis found that rich countries have bought enough doses to vaccinate their entire populations three times over if all of the vaccines are approved for use. Canada, for example, has ordered enough vaccines to protect each Canadian five times (even ten times according to some reports). The head of the World Health Organization, who warns of 'global moral failure', has criticised inequalities in the global vaccine roll-out, saying that it was 'not right' that younger adults in wealthy countries were getting vaccinated before older people or healthcare workers in poorer countries. He also hit out at the profiteering of drug companies, accusing vaccine makers of targeting locations where 'profits are highest' (ABC, 2021).

An over-enthusiastic free marketeer goes as far as claiming that without a free market the virus will win. Rasmussen (2020) uses a revolutionary language to talk about mobilisation to fight the disease and boost investment in healthcare, which sounds good except that he qualifies his statement by saying that 'free markets and working economies are absolutely essential in order to effectively mobilize the resources required to take on COVID-19 and other public health problems'. He proposes a 'visionary political program to deal with COVID-19 and future pandemics' – the requirement for that is to 'free up healthcare innovation and point out the life-threatening effects of totalitarianism and groupthink at home and abroad'. Such a programme, he argues, 'would make medical liberty a core pillar of an American-led liberal world order for the twenty-first century much like the United States organized and rallied the free world after World War II'.

This is truly amazing, five-star free market rhetoric! He implicitly claims that a working economy requires free markets and that only free markets can mobilise resources – any other line of thinking is totalitarianism and group-think. He seems to think that the world should follow America by adopting a system of 'if you cannot pay for treatment, you should die'. America cannot be a role model on how to tackle the virus – this is a rich country that has 4% of the world's population but 25% of the cases and 22% of deaths. As we are going to see, Rasmussen's programme is truly fascist in nature.

Rasmussen (2020) suggests nine elements to his programme of 'reform'. I will now list those elements with a comment on each one of them. The first element is about making a 'strong moral case for medical liberty, healthcare innovation, and healthcare investment as core pillars of democratic capitalism and a culture that values every human life'. I assume that 'medical liberty' means the liberty of choosing doctors, insurance companies and hospitals, but the millions of Americans who do not have health insurance do not have this liberty. The same is true of those who have insurance, but they are denied treatment on a technicality or required to make massive co-payments that they cannot afford. Since when do free marketeers believe in morality, given that markets are supposed to be efficient only because they have no morals? A culture that has no morals cannot value human life. What is moral about making a COVID-19 patient pay $50,000 for treatment, or else they are left to die? Free marketeers care more about capitalism than democracy – otherwise, the likes of Milton Friedman, Friedrich von Hayek and James Buchanan would not have celebrated the triumph of capitalism over democracy and human rights in Chile's 9/11 of 1973. Why is it that healthcare innovation and invest-ment can only be associated with the profit-maximising private sector and the oligarchy?

The second recommendation of Rasmussen (2020) is to 'reopen the econ-omies and borders of the world's democracies immediately while closely monitoring COVID-19 hot spots and applying locally driven restrictions as necessary'. This sounds like the usual 'West versus the Rest'. The problem is that on a global level, the COVID-19 hot spots are found in two of the 'world's democracies', the UK and US. Reopening economies and borders, while good for business, should be based on science (while taking into account economic considerations), not on free market rhetoric. We have seen that the initial containment of the virus in Europe was followed by a more devastating second wave caused by premature reopening. Australia and New Zealand have done much better by opening gradually. Remember that the place where someone is most likely to be infected is a crowded bar. Reopening the economy should be based on striking a balance between public health and the health of the economy.

It is noteworthy that the bosses of big businesses in the US have called for reopening the economy promptly at the early stages of the pandemic. Elon Musk told SpaceX employees that it is more dangerous to drive a car than to be exposed to coronavirus. Hobby Lobby founder, David Green, made headlines when he claimed that keeping his stores open was a part of God's plan, and initially defied state shutdowns. Corporate-funded conservative groups like Freedom Works were lobbying federal and state legislators and orchestrating anti-lockdown protests at state capitols. In April 2020 the CEOs of Amazon and Facebook (Jeff Bezos and Mark Zuckerberg) joined the president on phone calls to discuss reopening the economy as soon as possible (Núñez, 2020). Each one of these two gentlemen saw his net worth soar during the pandemic while practising social distancing by residing in their yachts or isolated holiday homes (perhaps some of them contemplated buying a $25 million ticket to the International Space Station).

The third recommendation is to 'prioritize supply-side tax cuts and deregulation over bailouts and unemployment benefits in order to quickly get the economy back on its feet'. This means that those who lost their jobs (and health insurance) as a result of the pandemic should be left to starve or die after contracting the virus. Tax cuts will benefit the super-rich and the corporate sector at the expense of those who have lost their jobs for no fault of their own. Rasmussen seems to be unaware of the basic contradiction in capitalism that wage earners are also the consumers who buy the goods and services produced by the private sector. Without income and health insurance, these consumers will die and the economy will not be back on its feet. Tax cuts do not pay for themselves and the benefits will not trickle down to everyone. They may also force the government to seek alternative financing modes such as debt accumulation and money printing, both of which can be detrimental to the health of the economy.

The fourth recommendation is to 'launch an ambitious free-market healthcare reform agenda, removing bureaucratic obstacles to private sector innovation and investment in healthcare'. This means privatisation of public hospitals and allowing private hospitals, health insurance companies and pharmaceutical companies to do as they please. Free marketeers always seek the commodification of healthcare and privatisation of the healthcare system for the benefit of the private healthcare establishment. In July 2019, the head of one of Australia's biggest health insurers called on the government to abolish Medicare and make private health insurance compulsory. The call was described as a 'radical solution to the growing crisis facing private health funds'. The move would 'allow the private sector to flourish without competition from Medicare', which he described as a 'government monopoly' (Fernyhough, 2019). For free marketeers, treating sick people and financing that through taxation is a sin, but using tax revenue to finance wars of aggression is fine, because the private military sector benefits enormously from war. The commodification of healthcare creates a profitable business because the demand for healthcare is price inelastic, except for those who choose to die because they cannot afford the free market price.

Recommendation number five is to 'create a transatlantic free trade area for healthcare, giving American healthcare innovators greater access to European and Canadian health systems and vice versa'. This sounds like a healthcare NATO, an arrangement that allows American 'healthcare innovators' to rip off America's allies. Despite American exceptionalism, America is not in a position to be a role model when it comes to the healthcare system. According to N. Moosa (2020), 'the US healthcare system fails to deliver services reliably to all of those who could benefit'. In particular, inadequate access to primary care has contributed to poor prevention and management of chronic diseases, delayed diagnoses, incomplete adherence to treatments, wasteful overuse of drugs and technologies, and problems pertaining to coordination and safety. I am sure that Canadians and Europeans do not want to emulate American exceptionalism with respect to the provision of healthcare services.

It may be worthwhile to give one example of those American healthcare 'innovators' who, according to Rasmussen, will save the world: Martin Shkreli. This is what what Matt Taibbi (2020a) says about Shkreli:

> Americans reacted in horror five years ago when a self-satisfied shark of an executive named Martin Shkreli, a.k.a. the 'Pharma Bro,' helped his company, Turing Pharmaceuticals, raise the price of lifesaving toxoplasmosis drug Daraprim from $13.50 to $750 per pill. Shkreli, who smirked throughout congressional testimony and tweeted that lawmakers were 'imbeciles,' was held up as a uniquely smug exemplar of corporate evil. On some level, though, he was right to roll his eyes at all the public outrage. Although he was convicted on unrelated corruption charges, little about his specific attitudes toward drug pricing was unusual. Really, the whole industry is one big Shkreli, and COVID-19 – a highly contagious virus with unique properties that may require generations of vaccinations and booster shots – looms now as the ultimate cash cow for lesser-known Pharma Bros.

In his sixth recommendation, Rasmussen wants to militarise healthcare and biotechnology by making them 'integral parts of NATO doctrine and preparedness, preventing totalitarian powers and terrorist organizations from deploying biological weapons and allowing military resources such as hospital ships and field hospitals to be deployed swiftly during future pandemics'. A better recommendation that would boost social welfare is to abolish NATO (which itself is a terrorist organisation), reduce international tension and channel a big part of military spending to healthcare and social services. The seventh recommendation is also intended to aggravate international tension as he calls for a 'global health summit of the world's democracies, calling out China and other totalitarian governments for their suppression of information and free inquiry on public health matters, including COVID-19'. Defeating the pandemic requires international co-operation, not rivalry and military provoca- tion. Australian politicians have seen the economic consequences of acting as a deputy sheriff and demanding an inquiry with a predetermined finding that China is responsible for the pandemic.

The last two recommendations are also motivated by the 'West versus the Rest' doctrine. Recommendation eight is to 'present a united front of democratic countries within the World Health Organization and build a new global health forum exclusively for democracies'. This simply means that when the US opposes China in the WHO, other 'Western' countries should be shoulder-to-shoulder with their American masters. After all, the West consists of America and the countries that say 'how high' when America says 'jump'. Last, but not least, Rasmussen wants to 'make medical liberty, doctors, and hospitals core pillars of a free-market development agenda for post-conflict zones, emerging democracies, and nations stuck in poverty'. The free market provision of healthcare means that those who cannot afford it should be left to die. In the COVID era, it means that those who cannot afford treatment should be allowed to infect others before they die.

In an interview with Matthew Rozsa, Richard Wolff makes the following comments on the healthcare industry in the US (Rozsa, 2020):

> There are four industry groups: doctors, number one, hospitals, number two, drug and device makers, number three, and medical insurance companies, number four. Those four together operate a conjoint monopoly. They are the only way to get the health care, one or another dimension of it, that is available. They operate as a monopoly. They help each other, coordinate their political and commercial lob- bying advertisements, and they have succeeded dramatically in the United States, particularly since World War II, in boosting the price of medical care far beyond what it would have been had there been genuine competition.

For free marketeers and right-wing commentators, Wolff is unpatriotic at best and a Communist at worst. They choose to overlook the fact that the found- ing fathers considered dissent to be a form of patriotism (see, for example, Matthews, 2017).

6.5   COVID PROFITEERING IN THE NAME OF THE FREE MARKET

Free marketers are proud of the market because it has no morals – it behaves according to the 'law' of supply and demand. It follows that profiteering during extraordinary circumstances is fine because it is all about supply and demand, which the government should not obstruct. In a general sense, the term 'profiteer' signifies the individual or business claiming profits beyond moral acceptability, while 'profiteering' denotes the act itself. In a pandemic, the biggest profiteers are pharmaceutical companies, which take public money to develop a vaccine then they charge unaffordable prices for it. In addition to profiteering from the vaccine, they also generate abnormal profit from treatment by raising the prices of prescription drugs.

Dyer (2021) describes cases of misconduct during the pandemic. In the first case, the profiteers were aided and abetted by a government agency, the Federal Personal Protective Equipment Taskforce. In a story published by the *Washington Post*, the Taskforce, led by Jared Kushner (Trump's son-in-law), was in charge of the procurement of PPE from abroad and bringing it quickly to the US. Rather than distributing the procured equipment to state governments that had a shortage, the Taskforce gave these supplies to six private medical supply companies to sell to the highest bidder, creating a bidding war among states (Brittain et al., 2020). Another case is that of two physician staffing companies that cut pay and benefits for clinicians treating COVID-19 patients while spending millions lobbying against legislation aimed at stopping 'surprise billing' for out-of-network care.

Some doctors took the opportunity to profiteer. A Californian doctor was criminally indicted for selling $4,000 'COVID-19 treatment packs', consisting of hydroxychloroquine, antibiotics, alprazolam (Xanax) and sildenafil (Viagra). A Connecticut internist used public COVID-19 testing sites to conduct unnecessary tests for at least 20 respiratory pathogens, billing up to $2,000 per person and charging insurers $480 to give patients test results by phone. Some hospitals punished doctors early in the pandemic for wearing PPE in front of patients (Richtel, 2020). Four California hospital systems, which had spare beds, denied requests from overflowing nearby hospitals to take uninsured patients or those on Medicaid (Evans et al., 2020).

In Australia, where the government firmly believes in the free market and the 'teachings' of Thatcher and Reagan and where price gouging is not illegal per se, a biosecurity law was issued to prohibit the selling or offering for sale of an 'essential' good at more than 120% of the value that the person bought the goods. Under this law, essential goods include masks, gloves, gowns, goggles, disinfectants and sanitiser. In Australia too, where following the big sister (America) is a favourite hobby for politicians, private health insurers have been raking in profits off the backs of Australian families struggling through the global health and economic crisis caused by COVID-19 (Medical Technology Association of Australia, 2020).

The Guardian reported that Australia's health regulator has fined dozens of companies more than $800,000 for unlawfully advertising or illegally importing health products to profit from the pandemic (Knaus, 2020). One business was fined for trying to sell a 'bionic air plasma' machine, promoted as a COVID preventing device for elderly patients. Other companies were fined for unlawfully advertising or importing masks, medical devices, disinfectants, hand sanitisers, peptide products and thermometers. One company advertised hyperbaric oxygen therapy chambers as a treatment for COVID-19. Another company pushed email advertising (targeting vulnerable groups, including seniors) about its 'bionic air plasma medical device', something it claimed could prevent COVID-19. Yet another company advertised a disinfectant as being a '99.9999% effective' against viruses, including Coronavirus.

Similar horror stories come from the UK. In April 2020 the BBC (2020b) reported that customers were seeing hand sanitiser being sold at £15 for 250 ml, toilet rolls for £1 each and pasta sold by the handful. Trading Standards officers in Swansea received complaints of Calpol sold for £10, loaves of bread doubling in price to £3, packs of toilet roll sold for £8.50, individual toilet rolls sold from a multi-pack and halal meat more than trebling in price to £11 per kilo.

The OECD (2020) reports similar stories from the rest of the world. In Spain the authorities looked into excessive pricing behaviour in sectors affected by the crisis, including funeral services. In Greece an inquiry was launched into possible price increases and output restrictions of healthcare materials and other products. Romania's competition authority investigated price hikes of sanitary products, protective equipment and disinfectants. Italy started an investigation into the prices charged by a private health and laboratory group for serological tests to identify COVID-19 antibodies. Kenya's competition authority sanctioned a supermarket for increasing excessively the prices of hand sanitisers. In South Africa, the government issued regulations that prohibit excessive prices for certain essential goods and services, ranging from foodstuff and medical supplies to masks and surgical gloves. The Indonesian competition authority looked into whether hospitals were overcharging for COVID-19 rapid tests. Thailand's authorities lodged a complaint over alleged inflated prices of surgical masks being sold on an online platform amid the outbreak of COVID-19. In Brazil the authorities carried out an investigation into whether companies were profiting unduly from an increase in the demand for pharmaceutical products connected to COVID-19. This is why some countries decided to regulate the prices of essential products in a way that did not involve competition authorities. It seems, therefore, that crisis profiteering is rampant, but that should be fine because the profiteers obey the 'law' of supply and demand! What is not fine, as far as free marketeers are concerned, is action taken by the government to prohibit profiteering during a health crisis.

6.6 KEYNES, MARX AND COVID-19

Following the global financial crisis and the resulting great recession, there was a worldwide resurgence of interest in Keynesian economics and a desire amongst policy-makers to implement the recommendations of J.M. Keynes in response to the Great Depression of the 1930s. Keynes' *General Theory* provided a conceptual justification for New Deal-type policies, which was lacking in the established economics of the day. Keynes believed that a contracting economy needed government intervention and deficit spending. From the end of the Great Depression until the early 1970s, Keynesian economics provided the main inspiration for economic policy-makers, but its influence waned in the 1970s as a result of stagflation and criticism from Friedrich von Hayek, Milton Friedman, Robert Lucas and other economists, who believed in the power of the market and opposed interventionist government policy. From the early 1980s to 2008, the normative consensus among economists was that fiscal stimulus is ineffective even in a recession. The underlying idea is that economies revert back to full employment if left alone and that markets, rather than governments, are capable of restoring economic stability following a shock.

The global financial crisis proved otherwise. If a person cuts himself while shaving, this person does not need the intervention of a surgeon because the body can heal itself. However, enduring a cut while shaving is a small 'shock' compared to the big 'shock' associated with shotgun wounds or injuries sustained in a major car accident. A big 'shock' like this requires the intervention of a surgeon to avoid death. The same is true of the economy where government intervention is needed to respond to a major shock like the global financial crisis and the COVID-19 pandemic. By early 2009 there was widespread acceptance among policy-makers of the need for fiscal stimulus, which is a Keynesian prescription. President Obama followed a Keynesian approach by enacting the American Recovery and Reinvestment Act of 2009, whereby the Congress allocated more than $800 billion to boost economic recovery.

Like Keynes, the teachings of Karl Marx started to attract interest. For some economists, Keynesian economics has some Marxist elements in it. For example, Mattick (1969, p. 30) says the following:

> The great economic and social upheavals of twentieth century capitalism destroyed confidence in laissez-faire's validity. Marx's critique of bourgeois society and its

economy could no longer be ignored. The overproduction of capital with its declining profitability, lack of investments, overproduction of commodities and growing unemployment, all predicted by Marx, was the undeniable reality and the obvious cause of the political upheavals of the time. To see these events as temporary dislocations that soon would dissolve themselves in an upward turn of capital production did not eliminate the urgent need for state interventions to reduce the depth of the depression and to secure some measure of social stability. Keynes' theory fitted this situation. It acknowledged Marx's economic predictions without acknowledging Marx himself, and represented, in its essentials and in bourgeois terms, a kind of weaker repetition of the Marxian critique; and, its purpose was to arrest capitalism's decline and prevent its possible collapse.

The global financial crisis was seen as a collapse of capitalism, which Marx criticised as a system with inherent contradictions. While Marx predicted the collapse of capitalism, Keynes suggested ways to preserve it via government intervention. The crisis led the general public to be interested in Marx's criticism of capitalism. In October 2008, booksellers in Germany reported massive sales of Marx's *Das Kapital*. Connolly (2008) quotes Jörn Schütrumpf, manager of the Berlin publishing house Karl-Dietz, which publishes the works of Marx and Engels in German, as saying that 'Marx is in fashion again' and that 'we're seeing a very distinct increase in demand for his books, a demand which we expect to rise even more steeply before the year's end'. According to Schütrumpf, readers are typically 'those of a young academic generation, who have come to recognise that the neoliberal promises of happiness have not proved to be true'.

In *Das Kapital*, Marx revealed the economic patterns underpinning the capitalist mode of production in contrast to classical political economists such as Adam Smith, Jean-Baptiste Say, David Ricardo and John Stuart Mill. Marx believed that capitalism is based on the exploitation of labour, whose unpaid work is the ultimate source of surplus value. Owners of the means of production claim the right to this surplus value because they are legally protected by the ruling regime through property rights and the legally established distribution of shares, which are by law distributed only to company owners and their board members. These rights were acquired mainly through plunder and conquest. In this system, commerce as a human activity implied no morality beyond that required to buy and sell goods and services. In the aftermath of the global financial crisis, Jones (2017) wrote the following in a review of *Das Kapital*:

> What is extraordinary about *Das Kapital* is that it offers a still-unrivalled picture of the dynamism of capitalism and its transformation of societies on a global scale. It firmly embedded concepts such as commodity and capital in the lexicon. And it highlights some of the vulnerabilities of capitalism, including its unsettling disruption of states and political systems. ... If *Das Kapital* has now emerged as one of

the great landmarks of nineteenth-century thought, it is [because it connects] critical analysis of the economy of his time with its historical roots. In doing so, he inaugurated a debate about how best to reform or transform politics and social relations, which has gone on ever since.

The 2008 crisis was a financial-economic crisis. This one is a health-economic crisis, but it is also attracting attention to the work of Keynes and Marx, at least because the fiscal response to the crisis is a Keynesian prescription. To paraphrase former European Central Bank president Mario Draghi (currently the Italian prime minister), rich countries are spending 'whatever it takes' while emerging and developing countries, with less ability to borrow, are spending 'whatever they can' (Velasco, 2020). The pandemic has caused a negative supply shock, in which case the absence of fiscal intervention would cause 'a demand-driven slump, give rise to a supply–demand doom loop, and open the door to stagnation traps induced by pessimistic animal spirits' (Fornaro and Wolf, 2020a). As Velasco (2020) puts it, 'we are all Keynesians again'.

Right-wing commentators do not like the Keynesian response, arguing against the presumption this would mitigate the economy-wide impact of the shock along Keynesian lines. Makin (2020) refers to the 'Keynesian fallacy', the 'notion that considerable government spending mitigates the macro-economic impact of a crisis' and warns of oblivion to 'harmful long-term consequences'. The alternative course of action, according to Makin, is to boost liquidity and loosen credit availability – meaning low interest rates. He seems to be oblivious to the fact that private-sector spending is not interest elastic but profit and economic outlook elastic, and this is why the monetary response to the crisis has been ineffective. Makin's prescription boosts asset markets and makes the rich richer while condemning to death the people who have lost their jobs. It is true that government spending has to be financed somehow but he does not mention the alternatives of cutting military spending, imposing a pandemic-related wealth tax on the super-rich and plugging tax loopholes.

As in the aftermath of the global financial crisis, the COVID crisis is giving rise to Marxist narratives. Giuliani (2020) asks the question whether or not the COVID crisis can help 'to promote an ideological shift towards a different type of capitalism'. For this purpose, she conducts a quantitative content analysis of the international press on the COVID-19 bailout conditionality debate, documenting three dominant narratives: the distributive justice, environmental justice and Marxist-type anti-capitalistic narratives. The Marxist-type narrative questions the legitimacy of the whole capitalistic system as reflected in this quote from *The Herald* on 7 May 2020:

> Perhaps, we need a new national flag. One that simply reads: 'Profit before People'. There's been plenty of stories about individual companies and bosses acting despicably during the outbreak – but don't be fooled into thinking this is about a few bad apples. The problem, the dysfunction, is systemic. The structures we have set in place around the economy allow the rich to sponge off the state when they need to, while simultaneously vilifying the poor and weak if they find themselves dependent on state support. It's a satanically sick joke; hypocrisy on an epic level.

The distributive justice narrative and the environmental justice narrative also call for a significant change from the current neoliberalism-based system. The distributive justice narrative centres on inequality, stigmatising companies for non-payment of taxes and denouncing their shareholders and executives for enriching themselves at a time when so many others are suffering. It also debunks preconceptions about the well-functioning of markets and the well-deserved payoffs of risk taking. As an example, the following was written in the 14 May 2020 issue of *The Washington Post*:

> The $2 trillion federal assistance package passed in March included hundreds of billions of dollars to prop up large corporations without questioning their commitment to workers or business practices. I understand the desire to keep businesses from failing, but doing so makes sense only if government funds are being used to support workers – not to enrich executives and shareholders. But that's what is happening.

In the 20 May issue of *The Times*, the following appeared:

> Some businesses receiving government cash and favourable loans are continuing to handsomely reward top executives and shareholders. Some are owned by wealthy individuals who for years have paid minimal tax personally and through their companies.

The environmental justice narrative focuses on bailouts, conditional on companies meeting certain environmental targets. Essentially, it portrays the COVID-19 crisis as an opportunity to start a new green transition towards a low-carbon economy. As an example, the following appeared in the 16 March 2020 issue of *The Guardian*:

> The economic challenge that represents the Coronavirus outbreak has also to be seen as an opportunity to undertake in the context of the EU Green deal an urgent reorientation of the EU economy as the current crisis reveals the fragility of a carbon-intensive system built on highly interconnected and specialised global supply chains.

No matter what the narrative is, it seems that non-free marketeers agree that it is time for change. We can only hope that something will happen to move away from an ideology that has inflicted significant socio-economic damage. This remains to be seen.

6.7 CONCLUDING REMARKS

The global financial crisis provided an opportunity to move away from the destructive ideology that has been used to manage economies for the benefit of the 1-percenters at the expense of the 99-percenters. Unfortunately, free marketeers proved to be resilient as they re-emerged with vengeance, claiming that the crisis was caused by the lack of free markets. The COVID-19 crisis is presenting us with a similar opportunity but free marketeers already claim that the way out of the crisis is by following the free market doctrine. This could not be further away from the truth.

In truth, the current crisis is presenting a choice to us as a society – a choice between continuing to distribute economic resources to the already-wealthy and well-connected and the alternative of redeploying resources into the fight against the pandemic and its adverse consequences, such as poverty, inequality and food insecurity. This is why Oxfam (2020) makes a recommendation that horrifies free marketeers: resurrecting an emergency tax tool used during World War II. Oxfam estimates that imposing a temporary tax on the excessive profits of the top 25 US companies could raise almost $80 billion that can be used to 're-invest in tackling COVID-19 inequalities across the US and around the world'. This is a far cry from what free marketeers aspire for: more tax cuts for the corporate sector, even when the pandemic has impoverished governments and ordinary people.

The coronavirus will not kill anywhere near as many people as the Black Death did, but it may well contribute to exposing the failures of free markets and the scandal of governments intervening in the economy on behalf of the one percenters. Feffer (2020) suggests that the pandemic is already undermining the 'small government canard', but he warns of the hazard of cosmetic changes by saying the following:

> The tweaking of markets to achieve optimal performance is much like the rejiggering of earth-centric models of the universe that took place in the Middle Ages. These models became more and more complex to account for new astronomical discoveries. Then along came Copernicus with a heliocentric model that accounted for all the new data. It took some time, however, for the old model to lose favor, despite its obvious failures. The global economy remains market-centered, even though the evidence has been mounting that these markets are failing us and the planet. Tweaking this model isn't good enough. We need a new Copernicus who will

provide a new theory that fits our unfolding reality, a new environment-centered economics that can maximize not profit but the well-being of living things.

Perhaps one such Copernicus is Richard Wolff (2020) who argues that 'the novel coronavirus pandemic has exposed many of the structural weaknesses in capitalism'. He tackles a number of issues, including how the US economy crashed (not because of a virus but because capitalism is incapable of coping with epidemics), how America's healthcare system is corrupt, and how income inequality caused immense suffering long before the pandemic. He suggests that capitalism is uniquely incapable of securing public health, which is a basic human need, because it is not profitable for a private, profit-maximising firm to produce masks, gloves and ventilators in anticipation of a pandemic.

7. Rethinking the principles of the Washington Consensus

7.1 AN OVERVIEW OF THE WASHINGTON CONSENSUS

The Washington Consensus is a set of ten principles and policy recommendations inspired by neoclassical economics and preached by the international financial institutions based in Washington DC (primarily, the IMF and the World Bank, which are effectively controlled and run by the US Treasury). The term was coined by John Williamson in 1989 when he was examining the principles of development economics that had guided economic policy in Latin America since the 1950s. Cohen-Setton (2016) describes the Washington Consensus by saying that 'John Williamson provided a list of ten policies that more or less everyone in Washington agreed were needed more or less everywhere in Latin America'. Williamson (2000) describes the Consensus as 'the lowest common denominator of policy advice being addressed by the Washington-based institutions to Latin American countries as of 1989'. At least for the critics, the Consensus is seen as synonymous with neoliberalism and globalisation.

In his original formulation, Williamson (1990) specified the ten principles of the Consensus, which can be classified under four pillars: fiscal reform, interest and exchange rate policies, liberalisation, and privatisation–deregulation. The Consensus can be summarised in terms of the slogan 'liberalise, deregulate and privatise'. For the purpose of the discussion here, we will concentrate on the policy recommendations that have been highlighted by the pandemic, which are the first principle of fiscal discipline, the second principle of redirecting public spending, the third principle of tax reform, and the principles pertaining to privatisation, deregulation and intellectual property rights.

The Consensus is intended to undermine the role of the state and glorify the role of the market, while the pandemic has shown the importance of the public sector. Lechini (2008) argues that 'one of the most important consequences of the introduction of the policies of the Washington Consensus has been the undermining of the state, an institution that was relentlessly demonized and attacked, and multiple efforts were made to de-legitimise it as a player in the development process'. More disturbing, according to Lechini (2008), is the 'systematic erosion of effective policy making and policy capacities and the relocation of key macro-economic decision making levers in the markets and in the hands of foreign international financial institutions, jeopardizing both democratic consolidation and development in the South'.

The Consensus has been described as a 'wonkish moniker' by Naim (1999) who wonders how and why it became so popular. To start with, the timing was great as the Consensus was 'invented' at a time to fill an ideological vacuum as communism was falling apart. The formulation of the Washington Consensus in the late 1980s coincided with the sudden collapse of the Soviet system and its ideological apparatus. At that time there was widespread revolt against socialist ideas and central planning – hence the search was on for an alternative set of ideas to organise economic and political life. It was relatively simple for politicians with little intellectual power or common sense to understand and use in speeches to promote neoliberalism as the path to the heavens. It provided a practical action plan with specific goals – for example, the efficiency associated with privatisation and deregulation. It was endorsed by prestigious institutions and individuals such as economists who could mobilise popular interest (Milton Friedman was one of them). Perhaps more importantly is that the Consensus promised the milk and honey to be provided by multilateral institutions and foreign investors.

Arguments against the Washington Consensus rest on several pillars. Some of the principles are not supported by good economics but rather by the stereotyped, ideologically driven argument that economic efficiency can be enhanced by reducing government intervention in the economy and that the benefits accruing to a minority trickle down to the rest of the society. Some of the principles imposed on developing countries are not practised by the preaching countries, either in the past (such as free trade) or at the present (such as free trade, competitive exchange rates, positive real interest rates and fiscal discipline). Some of the principles are stated but never put into practice – for example, pro-growth policies. In essence, the principles are designed to loot developing countries in need of financial assistance.

Proponents of the Consensus argue that the ten principles have considerable economic validity and can be justified in terms of 'good' economics where 'good' means neoclassical. For example, it is argued that broadening the tax base, investment in education, sustainable government borrowing and flexible exchange rates can boost economic welfare. However, broadening the tax base is typically intended to enable lower taxes for rich individuals and corporations, which amounts to a transfer of wealth from the poor to the rich. Yes, investment in education is conducive to growth because it boosts the quality of human capital, but the Washington Consensus, at least as practised by the IMF, does not encourage spending on health and education. Sustainable government borrowing is a good idea but strict limits on spending at any time, which is preached by the IMF, leads to poverty and inequality. As for whether or not flexible exchange rates boost welfare, the jury is still out, even though it is widely accepted that fixed exchange rates are more suitable for developing countries.

Glennie (2011), who argues that the Washington Consensus served rich country interests, is very critical of the arguments put forward to defend the Consensus. However, he senses a change of heart and return to reason amongst economists. This is what he says:

> The world of global development has seen the return of an important quality in people working on issues this complicated: humility. From the 1980s up to the early 2000s, hubris ruled. It was fairly common for people to be sure about the answer to growth and poverty reduction and to seek to impose it. But while there are still some true believers in the Washington Consensus, the majority of development experts are now far more circumspect about making grand claims.

In the following sections, the principles of the Washington Consensus highlighted by the pandemic will be discussed to show how a virus may have forced a rethink of the principles of neoclassical economics that are imposed on developing countries, particularly those requesting loans from the IMF and World Bank. We start with fiscal reform, which is very much relevant because the fiscal response to the pandemic has put the preachers of the Washington Consensus in a fiscal mess. Fiscal reform in relation to the pandemic is discussed in the following two sections.

7.2   FISCAL DISCIPLINE AND THE REDIRECTION OF PUBLIC SPENDING

Fiscal discipline pertains to reasonable levels of deficit to GDP and public debt to GDP. This principle has been imposed on developing countries by the IMF for the simple reason of demonising the public sector, portraying public spending as wasteful and inefficient. This happens despite the fact that the US, the custodian of the Washington Consensus, is one of the most fiscally undisciplined countries in the world. In Figure 7.1 we can see the US fiscal balance (deficit) and federal debt as a percentage of GDP.

COVID-19 has shattered fiscal discipline across the board, and justifiably so. In response to the crisis, governments around the world have ramped up their relief and stimulus spending to unprecedented levels, at a time when tax revenues slumped. The fiscal response to the pandemic was much more massive than the response to the global financial crisis as can be seen in Figure 7.2 according to figures provided by McKinsey and Company (Cassim et al., 2020). The result could be a worldwide deficit of $10 trillion in 2020

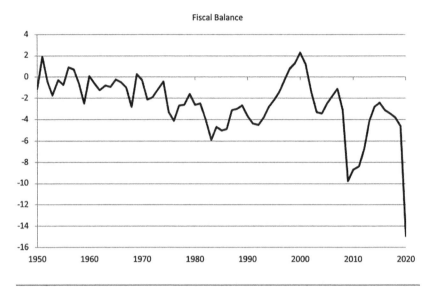

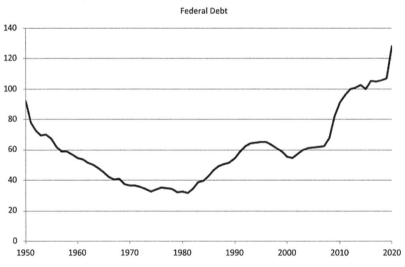

Figure 7.1   US deficit and federal debt

and a cumulative shortfall of up to $30 trillion by 2023 (Assi et al., 2020). As deficits mount, governments must consider a wide range of options. Some are, in effect, monetising their debt through central banks. Others lean on additional borrowing or are considering ways to reduce deficits or sell off assets. Whichever path governments choose, they face a tricky balancing act: managing record fiscal-deficit levels while restoring economic growth.

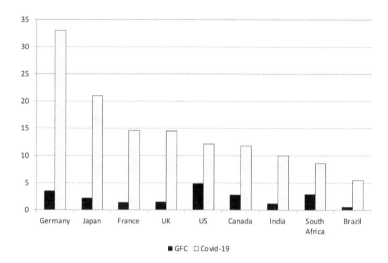

Figure 7.2   Fiscal response to the GFC and COVID-19 (% of GDP)

How will governments get out of this mess? Assi et al. (2020) suggest four different kinds of action that can be taken to correct the situation: (i) building excellence in debt issuance and management, (ii) unlocking funding potential of balance sheet assets, (iii) optimising revenue streams, and (iv) containing expenditure. These suggestions are, however, in line with the neoliberal thinking as reflected in the Washington Consensus. For example, unlocking funding potential of balance sheet assets means issuing more debt using assets as collateral, using public–private partnerships (PPP), selling 'non-strategic' assets, and privatising state-owned enterprises. Under (iii) they suggest improving fraud deterrence and tax collection. Under (iv) they recommend the reallocation of budget from 'non-core activities', reviewing staff utilisation and optimising social welfare policies.

In the Washington Consensus, public expenditure should be switched away from subsidies, never mind how that affects poverty. Nothing is said about switching away from military expenditure and corporate bailouts. Data provided by the Stockholm International Peace Research Institute (SIPRI) on the top ten military spenders show that the US spends more than the other nine countries by a factor of 1.7. Out of the world total, the US spends 38% compared to 36.8% for the other nine countries. If defence means defence, it should not cost this much to defend the homeland. German Chancellor Otto von Bismarck once famously said the following: 'The Americans are truly a lucky people. They are bordered to the north and south by weak neighbors and to the east and west by fish'. According to Reuter (2013), 'the Founding Fathers agreed'.

Waste in US military spending is monumental, to the extent that the Pentagon's 'missing trillions' has become a household expression. Lindorff (2018) analyses the 'Pentagon's massive accounting fraud', arguing that 'the DoD's leaders and accountants have been perpetrating a gigantic, uncon-stitutional accounting fraud, deliberately cooking the books to mislead the Congress and drive the DoD's budgets ever higher, regardless of military necessity'. Likewise, Turse (2018) wonders what happened to the $500 million, which was sent abroad for international drug wars, while Astore (2018) introduces 'the new, super-expensive stealth bomber the US doesn't need'. It seems that the Pentagon's job is not to defend the nation but to keep war profiteers happy and prosperous.

For the US and its allies (particularly the UK), the redirection of public spending should take the form of drastic cuts in military spending and using the savings to finance healthcare and reduce the deficit. For the developing countries under the hammer of the IMF, redirection of public spending should be away from debt service (by avoiding IMF loans, which has been done) to health, education and subsidies.

7.3   TAX REFORM

The third principle of tax reform is appropriate but not as recommended by the custodians of the Washington Consensus. Tax reform, according to Williamson (1990), involves the broadening of the tax base and keeping the marginal tax rates 'moderate'. Tax in this sense is income tax, because no tax reformer in the Washington tradition would dare entertain the idea of a wealth tax or tax on financial transactions. In the Washington Consensus, tax reform is structured in such a way as to benefit the corporate sector and the rich at the expense of the poor – it is a means whereby the rich get richer and the poor get poorer. The objective of broadening the tax base, while keeping marginal tax rates moderate, is to shift more of the tax burden onto middle- and low-income households.

We often hear about proposals to reduce the corporate tax rate because the business sector creates jobs. We often hear that cutting taxes boosts economic growth, and that the process is self-funding as growth produces a higher level of government revenue. And we often hear that cutting taxes for the rich is good for everyone because of the trickle-down effect. When applied to devel-oping countries, as recommended by the IMF, the objective of 'tax reform' is to enable multinationals to get away with minimal tax payments, if any at all. Nothing is said about closing loopholes in the tax collection system so that a rich person like Donald Trump pays more than $750 in tax for a whole year, as revealed by the *New York Times* in September 2020 (Buettner et al., 2020).

The third principle of the Washington Consensus does not consider the feasibility of introducing a wealth tax. Let us look at this issue in a crude manner first, by considering an individual who has amassed $50 billion by digging minerals from the ground and selling them for private profit. This person has this privilege only because his father or grandfather had struck a deal with a corrupt politician who happened to be in power at that time. The deal gives the family the right to extract minerals for 100 years in return for paying royalties amounting to a tiny fraction of the profits generated from this operation. In an ideal situation, mineral resources are placed under public ownership and the revenues are used for the purpose of being fiscally disciplined. Since this ideal situation cannot be found under the free market system, what is wrong with this person paying a 5% wealth tax? That will only reduce his wealth to $47.5 billion. This amount of tax revenue can be used to find accommodation for every homeless person on the land and more, but for this oligarch it is a small change.

What we see on the ground is exactly the opposite – that is, ordinary middle-class taxpayers subsidising the super-rich. A large number of the people working for the richest or second richest person on earth (Jeff Bezos) qualify for food stamps, which are financed by taxpayers. I. Khan (2020) suggests that much of the $80 trillion in cash or very liquid cash-like assets available worldwide is effectively untaxed. A levy of 2% on this amount would raise $1.6 trillion a year, which is adequate to eliminate world hunger 228 times. Khan also argues that support for wealth taxes is not meant to be an attack on capitalism, arguing that 'smart wealth taxes can preserve capitalism in its most sustainable and meritocratic forms by increasing innovation, entrepreneurship and wealth creation, rather than simply wealth preservation'.

COVID-19 has given rise to calls for the imposition of a wealth tax, particularly because the pandemic has affected the poor and vulnerable disproportionately. In South Africa, which has been hit hard by COVID-19, half of the adult population survives with near-zero savings, while 3,500 individuals own 15% of the country's wealth. This is why Chatterjee et al. (2020) propose a 'progressive solidarity wealth tax', which would put the fiscal burden of current interventions on those most capable of paying. Their estimates show that a wealth tax on the richest 354,000 individuals could raise at least $8.3 billion, about 29% of the announced $29.1 billion fiscal cost of the relief package. Likewise, Collins and Clemente (2020) call for a levy of a one-time pandemic wealth tax on billionaires' windfall gains realised during the pandemic. I. Khan (2020) argues that the ancient Greeks levied the eisphora wealth tax on the richest Athenians, particularly during times of war. Since the pandemic and the response resemble a war situation, perhaps there is a readiness for a modern day, post-COVID eisphora. It remains to say that a wealth tax already exists, except that it is not imposed on the wealth of the wealthy. A young couple who just bought their first home (with a massive mortgage) pay wealth tax on their home, and this tax is levied on the estimated value of the home rather than the couple's net equity. However, a billionaire with a stock portfolio of $20 billion does not pay wealth tax on this amount. The kind of wealth held by the not-so-wealthy (family home) is taxable, but the kind of wealth held by billionaires (financial assets) is not subject to wealth tax. This is a grotesquely twisted system.

The third principle of the Washington Consensus ignores other possible avenues for tax reform. For example, one way to broaden the tax base is to extend GST or VAT to cover financial transactions. As a matter of fact, it does not make any sense not to tax financial transactions when most of them are parasitic, conducted by (or on behalf of) people who can afford to pay extra tax. A better alternative that the Washington Consensus ignores is the imposition of a financial transactions tax (FTT), which is a type of excise tax imposed on trades of financial assets, including stocks, bonds and derivatives. It does not make sense to impose a massive stamp duty on a young couple buying their first home with a massive mortgage while billionaires are allowed to get away without paying taxes on stock transactions. The proponents of FTT highlight its progressivity (the rich pay more), its voluntary nature (don't want to pay? don't trade), and its ability to discourage unproductive high frequency trading.

The Washington Consensus has nothing to say about tax fraud, evasion and concessions. O'Hare (2019) compares estimates of international corporate tax avoidance and domestic government health expenditure for 2013 from 100 countries. She shows that revenues lost from corporate tax avoidance were bigger than government expenditure on healthcare. If the revenues lost to tax avoidance were allocated to the health sector, 'the annual government health expenditure could increase from $8 to $24 per capita in low-income countries and from $54 to $91 per capita in lower-middle-income countries'. In other words, if governments were to recover the revenue lost due to tax avoidance, they could fund public hospitals, improve the quality of healthcare, and improve the working conditions of health workers.

Gaspar (2020) examines the connection between COVID and taxation, arguing that 'COVID-19 will change taxation – in at least three important ways, with lasting implications'. He suggests that since vulnerability to COVID-19 and its economic impact are very different across social groups, taxation can correct this uneven playing field, which is an additional argument for progressive taxation. For the same reason, aggressive tax minimisation by large taxpayers (however legal it may appear) will become even more intolerable to the society at large. He also suggests that as the economies of the world recover, changes in the tax code may be necessary to deal with the fall in the tax revenue to GDP ratio. Sarin and Summers (2020) suggest that the Internal Revenue Service could generate over $100 billion annually by increasing audit rates substantially (with a focus on high-income individuals), improving third-party information reporting, and investing in better technology.

7.4 PRIVATISATION

The eighth principle of the Washington Consensus is privatisation, which is the transfer of government-owned businesses, operations, or assets to the private sector. The rationale for privatisation is based on the alleged efficiency of the private sector because (allegedly) those who work for the public sector are not as smart as those who work for the private sector. One of the pro-claimed benefits of privatisation, as identified by Williamson (1990), is that 'privatization may help relieve the pressure on the government budget, both in the short run by the revenue produced by the sale of the enterprise and in the longer run inasmuch as investment need no longer be financed by the govern-ment'. This argument, which is invalid theoretically and empirically, is used by right-wing governments and dictators to justify wholesale privatisation that benefits a minority of oligarchs. Yes, privatising a public hospital will save the government millions in running costs, but will taxpayers be better off? Unlikely, because they will still be paying taxes and now they have to pay for treatment in a private hospital that may cost $1,000 a night for bed only.

COVID-19 brought attention to the practices of private hospitals where profit comes before people. In June 2020, a leading private hospital in Delhi went viral on social media because of the sheer obscenity of the charges that it displayed for COVID patients. The costs for a bed ranged from $330 per day in a general ward (no private room, without isolation or ventilator) to $950 per day for an ICU bed with ventilator. Consequently, a petition was filed in the Supreme Court of India calling for price regulation (Contractor and Kakar, 2020).

An ignored facet of overcharging during the COVID-19 crisis is the rising cost of non-COVID treatment in private hospitals. As the number of cases has risen, more and more government hospitals have been converted entirely into 'COVID hospitals', leaving many non-COVID patients who are dependent on public hospitals (often due to economic reasons) for essential and life-saving treatments such as chemotherapy, radiation and dialysis. Patients needing these treatments are consequently forced to access care in private hospitals where the costs of treatment have been inflated. Private hospitals have been forcing patients to deposit hefty sums of money in order to gain access to non-COVID treatment. These deposits act as financial barriers to people in need of essential care. There have been instances where private hospitals compelled non-COVID patients to pay for a COVID-19 test in order to access services, even in cases where national testing guidelines do not permit a COVID test to be conducted. As an example, a dialysis dependent patient was forced to pay more than 15 times the cost of treatment in a private facility as the hospital insisted on doing the dialysis only in the ICU (Contractor and Kakar, 2020). Bertossa (2020) warns that if governments face spending constraints, then the last thing they should do is to encourage expensive private healthcare that crowds out more efficient public health and sends profits to tax havens.

It is not only private hospitals that have been engaged in malpractices – rather, it is private enterprise in general. According to one observer, 'the COVID crisis has shown how privatisation corrodes democracy' (Cordelli, 2020). She attributes the dismal failure of the UK in tackling the pandemic to outsourcing 'huge swathes of its pandemic response to the private sector'. She also describes as a fiasco the 'decision to outsource both testing and tracing, awarding contracts worth millions of pounds to companies such as Deloitte and Serco'. She goes on to say the following:

> The pandemic has refuted a myth sold to us since the reigns of Margaret Thatcher and Ronald Reagan: that private firms are more effective at delivering services than lumbering state bureaucracies. Over the past 40 years, governments have contracted out public services, from welfare benefits to prison management and public transport.

Cordelli puts forward the following argument for why privatisation erodes democracy:

> In a democracy, we want those delivering public services to make decisions in our name. When public services are outsourced, decisions are made by private companies (whether for-profit, or non-profit), rather than elected representatives. It's doubtful whether the private sector can ever act in a genuinely representative capacity – after all, we don't elect companies. Private firms aren't the same as civil servants; they have their own goals to pursue, as well as fiduciary obligations to shareholders. Indeed, acting out of private interest often just means not acting in the name of a democratic public.

Farha et al. (2020) do not only talk about healthcare, but about privatisation in general, suggesting that 'the COVID-19 pandemic has exposed the catastrophic fallout of decades of global privatisation and market competition'. They recommend a 'radical change in direction' as follows:

> For many years, vital public goods and services have been steadily outsourced to private companies. This has often resulted in inefficiency, corruption, dwindling quality, increasing costs and subsequent household debt, further marginalising

poorer people and undermining the social value of basic needs like housing and water. We need a radical change in direction.

Interestingly, pro-privatisation gurus argue against public enterprises on the grounds that they are inefficient, corrupt and produce low-quality products. Even a good capitalist like the French President Emmanuel Macron acknowledged on 12 March 2020 that 'the pandemic had revealed that there are goods and services that must be placed outside the laws of the market' (Farha et al., 2020). The effect of privatisation on democracy and human rights is identified by Farha et al. (2020) as follows:

> By continuing to opt for contracting out public goods and services, governments are paying lip service to their human rights obligations. Rights holders are transformed into the clients of private companies dedicated to profit maximisation and accountable not to the public but to shareholders. This affects the core of our democracies, contributes to exploding inequalities and generates unsustainable social segregation …. New alternatives are necessary. It is time to say it loud and clear: the commodification of health, education, housing, water, sanitation and other rights-related resources and services prices out the poor and may result in violations of human rights.

The second wave of COVID-19 in the Australian state of Victoria is attributed by Potter (2020) in part to privatisation as he argues that the link between privatisation and the outbreak is 'indisputable'. A judicial inquiry revealed that the outbreak has been traced in large part to breaches of quarantine security outsourced by the state government to private firms. Security workers were recruited through WhatsApp and employed as private contractors with minimal rights. They were neither trained properly nor supplied with adequate personal protective equipment.

Privatisation, we are told, promotes competition and eliminates corruption. In reality, however, the opposite is true because the beneficiaries of privatisation collude and commit fraud to maximise their net worth, to the detriment of the rest of the society. Privatisation aggravates the financial burdens of the public at large as a result of the use of monopolistic or oligopolistic pricing. Privatised firms tend to abuse market power for the sake of profit maximisation and in the name of free market pricing. Privatisation enriches the politically connected few who secure lucrative deals and acquire public assets at bargain prices – in the process, public interest is sacrificed for private profit. This is why Barwick (2020) describes privatisation as follows:

> Privatisation is not about more efficient delivery of public services – it is a mechanism to loot nations and concentrate profits into the hands of a select few, an extension of the corporatist (a.k.a. fascist) merger between governments and megabanks which caused the economic breakdown and financial crisis now sweeping the globe.

The pandemic has demonstrated very well that the arguments for privatisation are flawed. This is an opportunity for governments to reverse the trend of the last 40 years by nationalising basic services. This is not an easy task: just remember what happened to Jeremy Corbyn, the former leader of the opposition in the UK parliament, because he declared his intention of nationalising bits and pieces of the British economy if he were to become prime minister. We would need many more Jeremy Corbyns and less of his foes if things were to change.

7.5   DEREGULATION

Deregulation is the removal or reduction of restrictions on the operations of individuals and companies. It often takes the form of eliminating a regulation entirely or altering an existing regulation to reduce its impact. Measures of deregulation may include one or more of the following: (i) reducing restrictions on conduct; (ii) removing outdated, inconsistent, or otherwise unnecessary rules; (iii) eliminating particular disfavoured regulatory impacts; and (iv) boosting competition in a regulated market. Deregulation is described by Williamson (1990) as 'another way of promoting competition' – 'another' presumably means in addition to privatisation. However, deregulation may boost the monopolistic and oligopolistic powers of big firms to the extent that they can do what they like in the absence of restrictions on their operations. They find it easier, in the absence of regulation, to make it prohibitively expensive for new firms to enter the industry.

Three broad reasons can be presented for deregulation. The first is that the underlying regulation is no longer effective, in the sense that it no longer produces socially desirable outcomes. The second reason is ideology, which explains why wholesale deregulation took off on both sides of the Atlantic as a result of the advent of Reaganism–Thatcherism in the early 1980s, justified intellectually by the teachings of Milton Friedman and Friedrich von Hayek. The third reason is that a regulated industry might seek to bring about deregulation through lobbying and campaign donations. I have to emphasise that the term 'Reaganism–Thatcherism' does not imply any intellectual power on the part of originators. Rather, it represents an ideology that was used effectively to enrich themselves, their cronies and their sponsors at the expense of the public at large.

Regulation in general is needed to preserve social values and environmental standards – otherwise, the law of the jungle will prevail in a polluted environment. Regulation is needed in cases of market failure caused by monopoly, externalities, public goods, asymmetric information, etc. These are basic principles that students of economics learn at an early stage of their study of the 'dismal science'. Regulation is required for the attainment of collective desires as judged by a significant segment of the society. Regulation is required to deal with the problem of irreversibility that a certain type of conduct from current generations can result in outcomes from which future generations may not recover at all. Even though the proponents of deregulation argue that regulation stifles competition, regulation may actually create a level playing field and boost competition (for example, by ensuring that new electricity providers have competitive access to the national grid). Unlike the rhetoric, the oligarchy does not like competition and often indulges in anti-competitive behaviour for the sake of maximising profit, which can be achieved by cutting corners and swindling consumers, and this is why regulation is needed to protect consumers from fraud. Yet, free marketeers claim that the pandemic has taught us that more deregulation is needed for post-pandemic recovery (Hanrahan, 2020).

The pandemic created an opportunity for the Trump administration to pursue its deregulatory agenda. Wallach and Weissmann (2020) suggest that 'the Trump administration has pulled a fast one, pushing through its deregulatory agenda while the nation is distracted' and that 'the Trump administration is using our national emergency to advance corporate interests'. From its earliest days, the Trump administration has aggressively pursued a deregulatory agenda, with special emphasis on reversing some of the Obama administration's most ambitious environmental initiatives. One of the first things Donald Trump did as president was to tell a group of business leaders that his administration would 'cut regulations by 75 percent. Maybe more' (Wallach, 2019).

Free marketeers are asking for more deregulation and for temporary deregulation (intended to fight the pandemic) to be made permanent. In Australia, for example, the Institute of Company Directors called on the federal government to extend temporary COVID-19 regulatory relief including weaker personal responsibility for trading while insolvent and market disclosure requirements (Hanrahan, 2020). Pipes (2020) warns of the 'dangers posed by heavy-handed government regulation', which 'were clear from the first days of the coronavirus crisis'. For example, he argues that 'one of the chief reasons it took weeks to ramp up testing is that federal regulations prevented private laboratories from assisting in the effort'. On the other hand, the pandemic has demonstrated the importance of safeguards to protect the vulnerable. Regulation aimed at consumer protection is needed to protect people from price gouging. As the pandemic progressed, scams involving COVID-19 have become apparent.

The regulation of financial transactions is still needed to protect mums and dads from financial fraud. Financial regulation can be justified on several grounds, one of which is the objective of maintaining financial stability. If corruption and fraud cause financial boom and bust, regulation against malpractices and fraudulent behaviour in the financial sector can contribute to financial instability. Another motive for financial regulation in general is consumer protection – for example, protecting the public from those selling junk bonds as

AAA securities. The global financial crisis has taught us a lesson the hard way, the lesson that corruption, fraud and greed are rampant in the finance industry, which should be regulated to avoid another crisis. While the digitalisation of financial services was already progressing rapidly, the pandemic has escalated both the pace of change and the urgency to protect consumers, particularly those interacting with digital products for the first time.

Environmental regulation is still needed to protect people from pollution. Unregulated markets cannot protect the environment because it encompasses public goods (such as clean air) whose values are not well reflected by market processes. Persico and Johnson (2020) examine the proposition that pollution could cause additional or more severe infections from COVID-19, which typically manifests as a respiratory infection. Using variation in pollution induced by a rollback of enforcement of environmental regulations by the Environmental Protection Agency (EPA), they estimated the effects of increased pollution on county-level COVID-19 deaths and cases. Despite popular media coverage to the contrary, they find that higher levels of pollution are associated with increases in cases and deaths from COVID-19.

The regulatory debate should never be about regulation versus no regulation, but rather about good regulation versus bad regulation. Regulation is needed, but bad and unnecessary regulation should be avoided. Bad regulation is bad for economic growth but good regulation is good for economic growth. The pandemic has taught us that good regulation is needed.

7.6   INTELLECTUAL PROPERTY RIGHTS

The tenth principle of the Washington Consensus is to strengthen property rights. According to Williamson (1990), 'there is general acceptance that property rights do indeed matter'. This is right, and it is probably why the Industrial Revolution started in Britain not because of technology, but because of the establishment of a sophisticated system of property rights. The dark side of property rights is that they are used by the powerful to claim ownership of property extracted by force or by illegal or immoral means. European imperialism used property rights to claim ownership of whole countries and their resources (and people). King Leopold of Belgium claimed property rights to vast regions of the Congo. The East India Company claimed property rights to vast areas of East Asia. Britain until now claims property rights to the Falklands and Gibraltar. White settlers claimed property rights to farms and fertile land in Rhodesia and South Africa. Oligarchs claim property rights to the minerals that are supposed to belong to the people at large. Slave owners claimed property rights to slaves. Multinationals claim property rights to privatised assets that they acquired cheaply through extortion and bribery. Donald Trump has claimed property right to Syria's oil because he likes oil (his words, not mine). Property rights in the Washington Consensus are not about a system that is used to protect a family home from intruders but rather they are used to protect the interests of the oligarchs and multinationals from the rightful owners of the same property rights. The tenth principle works very well with privatisation, deregulation and liberalisation to accomplish the overall objective of 'liberalise, deregulate and privatise'.

In reference to COVID-19, what we are concerned with is intellectual property (IP) rights, which include patents, copyrights and industrial design rights. The founder of the Free Software Foundation, Richard Stallman, argues that although the term 'intellectual property' is widely used, it should be rejected altogether, because it is 'promoted by those who gain from this confusion' (Stallman, 2018). He asserts that the term 'operates as a catch-all to lump together disparate laws [which] originated separately, evolved differently, cover different activities, have different rules, and raise different public policy issues'. He goes on to argue that the term creates bias by confusing these monopolies with ownership of limited physical things, likening them to property rights. Likewise, Boldrin and Levine (2008) prefer to use the term 'intellectual monopoly' as a more appropriate and clear definition of the concept, which they argue is very dissimilar from property rights. They further argue that 'stronger patents do little or nothing to encourage innovation', mainly explained by its tendency to create market monopolies, thereby restricting further innovation and technology transfer.

Intellectual property is used for tax evasion by multinationals through profit shifting. Maney (2015) explains how patents kill innovation and hold tech companies back. Kinsella (2010) argues that 'people are literally dying because Fabrazyme is in short supply and the sole, monopolistic manufacturer, Genzyme, can't make enough quickly enough – and no one else is permitted to make it due to the patent'. He criticises what he calls the 'intellectual propagandists' who 'callously, arrogantly, and smugly retort that without patents, Genzyme would never have invented the drug in the first place', which would have resulted in the death of 20,000 rather than 5,000 people. He goes on to say the following:

> So saving 15,000 (I'm guessing at the numbers) is better than none, right? So the ones who die have no complaint about the patent system, since without it they'd die anyway. What a chilling mentality; and of course there is no reason to think drugs would not be invented absent patents.

The issue of IP rights re-emerged prominently during the pandemic, particularly with respect to vaccines. In a sign of their increasing frustration with global efforts to ensure that everyone everywhere will have access to vaccines, several developing countries have asked other members of the World Trade

Organization (WTO) to join them in a sweeping waiver of the intellectual property (IP) rights relating to those vaccines. Their waiver request rekindles the recurring debate within the WTO over the right balance between the protection of IP rights and access in poorer countries to urgently needed medicines. In early October 2020, India and South Africa asked members of the WTO to waive protections in WTO rules for patents, copyrights, industrial designs, and undisclosed information (trade secrets) in relation to the 'prevention, containment or treatment of COVID-19 ... until widespread vaccination is in place globally, and the majority of the world's population has developed immunity' (Council for Trade-Related Aspects of Intellectual Property Rights, 2020). India and South Africa wanted to give all WTO members the freedom to refuse to grant or enforce patents and other IP rights relating to COVID-19 vaccines, drugs, diagnostics, and other technologies for the duration of the pandemic.

In requesting the waiver, India and South Africa argued that 'an effective response to the COVID-19 pandemic requires rapid access to affordable medical products including diagnostic kits, medical masks, other personal protective equipment and ventilators, as well as vaccines and medicines for the prevention and treatment of patients in dire need'. They argued that 'as new diagnostics, therapeutics and vaccines for COVID-19 are developed, there are significant concerns on how these will be made available promptly, in sufficient quantities and at affordable prices to meet global demand'. In October 2020, members of the WTO failed to reach a consensus to move forward with the proposed waiver. The European Union, US and other 'Western' countries opposed the waiver request (Collis, 2020). One WTO delegate, from the UK, described it as 'an extreme measure to address an unproven problem' (UK Mission to the WTO, 2020). A spokesperson for the European Union noted that 'there is no evidence that intellectual property rights are a genuine barrier for accessibility of COVID-19-related medicines and technologies' (Collis, 2020). This is a clear case of the West versus the Rest and a repeat of the controversy regarding the HIV/AIDS drugs, which were unaffordable in Africa.

Typically, contradiction between the protection of intellectual property and the need to make and distribute affordable medicines is resolved through licensing, which allows a patent holder to permit others to make or trade the protected product – usually at a price determined by, and with some supervision from, the patent holder to ensure control. In public health emergencies, however, it may be impossible to obtain a licence. In such cases 'compulsory licenses' can be issued to local manufacturers, authorising them to make patented products or use patented processes even though they do not have the permission of the patent holders (on compulsory licensing, see Reinsch et al., 2020). Compulsory licensing of medicines is not popular with private pharmaceutical companies because it hurts their bottom lines. During the

COVID-19 pandemic, they expressed their opposition to the proposed waiver of IP rights for the duration of the pandemic, warning that allowing their vaccines to be copied without their permission through recourse to compulsory licensing 'would undermine innovation and raise the risk of unsafe viruses' (Shah, 2020). Since the start of the pandemic, pharmaceutical companies have continued with their 'business-as-usual' approaches, either by maintaining rigid control over their IP rights or by pursuing secretive and monopolistic commercial deals.

Bacchus (2020) argues that the primary justification for granting and protecting IP rights is that they provide incentives for innovation, which is the main source for long-term economic growth and enhancements in the quality of human life. Undermining private IP rights, he argues, would eliminate the incentives that inspire innovation, thus preventing the discovery and development of knowledge for new goods and services that the world needs. However, IP rights should never become legal obstacles to ensuring early access to affordable medicines for everyone in the world during a pandemic that had killed more than 4.3 million people by mid-August 2021 and threatens to kill millions more.

In a pandemic, no one is safe unless everyone is safe. No one says that pharmaceutical companies should not be allowed to recoup their costs and make a decent return, but IP rights should not be used to grant the CEO a bonus of $50 million while millions die because of the monopolistic power acquired through IP rights. The Office of the United Nations High Commissioner for Human Rights (2020) notes that 'there is no room for … profitability in decision-making about access to vaccines, essential tests and treatments, and all other medical goods, services and supplies that are at the heart of the right to the highest attainable standard of health for all'.

In 1742 Benjamin Franklin invented a new type of stove, for which he was offered a patent. He refused it, arguing in his autobiography that because 'we enjoy[ed] great advantages from the inventions of others, we should be glad of an opportunity to serve others by any invention of ours' (*The Economist*, 2014). Unfortunately, this is something that does not happen these days because it is not conducive to profit maximisation. This is altruism and compassion, which (unlike greed and selfishness) have no place in mainstream economic thinking.

7.7 CONCLUDING REMARKS

In Chapter 5 we saw how China looked more like a leader, partner and aid provider in the fight against COVID-19. As a result, some observers believe that we are witnessing the acceleration of a hegemonic transition between China and the US. This trend, however, was apparent before the advent of the pandemic, with the rise of the Beijing Consensus and the demise of the Washington Consensus.

The Beijing Consensus, a term coined by Ramo (2004), represents the Chinese approach to dealing with developing countries. Instead of prescribing rigid recommendations for the problems of developing countries, the Beijing Consensus is pragmatic and recognises the need for flexibility in solving multifarious problems. The Chinese approach involves substantial investment in infrastructure and public-sector assets. It is noteworthy that without the Washington Consensus, China has managed to raise more than 700 million people out of absolute poverty since the late 1970s. Over four decades, the country has transformed itself from a major recipient of foreign aid into a critical and global provider of investment and development resources.

The Chinese model works on the basis of 'quasi-barter' such that Chinese construction and engineering companies receive funding directly from the China Export–Import Bank. In return, the host country agrees to repay the Bank over several years in commodity terms, such as oil and iron ore, whose production and marketing may be facilitated by the construction project itself. This is vastly different from the 'Western' model, which starts by sending the air force to bomb the host country back to the Stone Age. Subsequently, the resources of the bombed country are confiscated to cover the cost of bombs and rockets and make some profit (Syria is the latest example). The pandemic will give a further boost to the Beijing Consensus.

8.   Rethinking healthcare and welfare

8.1   INTRODUCTION

The advent of COVID-19 has forced a rethinking of healthcare in the direction of aspiring to universal healthcare. In the US in particular, the healthcare system is brutal. With respect to health insurance, there are the haves and have-nots: the have-nots must pay for treatment or die whereas the haves may be denied coverage on a technicality or required to make co-payments that they cannot afford. A large number of haves have become have-nots as a result of losing their jobs because of the pandemic. In the US, those who are admitted to hospital with a coronavirus infection can expect to pay anywhere from \$42,486 to \$74,310 if they are uninsured or if they receive care that is deemed out-of-network by their insurance companies. For those who have insurance and use in-network providers, out-of-pocket costs are a portion of \$21,936 to \$38,755, depending on the cost-sharing provisions of their health plan (Leonhardt, 2020). This is why Glenza (2020) suggests that 'when most Americans are admitted to the hospital, one concern beyond health is usually at the top of patient's mind: the cost of their treatment'. The expression 'financial toxicity' refers to extraneous costs and the stress of not knowing who will pay them. It is often used in discussions of cancer treatment, which is so expensive that a remarkable 42.4% of American cancer patients deplete their entire life savings two years after a diagnosis (Glenza, 2020).

The COVID-19 pandemic has shed light on the systemic flaws within healthcare systems worldwide and enforced the belief that universal healthcare (UHC) is the key to pandemic management. Without universal coverage, at least with respect to COVID-19, the mortality and infection rates are bound to be higher. However, UHC on its own cannot alleviate the suffering caused by unemployment, poverty and food insecurity, which is why the pandemic has also attracted attention to the concept of universal basic income on a temporary or permanent basis. A widespread belief has arisen that what is needed is a new New Deal, following the original New Deal that was put in place during the Great Depression of the 1930s. The current economic crisis is comparable to the Great Depression, and if the original New Deal was good enough for the Great Depression, a new New Deal may be required to deal with the COVID depression. These issues are discussed in this chapter.

8.2   UNIVERSAL HEALTHCARE

Universal healthcare (or health coverage) means that all people have access to the healthcare services they need, when and where they need them, without having to endure financial hardship. According to the United Nations (2020a), UHC is intended to provide equity in access, in the sense that everyone who needs healthcare services (and not only those who can pay for them) should get them. It is also intended to provide healthcare services that are good enough to improve the health of those receiving the services without undue financial risk. The concept of UHC captures a common set of values, irrespective of the ability to pay: equity, shared responsibility, and quality healthcare delivery.

Since the 1970s, there has been a near consensus among the public health community that UHC should be a fundamental objective that countries must strive to accomplish. At the 1978 conference in Alma-Ata, and subsequently in Ottawa in 1986, commitments were made to pursue equitable healthcare systems, which would provide access to all for point-of-entry healthcare services. Unfortunately, progress has been elusive, as the tendency has been to promote 'selective healthcare models', with substantial private-sector involvement – all in the name of the free market and the alleged efficiency of the private sector. Achieving UHC is one of the targets set when adopting the Sustainable Development Goals in 2015. UHC is implemented through legislation, regulation and taxation for the purpose of directing the services to be provided, to whom, and on what basis.

The case put for UHC by the World Health Organization (2019b) is that 'protecting people from the financial consequences of paying for health services out of their own pockets reduces the risk that people will be pushed into poverty because unexpected illness requires them to use up their life savings, sell assets, or borrow – destroying their futures and often those of their children'. When people have to pay most of the cost for health services out of their own pockets, the poor are often unable to obtain many of the services they need, and even the rich may be exposed to financial hardship in the event of severe or long-term illness.

Achieving UHC requires investment in primary healthcare, which is defined by the World Health Organization (2019b) as encompassing three components. The first is to ensure that health problems are addressed throughout the life course. The second is to address the broader determinants of health. The third is to empower individuals, families and communities to optimise their health. As such, it is suggested that primary healthcare is 'the most efficient and cost effective way to achieve universal health coverage'. Progress towards UHC can be measured in terms of the proportion of a population that can access essential quality health services and the proportion of the population that spends a large amount of household income on health. The decision to adopt UHC or otherwise is primarily political. In the absence of severe financial constraints, the adoption of UHC is more likely in the presence of strong social democratic parties and labour movement. While poverty may act as an obstacle, political commitment is conducive to UHC. Militarism is an obstacle in countries allocating huge proportions of their financial resources to the military, which deprives the healthcare system from the financial resources required to commit to UHC.

The debate on the pros and cons of UHC precedes COVID-19. The main advantage of UHC is that it is a conduit to the realisation of a human right, the right to access healthcare without ending up bankrupt or dead. UHC reduces healthcare costs as the government controls the price of healthcare services through negotiation and regulation. Naturally, free marketeers reject this perceived advantage because prices should not be controlled and regulation should be forbidden. UHC eliminates the administrative costs of dealing with different private health insurance companies and leads to a standardisation of billing procedures and coverage rules. It forces hospitals and doctors to provide the same standard of service at a low cost, which again is rejected by free marketeers on the grounds that standardisation kills innovation. UHC creates a healthier labour force because preventive care reduces the need for expensive emergency room usage. This advantage pertains to the positive effect of good health on economic growth. Another advantage of UHC is that early childhood care prevents or reduces the extent of consequences such as crime, welfare dependency, and health issues.

On the other hand, the first perceived disadvantage of UHC is that healthy people are forced to pay for others' medical care. The argument goes as follows: why would healthy people, who are healthy because they choose a healthy life style, pay for unhealthy people, who are unhealthy because they choose an unhealthy life style? There is an element of truth in this argument, but what about someone with a healthy life style who gets injured in an accident? And what about people who get sick because of pollution? Furthermore, why is that everyone contributes to the cost of militarism, which benefits a few war profiteers? Naturally, someone who wants cosmetic surgery because they do not like how their nose looks should pay for that themselves.

Another perceived disadvantage is that free healthcare encourages people to be less careful about their health because they do not have the financial incentive to do so. It also provides an incentive to overuse emergency rooms and doctors. This, however, is unlikely to be the case because most people hate to go to doctors and they do so only when they have to. It is bizarre to think that people enjoy, amongst medical activities, ambulance rides, colonoscopies, or the manual prostate 'test'. In any case, co-payments can be used to circumvent this problem.

Most UHC systems report long waiting times for elective procedures. That is right, but the solution is to divert more resources to healthcare (preferably from the military). In any case, nothing is wrong with waiting if the situation is not life threatening or not painful. Another alleged disadvantage is that government-imposed limits on payments, to keep costs low, make doctors less inclined to provide high-quality service and more inclined to spend less time per patient. This is an issue of consumer protection, which is not unique to healthcare. The opponents of UHC also believe that healthcare costs overwhelm government budgets, which reduces funding for other programmes like education and infrastructure. Naturally, no one talks about the resources allocated to militarism, bailouts or tax cuts for the rich.

The last point is that to cut costs, the government may limit services with a low probability of success by excluding drugs for rare conditions and prioritising palliative care over expensive end-of-life care. There is nothing wrong here – this is a general problem related to scarcity and choice where choice should be made for the benefit of the majority of the population. Free flu shots are more effective than a $10,000 pill that may or may not prevent death at an old age from a rare disease.

The fact of the matter is that universal healthcare is opposed because healthcare is a very profitable business, since we are talking about the provision of goods and services with very low price and income elasticities of demand. Naturally, this is not what free marketeers and the private healthcare industry say. Some 20 years before he became president, Ronald Reagan (who is famous for saying that the government cannot solve a problem because the government is the problem) argued against any role for the government in the provision of healthcare. In a radio address on the so-called 'socialised medicine', he suggested that 'one of the traditional methods of imposing statism or socialism on a people has been by way of medicine'. He described the movement towards universal healthcare as the 'most imminent threat' to the American people and insisted that the free enterprise system had it all: 'the privacy, the care that is given to a person, the right to choose a doctor, the right to go from one doctor to the other' (Reagan, 1961). In 2012, Mitt Romney argued that healthcare should 'act more like a consumer market, meaning like the things we deal with every day in our lives: the purchases of tires, of automobiles, of air filters, of all sorts of products' because 'consumer markets tend to work very well – keep the costs down and the quality up' (Romney, 2012).

The use of expressions like 'socialism' and 'statism' is meant to instil fear in the community. How can UHC be a threat to the American people when thousands of them die every year, either because they do not have health insurance or because they are refused coverage on a technicality? How can it be a threat when the alternative is to choose between bankruptcy and death, except for a minority? Yes, someone who can afford a private suite in a private hospital will get five-star care, but how many people can afford that? Who says that under UHC you cannot choose a doctor? The rich Romney advocates the commodification of healthcare like anything else in the free market system. It seems that Romney has not seen any statistics on the rising costs of healthcare, which is why he makes the heroic and dishonest statement that private health-care costs are going down. Remember that this market is characterised by oligopolistic competition for goods and services with low elasticity of demand.

The advent of COVID-19 has revealed the inadequacy of healthcare systems worldwide because the absence of universal coverage has caused so much pain and suffering. The fragility of healthcare systems is evident by the failure to contain the virus and treat infected patients. The crisis has highlighted and amplified gaps in access to quality healthcare systems between and within countries. When COVID-19 emerged in Kenya, rich people sent samples through private labs to South Africa for testing whereas poor people had no choice but to wait for the public healthcare system to provide tests. Inequity is evident not only in terms of testing but also in terms of treatment and vacci-nation. The crisis has also shown that providing quality healthcare to the poor and unprivileged is important, not only for social justice, but also for disease containment. Furthermore, the COVID-19 crisis has highlighted the links between health and other sectors of the economy. There can no longer be any question about the links between public health and the broader resilience of economies and societies. COVID-19 has reinforced existing evidence for the proposition that investment in healthcare produces long-term returns, while underinvestment has devastating large-scale social and economic effects that could last for years.

COVID-19 has reinforced the belief that financial barriers should be removed from individuals' decisions about whether or not to seek care. In a pandemic, patients should not pay at the point of care for essential services because the expectation of payment may pose a substantial barrier to seeking and receiving the needed care. While this is generally a concern for ensuring equitable access, it takes on additional importance in the context of a highly communicable disease, affecting not only the person who might need care but others who might be affected by that person. The pandemic has also reinforced messages about the financing of UHC. If health coverage is linked to employ-ment, an economic shock that leads to job losses has negative consequences for health coverage, which is at odds with the proposition that the right to health coverage is not a mere employee benefit. Therefore, in countries that rely on contributory, employment-linked coverage, it is essential to inject general budget revenues into the system, both to reduce the vulnerability of the system to job losses and to ensure that the essential actions needed to respond to the pandemic can be implemented.

The proposition that countries with universal healthcare systems are in a better position to deal with the pandemic has been recognised by the United Nations (2020a). With universal health coverage in place, countries could address more effectively and efficiently the three ways in which the pandemic is directly and indirectly causing morbidity and mortality: the first is due to the virus itself, the second is due to the inability of healthcare systems to provide ongoing essential services, and the third is linked to its socio-economic impact. The lessons learned call for a healthcare system that ensures equal access to quality healthcare without financial risks for everyone and a system that effectively protects societies from a health crisis that has devastating effects on lives and livelihoods.

Tediosi et al. (2020) argue that the COVID-19 pandemic further highlighted the importance of UHC that should be promoted with better governance and linkages to social protection systems. They put forward four propositions on how to move forward. The first is that moving towards and sustaining UHC is required for the purpose of building resilient healthcare systems and to promote more inclusive and fairer societies. The second proposition is that the progressive realisation of UHC requires good governance and linkages with social protection systems. The third is that UHC policies should be coordinated with social protection systems to provide social safety nets. Last, but not least, system-wide social and healthcare policies break the boundaries of traditionally fragmented welfare systems and global health programmes.

Let us consider some events, facts and figures that show how vital UHC is. The first is a story that is not related to COVID-19, but it serves the purpose of demonstrating that UHC is important even without COVID. The story, told by the World Health Organization (2010), is that of a motorcycle accident that took place somewhere in Thailand on 7 October 2006 involving Narin Pintalakarn, an ordinary citizen earning $5 a day, whose life was saved even though he sustained horrific injuries. As he struck a tree, his unprotected head took the full force of the impact. Passing motorists found him some time later and took him to a nearby hospital. Doctors diagnosed severe head injury and referred him to the trauma centre, 65 km away, where the diagnosis was confirmed. A scan showed subdural haematoma with subfalcine and uncal herniation. Pintalakarn's skull had fractured in several places, and his brain had bulged and shifted. He was taken to an emergency department where a surgeon removed part of his skull to relieve pressure. A blood clot was also removed. Five hours later, the patient was put on a respirator and taken to the intensive care unit where he stayed for 21 days. Thirty-nine days after being admitted to hospital, he had recovered sufficiently to be discharged. And he did not have to pay anything. He received the treatment because Thai legislation demands that all injured patients be taken care of with a standard procedure, no matter what their status is. He would have probably (or most likely) died, had the accident occurred in a country where healthcare is financed by private insurance.

Now consider the following story as told by Beaumont (2020). In mid-March 2020, American comedian Baten Phillips tested positive for COVID-19. He fought for his life in the intensive care unit for six weeks, at which point the hospital gave him a choice: stay longer and add to his bill, or leave and pay for oxygen at a lower cost. Phillips has diabetes, making his COVID-19 infection more severe, and with no health insurance, he pays for medication and hospital costs out-of-pocket. He chose to leave, but he still incurred $14,000 in medical bills even though that hospital had received $145 million through the CARES Act that was supposed to provide aid to hospitals hit hard by COVID-19 (not sure what this means because COVID is a blessing for a profit-maximising hospital seeking paying customers). The hospital claimed that the aid did not cover its entire financial gap. Beaumont (2020) also tells the story of a COVID-19 survivor who was billed $1.1 million by a hospital in Seattle.

On the other hand, Kliff (2020) tells the story of another COVID survivor, Donald J. Trump, who did not have to worry about the cost of his treatment. For the nearly half a million other Americans to have been admitted to hospital with COVID-19, it is a different story. He did not have to worry about surprise bills and medical debt, even after health insurance paid its share. The former president's treatment was paid for in full by taxpayers. This is why he was impressed as he praised the high-quality care he received at the Walter Reed National Military Medical Center. When he recovered, he told the taxpayers who paid for his treatment not to be afraid of the virus. In a tweet, he said the following to those who could not afford the treatment: 'Don't be afraid of COVID'. That was quite reassuring for those who lost loved ones to the virus.

8.3 UNIVERSAL BASIC INCOME

In his 1516 fictional work, *Utopia*, the philosopher Thomas More described a conversation between a Portuguese traveller, Raphael Nonsenso, and the Archbishop of Canterbury, John Morton, in which the former argued that cash handouts provided by the state could reduce theft in the city of Antwerp. According to More, Nonsenso declared that no penalty, no matter how severe, would stop people from stealing, if it is their only way of getting food and that it would be a good idea to provide everyone with some means of livelihood. According to Gifford (2020), 'this is thought to be the earliest written example of a concept that's still considered radical today: universal basic income'.

Under a universal basic income (UBI) scheme, payments are disbursed by the government to citizens to provide a secure income. Such a scheme should meet the following criteria: (i) the payments are distributed to individuals, (ii) it does not involve means testing, (iii) the payments are unconditional (for example, the requirement that the recipient seeks employment or attends school), (iv) the payments are made at regular intervals, and (v) the recipient has the freedom to choose how the money is spent. UBI is intended to alleviate mass poverty or financial hardship resulting, for example, from unemployment. In other words, a universal basic income scheme has five key characteristics: it is regular, paid in cash, provided to individuals, universal with no means test, and it is unconditional with no requirement to work or seek work.

At the onset of the COVID-19 pandemic, governments struggled to address both the healthcare crisis and rapidly deteriorating economic conditions. In response, governments worldwide adopted large economic relief programmes to help those in need. On 11 March 2021, President Joseph Biden signed a $1.9 trillion relief package into law, authorising a massive infusion of federal aid aimed primarily at working families. On that occasion, Biden said that 'this historic legislation is about rebuilding the backbone of this country and giving people in this nation, working people, middle class folks, the people who built this country, a fighting chance' (Stokols, 2021). The relief package includes a one-off $1,400-per-person stimulus payment to about 90% of households and a $300 federal boost to weekly jobless benefits.

While this is commendable, the lesson learned from previous occasions is that most families spend their one-time cash payment on rent and food during the month it is provided, leaving them with an uncertain future as their ability to earn an income diminishes and the promise of additional relief wanes. Even worse, most of those living in rental accommodation and who lost their jobs are in arrears, which means that this payment will not save them from eviction. This is why over 500 academics and public figures from around the globe signed an open letter in March 2020, urging governments to enact emergency basic income during the pandemic on the grounds that it could provide vital support to small businesses and the self-employed, many of whom have been neglected in governments' financial stimulus packages during the pandemic (Gifford, 2020). It is plausible to suggest that UBI could limit the virus's spread by making social distancing more feasible and that without the need to work, fewer vulnerable people would put themselves at the risk of contracting the disease.

Some countries are already taking the idea seriously. On 15 June 2020, Spain (one of the hardest-hit countries at the start of the pandemic) offered monthly payments of €1,015 to the poorest families. In August 2020 Germany announced that it was experimenting with such a system in a three-year study, giving monthly payments of €1,200 to 120 Germans and aiming to compare the results with 1,380 people who do not receive the payments (Gifford, 2020).

While universal basic income has been a debatable topic for a long time, the advent of the pandemic has revived the debate on the pros, cons and alternatives. The first argument for UBI is that it is needed to provide freedom for all.

This is not the same freedom that free marketeers brag about – the freedom of the business sector to operate without restrictions. Rather, it is freedom from poverty, which free marketeers never talk about (they do not recognise the difference between 'freedom to' and 'freedom from'). A related point is that UBI can potentially empower workers to refuse bad or unsafe jobs. In such instances, it could facilitate people's efforts to seek different employment or start a new career. UBI would free people to pursue creative ideas or to take up volunteering or entrepreneurial roles that offer meaning but which are not financially sustainable.

UBI offers financial stability, which is particularly beneficial for disadvantaged workers, such as people taking precarious jobs or temporary positions (the gig economy). In cases like these, UBI would reduce the stress of irregular income or losing one's income. It could also serve as a safety net for those who do not qualify for other benefits due to weak employment status, without stigmatising the recipients. Under COVID-19, UBI would support temporary workers who see their livelihood vanish with the crumbling economy. It could also improve people's lives significantly, by providing them with more income to spend on diet and by potentially eliminating homelessness.

One argument that has been put forward in defence of UBI is the impact of automation on employment. The underlying idea is that the corporate sector uses automation to boost profit by reducing labour cost. The proponents of UBI argue that although automation displaces jobs, it also creates surplus within the economy. This surplus, they assert, should be shared by the society through a universal basic income (for example, Susskind, 2020a, 2020b). This point is relevant to the basic contradiction in capitalism that workers are also consumers. Reducing labour cost by firing workers means that those workers will not have income to spend on the goods and services produced by robots, in which case UBI may be useful for the corporate sector. In fact, UBI could preserve capitalism.

A related point is that of under-consumption. When income and wealth are concentrated in a small minority of the population, consumption will be low because there is a limit on the items purchased by rich people. Someone on a million dollar annual income does not buy 20 times the number of burgers bought by 20 people on $50,000 each. In an expanding economy, production tends to grow more rapidly than consumption as a result of unequal distribution of income, which pushes the economy into recession. A 2017 study by the Roosevelt Institute found that giving every adult in the US $1,000 a month could add $2.5 trillion to the economy by 2025 (Gifford, 2020).

Libertarians who aspire for small governments may be in favour of UBI on the grounds that the government can reduce or eliminate other forms of welfare payments, thereby reducing bureaucracy. The underlying idea is that people know best how to spend their money and are free to buy the services they want, liberating governments from the need to provide free or subsidised services. Milton Friedman's advocacy of negative income tax falls in this domain as suggested by Milton and Rose Friedman in a brief section of their book *Capitalism and Freedom* (Friedman and Friedman, 1962). In his 1966 paper, *View from the Right*, Friedman remarked that his proposal 'has been greeted with considerable (though far from unanimous) enthusiasm on the left and with considerable (though again far from unanimous) hostility on the right'. He argued that 'the negative income tax is more compatible with the philosophy and aims of the proponents of limited government and maximum individual freedom than with the philosophy and aims of the proponents of the welfare state and greater government control of the economy' (Friedman, 1966). In their book, *Free to Choose*, the Friedmans promoted the idea to a wider audience, arguing that the proposal has the advantages of alleviating poverty, eliminating the 'welfare trap' and streamlining the benefits system (Friedman and Friedman, 1980).

The common wealth argument is also put forward to advocate UBI. According to this argument, which is based on Thomas Paine's 'Rights of Man' school of thought (Paine, 1791), the earth's resources should be shared fairly, in which case UBI would be a way for everyone to share in the proceeds of public goods. Naturally, this idea is opposed by the mining cabal on the grounds that resource exploitation requires individual risk taking and that common ownership of resources takes us on a route to communism. So, it is communism if natural resources are publicly owned and the revenues derived from those resources are used to finance public welfare. And it is freedom and democracy if resources are extracted and sold for private profit (without paying taxes) by a Mafia of oligarchs with close connections to the people in power.

The last argument for UBI is that it is a means of income redistribution that can help reduce the extent of inequality, which has been made much worse by the pandemic. In recent decades, particularly since the *laissez faire* revolution of the 1980s, the share of the wealth generated by the society has disproportionally benefited the super-rich, while real wages have stagnated. UBI can address skewed wealth and income distributions, which would lead to less divided societies.

The main argument against UBI is affordability, which is put forward succinctly by Martinelli (2017) who argues that 'an affordable UBI is inadequate, and an adequate UBI is unaffordable'. This is the same argument put forward against universal healthcare and housing the homeless – that they are unaffordable. The fact of the matter is that UBI is unaffordable because it is a matter of choice and that it can be financed in a number of ways. The first is to divert resources away from the military, the resources that are not needed to defend the homeland but to benefit the military-industrial complex.

The US, for example, can defend the homeland with one-fifth of the trillion dollars spent on the military every year. If the objective of the military is to save lives, social welfare can save more lives than nuclear submarines and ballistic missiles. The second means is to plug loopholes in the tax system and force the corporate sector and the super-rich to pay their dues. One idea is to impose a tax on the purchase of luxury goods. Someone paying $100 million for a yacht or a private jet can afford to pay $120 million. The third means of financing, as argued earlier, is nationalising the mining sector in resource-rich countries such as Australia. It does not make any sense that the resources underneath are extracted and sold for private profit by individuals and companies because at one time they struck a deal to do so with a corrupt politician.

The proponents of UBI argue that it is much more affordable than people think. In a working paper for the United Nations Development Programme, Molina and Ortiz-Juarez (2020) estimate the cost of providing temporary basic income to all people living below the poverty line could cost between $200 billion and $465 billion per month (depending on the specific policy) which is reasonable, given that it could keep 2.78 billion people out of poverty. Gifford (2020) quotes the economist Karl Widerquist as saying that to fund a UBI of $12,000 per adult and $6,000 per child annually, the US would have to raise an additional $539 billion a year, which is much less than the alleged trillions of dollars suggested by the opponents. It is also half the amount allocated to the war machine. It is typically the case that the opponents exaggerate the cost of UBI (just like the amounts spent by Big Pharma on research and development).

The second argument against UBI is the availability of better, more feasible alternatives. The critics suggest that a universal basic income distracts time and resources from pursuing these other policies (for example, Piachaud, 2018; Haagh, 2019). Some alternatives, which make a lot of sense, can be suggested. The first is to consider universality versus targeting because it has been established that the low-paid are among those hit worst by the lockdown (Joyce and Xu, 2020). Clearly, poor households are in greater need of help than rich ones for coping with COVID-19. This suggests that targeted income support may be the priority rather than universal income payments. The second alternative is the provision of universal basic services, including healthcare, education, shelter, food, transport, legal and information. These services can be funded publicly and made available free of charge at the point of delivery. Another alternative is a temporary variety of UBI to overcome the hardship instigated by COVID-19. Several benefits can be envisaged from such a scheme: (i) it serves as a cushion for people who are unemployed or under-employed during the crisis; (ii) it serves as a cushion for essential workers who typically earn very low wages and could benefit from a bonus that recognises their contribution to society; (iii) it serves as a stimulus for the economy as a whole; and (iv) it is simpler than other policies, as it involves lower transaction costs and less bureaucracy (such as delays due to determining eligibility).

Yet another argument against UBI is that it would dampen the incentive to work. However, it has been demonstrated that UBI has no or limited adverse effect on labour force participation (Bregman, 2017; Calnitsky and Latner 2017; Standing, 2017). Furthermore, it has been suggested that a decline in employment, should it occur in the presence of UBI, would not necessarily be a negative outcome because full employment is an uncertain ideal in a context where automation has caused many jobs to disappear and where unemployment rates are generally higher today than in previous decades (OECD, 2018).

UBI may actually boost labour participation by alleviating the many different 'policy traps' that limit people's ability to participate in the labour force. These include the poverty and unemployment traps of being caught in social assistance or unemployment benefits, because receiving an income from work reduces the benefit award or amount. Another is the employment trap, when people are caught in low-wage jobs in order to survive, which makes it impossible to invest time or income into things such as childcare and education that might, in the long run, prove beneficial to employment (Van Parijs and Vanderborght, 2017). The 'disability trap' arises when income support depends on individuals' ability to prove their inability to work due to injury or illness. This takes time away from actual rehabilitation and may provide a disincentive for attempting to overcome disability.

The empirical evidence on the hypothesis that universal basic income could make people lazy is at best mixed. When Finland experimented with UBI for nearly two years between January 2017 and December 2018, the researchers concluded that while it made unemployed people happier, it did not lead to increased employment (Gifford, 2020). However, the trial involved only 2,000 people who had to take cuts to other forms of government support. Gifford (2020) quotes Liz Fouksman of the University of Oxford as saying that 'we actually know from tonnes of randomised control trials experiments and pilot programmes around the world dating back as far as the 1960s that when people have a guaranteed income, actually, most of the time their participation in the economy increases'. This happens because the ability of workers to find jobs gets bigger, as they can migrate to places where jobs are available or because they are in a position to finish their education and apply for more skill-intensive jobs. It also happens because UBI puts them in a better position to take a risk and start their own businesses.

The money for nothing argument is also used against UBI. This mentality is deeply ingrained within capitalist society and neoliberal thinking where it is customary to demonise the victim. Why is it that when a poor person gets $1,000 a month in UBI, it is money for nothing, but when the executives of failed banks get bonuses and golden parachutes out of taxpayers' money, it is well deserved as a reward for their 'achievements'? What about getting the same out of depositors' money, when a failed bank demands the implementation of bail-in legislation, which enables banks to confiscate deposits? What about someone who becomes a billionaire by extracting and selling for private profit natural resources that in theory belong to the people at large?

Right now there are those who believe that universal basic income should be much more than an emergency response to the pandemic. They would like to see UBI become integrated into economic systems around the world. However, there are those who cannot accept the proposition that UBI is a fundamental right, but rather another 'handout'. A change of heart would require a huge shift within the belief system of capitalist society, and now could be the right time for that shift in perception. It is not unfeasible that universal basic income could become part of the legacy that the pandemic leaves behind, even though better alternatives are available.

8.4 FOOD INSECURITY

Food security refers to the physical availability of food, and to whether or not people have the resources and opportunity to gain reliable access to it. Thus, food insecurity is represented by limited or uncertain access to sufficient, nutritious food for a healthy life. The 1996 World Food Summit defines food security as a situation 'when all people, at all times, have physical and economic access to sufficient, safe and nutritious food to meet their dietary needs and food preferences for an active and healthy life' (FAO, 1996). The four pillars of food security, as identified by FAO (2006), are availability, access, utilisation and stability of supply. A food-insecure household lacks sufficient resources to provide adequate nutrition to its members.

People experiencing severe food insecurity skip meals or go hungry, either because they cannot afford food or because they lack access to it. The experience of food insecurity is stressful, and it is associated with numerous harmful physical and mental health outcomes in the short as well as the long run. Among children, food insecurity is also associated with adverse behavioural and learning outcomes. Children born into food-insecure households risk birth defects and those living in food-insecure households tend to have a lower health-related quality of life as well as cognitive and behavioural problems that affect wellbeing and school performance.

The COVID-19 pandemic is having diverse and multi-faceted impacts on the global food system. Reduced productivity, breakdown of distribution chains, changes in demand, supply chain restrictions and trade measures brought in to deal with these problems have far-reaching consequences, which can cascade through food systems, potentially affecting people and societies far from the sites of primary impacts. The effect of the pandemic on food security runs through the negative effect on incomes and supply chains, which affects food production. Even before the advent of the pandemic, hunger was on the rise as a result of conflict, deteriorating socio-economic conditions, natural disasters, climate change and the prevalence of pests. Because of COVID-19, the year 2020 marks a catastrophic rise in food insecurity worldwide, impacting particularly vulnerable families in almost every country.

Border closures, trade restrictions and confinement measures have been preventing farmers from accessing markets to buy inputs and sell their produce. The same factors have been preventing agricultural workers from harvesting crops, thus disrupting domestic and international food supply chains and reducing access to healthy, safe and diverse diets. According to the United Nations (2020b) measures taken to control or mitigate the pandemic are already affecting global food supply chains. Border restrictions and lockdowns are, for example, slowing harvests in some parts of the world, leaving millions of seasonal workers without work, while also constraining the transport of food to markets. Meat processing plants and food markets have been forced to close in many locations due to serious outbreaks among workers. Farmers have been burying perishable produce or dumping milk as a result of supply chain disruption. Consequently, many people in urban centres struggle to access fresh fruits and vegetables, dairy, meat and fish. Mundell (2020) points out that in many countries, the threat of hunger and malnutrition as a result of COVID-19 is greater than the virus itself.

Even though global food prices are stable, a large number of countries are experiencing food price inflation at the retail level, reflecting pandemic-instigated supply disruptions. Higher retail prices and reduced incomes mean that households have to cut down on the quantity and quality of their food consumption. The World Food Programme (2020) estimated that 271.8 million people in countries where it operates are 'acutely food insecure or directly at the risk of becoming so'. According to the United Nations (2020b) the food security of 135 million people can be categorised as crisis level or worse.

The current food insecurity is not driven by food shortages, but rather by supply disruptions and inflation affecting key agricultural inputs such as fertilisers and seeds, or prolonged labour shortages that could diminish next season's crop. If farmers are experiencing acute hunger, they may prioritise consuming seeds as food today over planting seeds for tomorrow, raising the threat of food shortages later on. The World Bank (2020) identifies 'food security hot spots' as the following: (i) fragile and conflict-affected states, where logistics and distribution are difficult even without morbidity and social distancing; (ii) countries affected by multiple crises resulting from more frequent extreme weather events (floods, droughts and pests); (iii) the poor and vulnerable, including the 690 million people who were already chronically or acutely food-insecure before the COVID-19 crisis; (iv) countries with significant currency depreciation (driving up the cost of imported food); and (v) countries experiencing a collapse of commodity prices (reducing their capacity to import food).

Food insecurity is not observed in developing countries only. Pollard and Booth (2019) point out that 'household food insecurity is a serious public health concern in rich countries with developed economies closely associated with inequality'. They put the prevalence of household food insecurity in some developed countries in the range of 8–20% of the population. Wolfson and Leung (2020) suggest that the disruptions to daily life generated by COVID-19 have created unique hardships, particularly for low-income Americans and communities of colour, who are historically at higher risk for food insecurity, and who are also at disproportionately higher risk for negative health and economic outcomes associated with the pandemic. Likewise, Bauer (2020) points out that since the onset of the pandemic, food insecurity has risen in the US. The same goes for the UK, as Butler (2020) notes that the pandemic has had a catastrophic effect on the nutritional health of the UK's poorest citizens with as many as one in ten forced to use food banks, and vast numbers skipping meals and going hungry.

Food insecurity is a problem that has been aggravated by the pandemic all over the world. It warrants some action since the market mechanism cannot relieve the pain and suffering of those who are food-insecure. Perhaps universal basic income or one of the viable alternatives would help in this matter. What should change is the free market mentality that those who cannot pay for food should be condemned to starvation.

8.5   HOMELESSNESS

One tends to think that the homeless are those who sleep rough; those whom wc see sleep on the street and beg for help. The fact of the matter is that those who sleep on the street represent a small fraction of the homeless. The majority of the homeless are the 'hidden' homeless, those who may be staying in temporary accommodation, sleeping in cars or caravans or the so-called 'sofa surfers' – those who are allowed to sleep on someone's sofa on a temporary basis.

Fondeville and Ward (2011) classify the homeless into the following categories: (i) people without a roof over their heads who sleep rough or in overnight shelters; (ii) people without a home who have a roof over their heads but they are excluded from the legal rights of occupancy and do not have a place to pursue normal social relations (such as those living in hostels or temporary accommodation for the homeless, women living in refuge accommodation, migrants living in specific accommodation and people living in institutions);

(iii) people living in insecure housing who do not have a secure tenancy and/ or are threatened with eviction; (iv) people living in inadequate housing conditions (with friends or relatives, in squats, in caravans or illegal campsites, in conditions of extreme over-crowding and in other generally unsuitable places). On the other hand, Bainbridge and Carrizales (2017) distinguish between rooflessness (without a shelter of any kind, sleeping rough) and houselessness (with a place to sleep but temporary in institutions or shelter).

When the pandemic forced countries into lockdown and confined people to their homes, governments had to confront an urgent question: how do stay-at-home orders apply to someone without a home? The answer is simple: provide them with accommodation, and this is what some governments did. Within days of imposing the first national lockdown in the UK on 23 March 2020, the government told local authorities to shelter any person in need of accommodation. As a result, thousands of homeless people were placed in vacant hotel rooms, student dormitories and other forms of temporary housing. While the exercise was costly, the alternative would have been failure to contain the virus. The homeless have lower life expectancy, suffer from addiction and have underlying health conditions that put them at greater risk if (or when) they catch the virus.

A report, published by the non-profit National Alliance to End Homelessness, projects that the homeless population in the US 'will be twice as likely to be hospitalized, two to four times as likely to require critical care, and two to three times as likely to die as the general population' (Culhane et al., 2020). The report raises concern about the potential for widespread transmission of COVID-19 within the homeless population due to inadequate access to hygiene and sanitation and the difficulty of early detection among a population isolated from healthcare. The report finds that that 21,295 homeless people, or 4.3% of the US homeless population, could be admitted to hospital at the peak infection rate. The second finding is that critical care needs could range from 0.6% to 4.2%, with the midpoint scenario indicating 7,145 in critical care nationwide. The third finding is a wide range (0.3% to 1.9%) of potential mortality rates, with the central estimate of 0.7%, implying 3,454 homeless deaths. The authors of the report warn that 'the true likely fatality outcome would be on the higher end of this range given the challenge of actually getting homeless clients to the hospital, especially when they are unsheltered, as well as the unusually high mortality risks that prevail among the homeless population'.

Housing the homeless during the pandemic was a good step, both as a humanitarian gesture and a public health measure. The question is what will happen when the pandemic is over? Will the homeless return to the street? This is so much the case because the pandemic must have caused an increase in the number of the homeless, given the inability of millions of people to pay rent or mortgage as a result of losing their jobs. The same happened during the global financial crisis as the number of families entering the New York City homeless shelters jumped by 40% during the period July–November 2008 compared with the same period of 2007 (Sard, 2009).

Housing the homeless permanently will be impeded by the issue of affordability (real or imaginary) or the other issue that no one should get anything for nothing. However, it has been found that it is significantly cheaper for governments to provide housing than to have people continuing to sleep on the street. For example, the cost of homelessness in the Australian state of Victoria has been estimated at $25,615 per person per year, covering health, crime and other factors. With 7,600 Victorians living on the street, that represents an annual cost of $194 million, which would produce savings of $10,800 per year when calculated over 20 years (Stayner, 2017). This is because when the homeless are provided with a roof over their heads, the demand for emergency services will decline because of the consequent reduction in crime. As Skinner and Carnemolla (2020) put it, 'beyond the human tragedy, what most passers-by fail to see is the cost of homelessness to us all', which includes 'the bills for police and ambulance call-outs, prison nights, visits to emergency departments, hospital stays and mental health and drying out clinics'. It would also improve the quality of life of the people involved.

For the US, it is estimated that the cost of eradicating homelessness is $20 billion which is slightly less than what Americans spend on Christmas decorations. It is less than taxpayer subsidies for the oil industry. It is much less than the savings realised by responsibly cutting spending on nuclear weapons. It is about one-third of the amount that can be saved by eliminating corporate meals and entertainment write-offs. And it is by far less than the amount that can be saved by eliminating capital gains tax cuts (Kavoussi, 2012). Skinner and Carnemolla (2020) tell a story of two Nevada police officers who spent much of their time dealing with homeless people. The bills of one particular homeless person were so legendary that it would have been cheaper to put him in a hotel with a private nurse. The conclusion was that 'the kind of money it would take to solve the homeless problem could well be less than the kind of money it took to ignore it'.

COVID-19 has shown us that the homeless problem is solvable and that the solution could actually provide some savings. Let us hope that the response to homelessness during the pandemic becomes permanent and that the homelessness problem is solved once and for all. This is how Skinner and Carnemolla (2020) put it:

> Our review found a clear economic case for governments to take a systematic approach to ending homelessness. While this argument might be seen as a capitulation to the 'financialisation of everything', the darkening economic cloud of the

pandemic might provide just the right cover for government decision-makers to act on the catastrophe of homelessness.

Even on cost considerations alone, housing the homeless pays off. It pays off more so in terms of social costs and benefits.

8.6   CONCLUDING REMARKS: NEW DEAL 2.0?

In his address at the Democratic National Convention in 1932, Franklin D. Roosevelt (FDR) declared that 'economic laws are not made by nature', but rather 'they are made by human beings'. He saw the solution in the New Deal, a series of programmes, public work projects, financial reforms, and regulatory measures that were enacted by the FDR administration between 1933 and 1939. New constraints and safeguards were introduced to reduce the power of bankers, including the Glass–Steagall Act which separated investment banking from commercial banking. The programmes were implemented according to laws passed by Congress and presidential executive orders. The main drive was to provide relief for the unemployed and poor, support economic recovery, and reform of the financial system as a financial collapse was a precursor to the Great Depression.

The COVID-19 pandemic has produced a blueprint for the next New Deal as envisaged by the Roosevelt Institute, a think tank that is affiliated with the Franklin D. Roosevelt Presidential Library. In a report entitled *A True New Deal: Building an Inclusive Economy in the COVID-19 Era*, inspiration from FDR is spelled out as follows (Roosevelt Institute, 2020):

> As FDR proved, in providing the immediate relief our country needs, we can also confront broken power structures head-on; by curbing excess concentrations of corporate power and reviving the use of public power in our response to crisis, we can build a more inclusive economy that is more resilient to the challenges we will face in the years and decades to come.

The new New Deal as outlined in the report consists of nine essential policies: (i) cancelling student, housing and medical debts – and implementing structural change to address the accumulation of debt; (ii) creating a federal jobs guarantee; (iii) federalising and expanding unemployment insurance; (iv) building a modern reconstruction finance corporation; (v) guaranteeing universal childcare; (vi) mandating sectoral bargaining; (vii) ensuring corporate accountability through federal chartering; (viii) reinvigorating antitrust law for real trust-busting; and (ix) rebalancing political power through institutional reform. These policies are described as being 'particularly important because they target not only the effects of COVID-19 but the broken economic system that has amplified them'. Some policy-makers may argue that the most pressing problems at hand must be dealt with immediately while others can wait. The report responds to this point by suggesting that 'the policies proposed here show that this is a false choice' because 'we can address the pandemic while also dismantling systemic racism, strengthening democracy, diminishing outsize corporate power, creating better jobs, and building worker power'.

The new New Deal is not an idea that is entertained in the US only. In a report published by the UK House of Lords (2020), entitled *Employment and COVID-19: Time for a New Deal*, three main recommendations are made in a plan for recovery: redirecting investment towards creating jobs; introducing a new job, skills and training guarantee; and enhancing existing skills, training and employment support policies. Likewise, South Korea's President Moon Jae-in has proposed a Korean version of the New Deal to combat the economic setbacks caused by the pandemic and sharply declining exports of Korean manufactured goods (Kirk, 2020). Moon promised what he said would be 'unprecedented investment in the Korean version of the New Deal', placing great emphasis on the need to provide work for jobless people.

A new New Deal will address most of the concerns highlighted in this chapter. The obstacle to the development and implementation of a new New Deal is that no contemporary political leader is a Franklin D. Roosevelt in terms of vision and courage. Unlike FDR, contemporary political leaders believe that economic laws are made by the almighty market, and the market cannot be wrong. Free marketeers do not like anything that remotely resembles FDR's New Deal.

9.   Rethinking the status quo

9.1   INTRODUCTION

Under the status quo and the dominance of neoliberal thinking, some propositions are accepted as undisputed facts of life and the outcomes as inevitable. Globalisation is necessary and beneficial. Deindustrialisation is a natural outcome of progression. Financialisation is another outcome of natural progression. Inequality is acceptable. Poverty is inevitable. Minimum wages are bad for the economy and so are maximum wages. These propositions are acceptable because they are determined by market outcomes, and the market cannot be wrong. If anything, COVID-19 is a neoliberal pandemic as correctly argued and rationalised by Šumonja (2020).

COVID-19 has implications for all of these 'undisputed facts of life'. Globalisation must be handled with care and it must not follow a unified model. Deindustrialisation to the core may not be a good idea because it instils economic vulnerability. Financialisation has led to the creation of a paper economy without much wealth creation but rampant wealth transfer from Main Street to Wall Street. Poverty is not inevitable and a social safety net is warranted. The pandemic has shown that minimum wages can go a long way towards sheltering people from poverty, and that they are good for the economy. The heroes of the pandemic, health workers and otherwise, have demonstrated how valuable they are to our wellbeing, in which case they deserve better pay at a time when a CEO gets hundreds of multiples of the wage earned by an ordinary worker.

These issues are discussed in this chapter to find out how the pandemic may have forced rethinking of the status quo. We will find out that changing the status quo will not be easy in the presence of powerful beneficiaries who oppose changes that undermine their power and privileges (and their ability to accumulate more wealth). Those beneficiaries, who practise 'scratch my back and I will scratch yours', belong to the alliance between a bad government and the oligarchy.

9.2   GLOBALISATION

Scholars have come up with various definitions of globalisation. Albrow and King (1990) define the term as 'all those processes by which the people of the world are incorporated into a single world society'. Giddens (1990) describes globalisation as 'the intensification of worldwide social relations which link distant localities in such a way that local happenings are shaped by events occurring many miles away and vice versa'. For Robertson (1992), globalisation is the 'compression of the world and the intensification of the consciousness of the world as a whole'. Held et al. (1999) define it as a 'continuum with the local, national and regional', referring to 'those spatial-temporal processes of change which underpin a transformation in the organization of human affairs by linking together and expanding human activity across regions and continents'. James (2005) describes globalisation as 'the extension of social relations across world-space, defining that world-space in terms of the historically variable ways that it has been practiced and socially understood through changing world-time'. The Peterson Institute for International Economics (2018) defines globalisation as 'the word used to describe the growing interdependence of the world's economies, cultures, and populations, brought about by cross-border trade in goods and services, technology, and flows of investment, people, and information'.

Distinction can be made amongst four kinds of globalisation: economic, business, cultural and political. Economic globalisation is the increasing economic interdependence of national economies across the world as a result of the growth of cross-border movement of goods, services, technology and capital. It comprises the globalisation of production, which refers to the act of obtaining goods and services from locations around the world, and the globalisation of markets, which is the union of different and separate markets into a massive global market. The globalisation of business, on the other hand, is centred on the liberalisation of international trade and foreign direct investment, leading to the emergence of multinational firms. Cultural globalisation is the transmission of ideas and values around the world to extend and intensify social relations. This process has been aided by the internet, popular culture media and international travel. Political globalisation refers to the growth of the worldwide political system, both in size and complexity, including inter-governmental organisations, international non-governmental organisations and social movement organisations. Thompson (2008) defines political globalisation as 'the expansion of a global political system, and its institutions, in which inter-regional transactions (including, but certainly not limited to, trade) are managed'.

Other dimensions of globalisation that have been identified by Steger (2009) include the ecological and ideological dimensions. The ecological, or environmental, dimension pertains to ecological problems, including resource and food shortages, overpopulation, shrinking biodiversity, pollution, and climate change, which are global in nature. Ideological globalisation pertains to the norms, claims, beliefs and narratives about the phenomenon itself. Yet another dimension is legal globalisation, which pertains to how international law is created and enforced. Halliday and Osinsky (2006) define the globalisation of law as the 'worldwide progression of transnational legal structures and discourses along the dimensions of extensity, intensity, velocity, and impact'.

The dark side of globalisation is that it is a creation of European imperialism. The first wave of globalisation was propelled by steamships, railways, the telegraph and other technological breakthroughs, and also by increasing 'economic co-operation' among countries, a term that is used to mask the exploitation of colonies. The trend was interrupted by World War I, post-war protectionism, the Great Depression and World War II. The second wave of globalisation started in the post-war period as the US dominated the world economy. This wave can be described as the 'Americanisation' or 'McDonaldisation' of the world. Even though the beneficiaries claim that the whole world has benefited from globalisation, the feelings are mixed. According to the IMF (2000):

> The term 'globalization' has acquired considerable emotive force. Some view it as a process that is beneficial – a key to future world economic development – and also inevitable and irreversible. Others regard it with hostility, even fear, believing that it increases inequality within and between nations, threatens employment and living standards and thwarts social progress.

Yap and Huan (2018) talk about the good, bad and ugly sides of globalisation. The good side is that it creates new jobs and supports manufacturing industry, boosting economic growth. Benefits accrue from technological advancement, foreign direct investment, information exchange and the development of skills and knowledge. The bad side lies in the by-products of interdependence and interconnectivity, including the spread of environmental pollution, diseases, cross-border crime, international terrorism and financial crises. The ugly side is the consequence of rising inequality, which brings about huge social costs.

The backlash against globalisation started before the advent of COVID-19. The anti-globalisation, or counter-globalisation, movement (also known as alter-globalisation movement, anti-globalist movement, anti-corporate globalisation movement, and movement against neoliberal globalisation) is based on a number of criticisms of globalisation, but the main criticism is that globalisation boosts corporate capitalism. The opponents of globalisation correctly argue that there is unequal power and respect in terms of international trade between developed and underdeveloped countries. The diverse subgroups that make up this movement include some of the following: trade unionists, environmentalists, anarchists, land rights and Indigenous rights activists, organisations promoting human rights and sustainable development, opponents of privatisation, and anti-sweatshop campaigners. For the globalists, these are 'bad guys', 'lunatics', 'unpatriotic', 'lefties', etc.

The proponents of globalisation claim that it allows developing countries to catch up to developed countries by boosting manufacturing industry, diversification, economic growth and the standards of living. They attribute the decline in poverty in part to the growth in trade and investment flows that accompany globalisation. However, the rules of globalisation are written by developed countries, for the benefit of multinational firms, at the expense of developing countries. Growth was much faster in the 1950s and 1960s than now, even though the world was less globalised than it is now. China has the best record in poverty reduction, not because it embraced the rules of globalisation as written by the 'West', but because China chose a path of interaction with the outside world that benefits its economy. This is the essence of the Stiglitz critique, as we are going to see. The second alleged benefit is that outsourcing by companies brings jobs and technology to developing countries, which help them grow their economies. The fact of the matter is that outsourcing is not motivated by the altruistic endeavour of helping developing countries but by the desire to take advantage of low wages and lax environmental standards.

The most ludicrous claim in favour of globalisation is that it has advanced social justice on an international level by focusing attention on human rights worldwide that might have otherwise been ignored on a large scale. This means that the world is a better place, now that there is a global cop, be it the USA or NATO, although the difference between them is subtle. Look no further than Iraq, Afghanistan, Libya, Syria and Venezuela. In this globalised world, the US and its allies (read 'subordinates') in NATO watch dictators who 'kill their own people', preferably in resource-rich countries. To protect the civilian population from the dictator, they bomb the country back to the Stone Age, and in some cases they invade and occupy the country. In the process they kill more people than the dictator by a factor of 100 (through bombing, assassination, torture, dawn raids and indiscriminate arrests) and steal the wealth of those nations. Donald Trump is known to have said the following about the US 'humanitarian' mission in Syria and why US troops are stationed in Syria illegally: 'We're keeping the oil. We have the oil. The oil is secure. We left troops behind only for the oil' (Borger, 2019). The chief cop gets the lion's share of the heist while the subordinates get some 'breadcrumbs'.

Furthermore, the 'West' is selective in defending human rights in 'non-Western' countries, which sometimes amounts to defending the oppressor rather than the oppressed. The 'West' condemns the Chinese leadership for violating the human rights of the Uighurs Muslims, yet the same 'West' shouts 'foul' at the arrest of Aung San Suu Kyi by the generals of Myanmar, even though she defended those same generals when they were accused of committing crimes against the Rohingya Muslims. And no one says anything about Modi's India, which has become a very dangerous place for Muslims to live in, thanks mainly to his Hindu nationalism. For Uncle Sam, the Sunni are the bad guys and the Shiite are the good guys in Iraq – in Syria, however, the Sunni are the good guys and the Shiite are the bad guys. Globalisation, which is a phenomenon of the American Empire, has created a bad global cop that lacks impartiality. The so-called 'defence of human rights' by the 'West' (sometimes by bombing and torturing the same humans) is the very reason for the rise of the slogan 'Yankees go home', which is an anti-globalisation slogan.

The opponents of globalisation make several points. The first is that a consequence of globalisation is economic contagion as an economic downturn in one country can create a domino effect through trade and capital flows. In this sense, globalisation aggravates systemic risk. Globalisation has led to a concentration of wealth and power in the hands of a small corporate elite with a grotesque level of income and wealth inequality. Globalisation has been harmful to the working and middle class in the US itself as entire industries have moved to new locations abroad. Globalisation has killed local cultures and made the world less diverse, as it has caused the spread of the junk food industry to all corners of the world. The sheer size and reach of the US have made the cultural exchange among nations largely a one-sided affair. Globalisation can also have negative environmental impacts due to rapid economic development, industrialisation, and international travel.

In his brilliant book, *Globalization and its Discontents*, Stiglitz (2000) argues that globalisation could be good or bad, depending on its management. It is good when it is managed by national government that embraces the characteristics of the country, but it is bad when it is managed by international institutions, such as the IMF and World Bank, according to the prescriptions of the Washington Consensus. In other words, Stiglitz argues that countries should embrace globalisation on their own terms, taking into account their history, culture and traditions. The problem, according to Stiglitz, is that globalisation has not been pushed carefully or fairly. On the contrary, liberalisation policies have been implemented too quickly, in the wrong order, and often using inadequate (or plainly wrong) economic analysis. As a consequence, he argues, 'we now face terrible results, including increases in destitution and social conflict, and generalized frustration'.

A two-way interaction between globalisation and COVID-19 can be observed. The spread of the virus has been aided by international travel, but the pandemic itself has caused the largest and fastest decline in international flows in modern history (including trade, foreign direct investment, and international travel). The relation between travel and the spread of disease has been known for a long time, and this is why countries closed their borders or imposed restrictions of varying degrees of severity. The Bubonic Plague was transmitted from China to Europe through trade routes. Likewise, the influenza pandemic of 1918–20, which led to over 50 million deaths worldwide, spread mainly through the movement of armies in World War I. More recently, the Asian flu of 1957 (influenza A H2N2) was reported in 20 countries and primarily spread via land and sea travel. The Hong Kong flu pandemic (influenza A H3N2) spread extensively through air travel.

On the other hand, it is believed that the pandemic has not been good for globalisation. The US National Intelligence Council (2004, p. 30) warned of the adverse effect of a potential pandemic on globalisation:

> Some experts believe that it is only a matter of time before a new pandemic appears, such as the Spanish Flu …. From mega-cities in the developing world with poor health systems …, such a pandemic would be devastating and could spread rapidly around the world. Globalization would be in jeopardy if the death toll were counted in the millions in major countries and the spread of the disease would put a halt to global trade and travel for an extended period of time, forcing governments to spend enormous resources on exhausted health systems.

The pandemic is likely to force a rethinking of the benefits and costs of globalisation for at least two reasons. The first is that the collapse of supply chains may force companies to look for domestic suppliers to avoid interruption. The second pertains to the importance of the domestic production of medical goods, which has been recognised following the scramble for PPE and the price gouging events of the early stages of the pandemic. This is why Gray (2020) believes that 'the era of peak globalisation is over', describing the impact of the pandemic as 'not a temporary rupture in an otherwise stable equilibrium' and that 'the crisis through which we are living is a turning point in history'. Therefore, he expects a 'more fragmented world that in some ways may be more resilient' to come into being.

Likewise, Darius (2021) thinks that the pandemic will propel anti-globalist political forces, with a shift towards the era of deglobalisation, suggesting two reasons for the shift. The first is that the pandemic itself adheres to the central narrative that has instigated anti-globalist political movements and policies throughout the world: the vulnerability of the domestic populace to nefarious foreign elements. The second reason for the shift in favour of deglobalisation pertains to the measures that countries have taken in response to the pandemic. For some time now, the prevailing narrative amongst political leaders in relation to globalisation is that it is the phenomenon of our time that both policy-makers and the electorate have to contend with in all its forms: the good, the bad, and the ugly.

9.3   DEINDUSTRIALISATION

Deindustrialisation is a process of economic and social change that is characterised by: (i) a long-term decline in the output and employment of manufacturing industry; (ii) a shift to the service sectors, so that manufacturing output has a lower share of total GDP and employment; and (iii) a persistent trade deficit. The term 'deindustrialisation crisis' is used to describe the decline of labour-intensive industry, such as manufacturing industry, in a number of countries and the flight of jobs away from cities. The free-trade agreements concluded between the West and the Rest in the 1980s and 1990s have led to the relocation of labour-intensive manufacturing industry to developing countries, seeking low costs of production and lax environmental standards, without having to worry about trade restrictions. Employment in manufacturing industry has also been affected adversely by technological progress as robots and computers have been taking over from humans and eliminating many manufacturing jobs.

In Figure 9.1 we can see all symptoms of American deindustrialisation over the period 1998–2020. In terms of output, the share of manufacturing output in GDP has been declining while the share of service output has been rising. The same is observed about the employment shares of manufacturing and services. The balance of trade in goods has become increasingly negative while the balance of trade in services has been in surplus. The US trade deficit is an American problem that can be attributed partly to deindustrialisation, not a problem that is allegedly caused by the undervaluation of the Chinese currency. The US no longer produces the manufactured goods imported from China due to the erosion of the industrial base, which free marketeers consider to be 'natural' as a phase of economic evolution.

Jagdish Bhagwati thinks that those who argue for boosting manufacturing output suffer from 'manufacturing fetishism', arguing that the service industry is as good as manufacturing in generating jobs and boosting exports (*The Economist*, 2011). This claim, however, is not supported by simple observable facts such as jobless growth, a state of affairs where high unemployment co-exists with an expansion in GDP. This state of affairs can be attributed to structural changes in the economy rather than a cyclical recovery – one form of this structural change is deindustrialisation. Since job-generating growth is preferable to jobless growth, Bhagwati must be wrong in thinking that the service industry is as good as manufacturing in generating jobs.

Manufacturing fetishism, which is the idea that manufacturing is the central economic activity and everything else is somehow subordinate, is not as bad

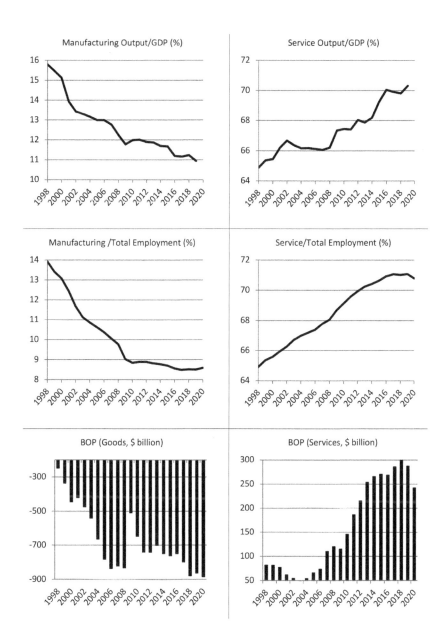

Figure 9.1   Indicators of US deindustrialisation

as Bhagwati thinks. Advanced countries have become advanced only because of industrialisation. Those who resent manufacturing fetishism and argue that services are just as important seem to be oblivious to the line separating manufacturing industry from services. For example, design is part of the manufacturing process – it is not a 'service'. When we fly across continents, the plane is a manufactured product and so is the fuel, but we get served by the crew who provide meals and drinks, with a big smile (if you are in business class). Without the plane and fuel, we cannot fly, despite the excellent service provided by the crew. Manufacturing fetishism can be justified. It seems that Bhagwati suffers from 'services fetishism', thinking that manicure and massage are as good for the economy as manufacturing PPE to combat the virus. He may also think that the so-called 'financial engineering' contributes as much to the economy as traditional mechanical and electrical engineering. While traditional engineers create the infrastructure and means of transportation, financial engineers invent financial products and services (such as collateralised debt obligations) that end up destroying the world economy.

Friedman (2002) disagrees with the proposition that it is natural for services to replace manufacturing industry by arguing along the following lines:

> Such beliefs were plausible in 1994–1998, when business-service employment was booming. As millions of jobs in technically demanding work – programming computers, setting up communications systems, for example – were created, business services offset slower growth or job losses in manufacturing. But when manufacturing went into a tailspin in the later 1990s, the business-service growth that powered the healthiest phases of the decade's boom slowed too. Rather than supplant manufacturing, business-service enterprises depended on healthy factories, which, after all, were among their biggest clients.

Friedman is justifiably sarcastic when he points out that 'it's hard to imagine how service-sector expansion can play a role in wealth creation if growth in, say, manicurists exceeds that of engineers'. And while manufacturing industry lends itself to specialisation and economies of scale (hence, rising productivity) the service industry kills productivity because of the lack of potential for the exploitation of economies of scale and exports. This is why Spence and Hlatshwayo (2011) call for the US economy to find ways to expand employment in traded goods (mostly the output of manufacturing industry), arguing that the demand for non-traded goods may not continue to grow at the pace of recent decades. Again, I am not sure why setting up communication systems is a 'service' when those systems are products of manufacturing industry.

Labour-intensive manufacturing industry has been affected adversely by COVID-19. On the other hand, it is likely that the advent of the pandemic will force a rethink of deindustrialisation. Perhaps one important development is the scramble for personal protective equipment (PPE), a term that was hardly known to people outside the healthcare industry. Most countries went into the pandemic without an adequate supply. According to the *Financial Times*, 'the UK government's belated efforts to secure personal protective equipment for health workers during the COVID-19 pandemic led to huge extra costs to the taxpayer' (Thomas, 2020). Between February and July 2020, the health department spent £12.5 billion on 32 billion items of PPE, but this would have cost just £2.5 billion at 2019 prices. Jacob Rees-Mogg, a British MP and the Commons Leader, has compared the government's scramble for equipment during the COVID-19 pandemic to calling out an emergency plumber (Mellor, 2020). He described the situation as 'having a leak at two in the morning'.

The scramble for PPE led to international acts of piracy. In April 2020, *The Guardian* reported on how the US managed to acquire a consignment of masks as it was about to be dispatched from China to one of the worst-hit coronavirus regions of France (Willsher et al., 2020). The masks were on a plane at Shanghai airport that was ready to take off when the US buyers turned up and offered three times what their French counterparts were paying. Jean Rottner, a doctor and president of the Grand Est regional council, summarised what happened as follows: 'On the tarmac, they arrive, get the cash out … so we really have to fight'. Rottner would not identify the buyers, who they were working for, or which US state the cargo was flown to, but another French official (also involved in procuring masks from China) said that the group were acting for the US government.

Some observers use national security as an argument against deindustrialisation. Lincicome (2021) makes this point as follows:

'Free markets' and a lack of government support for the manufacturing sector are alleged to have crippled the U.S. defense industrial base's ability to supply 'essential' goods during war or other emergencies, thus imperiling national security and demanding a fundamental rethink of U.S. trade and manufacturing policy. The COVID-19 crisis and U.S.–China tensions have amplified these claims.

In an op-ed, Senator Marco Rubio advocated reindustrialisation as follows (Rubio, 2020):

Any prudent policymaker should recognize that both efficiency and resiliency are values we should prioritize and seek to balance. But that's not what we have done in recent decades. [U.S. economic policy] choices, from offshoring to building an economy based on finance and service, have produced one of the most efficient economic engines of all time. But a pendulum can swing too far in one direction. And when an economy lacks resiliency, it can be devastating in a crisis …. Today, the result of these failed policy choices is that our manufacturing base is severely diminished, and millions of productive jobs that relied on it are gone. The American domestic supply chain devoted to producing vital medical supplies like generic pharmaceuticals and respirators has withered.

Rubio goes on to claim that these problems require 'a new vision to create a more resilient economy' and proposes a 'sweeping pro-American industrial policy' that involves 're-shoring of supply chains integral to our national interest – everything from basic medicines and equipment to vital rare-earth minerals and technologies of the future'. He is not alone: according to Lincicome (2021), 'prominent politicians and pundits on the right and left routinely lament the harms that deindustrialization has imposed on U.S. national and economic security and propose "sweeping" programs (protectionism, domestic procurement mandates, subsidies, etc.) to fix this alleged problem'.

9.4   FINANCIALISATION

Financialisation is a term that describes the dominance of the financial sector over other sectors of the economy, including manufacturing industry and agriculture. It refers to 'the increasing importance of financial markets, financial motives, financial institutions, and financial elites in the operation of the economy and its governing institutions, both at the national and international levels' (Epstein, 2002). The financialisation process began during the 1980s and took hold during the 1990s and 2000s, as financial markets decoupled from the underlying real economy in a series of debt-driven boom–bust cycles. Prior to 1980, the speculative use of debt was constrained under the financial framework adopted during the New Deal. Interest rates were regulated (Regulation Q) and the Glass–Steagall Act separated commercial from investment banking.

Financial deregulation resulted in the abolition of Regulation Q and the Glass–Steagall Act, as well as the removal of regulation prohibiting corporate stock buy-backs, subjecting credit default swaps to federal scrutiny and permitting corporations to grant stock options. In this sense, deregulation has led to extensive financialisation by allowing financial institutions to do as they please, aided and abetted by central bankers, policy-makers and financial regulators (rather, deregulators). Balder (2020) argues that the Fed has been complicit in the financialisation process even though it is not entirely clear whether this was attributable to regulatory capture, ideology or more than likely, a combination of both. In a speech entitled *The Great Moderation* (more correctly, the great illusion) delivered by Ben Bernanke in February 2004, he said that markets were efficient and rational, in the sense that they cannot be wrong (Bernanke, 2004).

Like deindustrialisation, financialisation is believed by some observers to come naturally as the economy moves away from manufacturing industry to services (hence the term 'financial services', which are largely useless at best and fraudulent at worst). However, it is far away from being a 'natural development'. Rather, as Witko (2016) argues, it is a consequence of public policy choices that occur when large firms in the FIRE (finance, insurance and real estate) sector are active in politics. Financialisation, therefore, represents regulatory and political capture. David Stockman, a former director of the Office of Management and Budget once described financialisation as 'corrosive', arguing that it had turned the economy into a 'giant casino' where banks skim an oversize share of profits (Bartlett, 2013).

Numerous studies have demonstrated the adverse consequences of finicialisation, particularly the retardation of growth and intensification of inequality, which are arguably related in the sense that inequality itself retards growth. For example, Bartlett (2013) suggests that 'financialization is also an important factor in the growth of income inequality, which is also a culprit in slow growth'. Cushen (2013) explores how the workplace outcomes associated with financialisation render employees insecure and angry. Black (2011) lists the ways in which the financial sector harms the real economy, describing the financial sector functions as 'the sharp canines that the predator state uses to rend the nation'. The adverse effects of financialisation have been widely recognised as being mostly related to the accumulation of debt, which leads to a diversion of increasing portions of the financial resources of the corporate and household sectors to debt service. This point is emphasised by Balder (2020).

Financialisation has adverse macroeconomic consequences because it makes the financial system weaker by boosting leverage, opacity, complexity, spillover effects within and outside financial institutions, and by accelerating debt deflation (Sinapi, 2014). Furthermore, the dominance of finance fuels asset price inflation as suggested by Bellofiore (2013). Financialisation has a depressive effect on productive investment, consumption and aggregate demand. For example, Lavoie (2012) associates financialisation with the development of a consumption-led accumulation regime fuelled by increasing household debt as households strive to compensate for their stagnating purchasing power. Given that financial crises cause subsequent recessions and that financialisation leads to a bigger and more unstable financial sector, the link between financialisation and output becomes conspicuous. According to the IMF (2009), recessions associated with financial crises last on average 18 months longer than other recessions and take almost three years to go back to pre-recession output levels. According to Crotty (1990, 2009) the financial sector has grown so fast that it poses a threat to the growth of the real economy by generating endogenous financial instability and exerting a depressive impact on the real sector.

The literature suggests that financialisation has adverse effects on living standards, capital accumulation, consumption, productivity, aggregate demand, value added, income distribution, employment, wages, tax revenue, asset price inflation, financial stability, and the opacity and complexity of the financial sector. It is intuitive to suggest that some of these effects imply adverse consequences for aggregate output and economic growth. Other transmission mechanisms whereby financialisation impinges upon the real economy include competition with the real sector for resources, the brain drain, the Dutch disease and the dominance of a mentality of trading for short-term gains. Moosa (2018) presents empirical evidence on the relation between economic growth and financialisation as measured by the ratio of credit to GDP and the ratio of publicly traded shares to GDP.

According to Balder (2020) the COVID-19 pandemic has revealed the extreme income and wealth inequality that has undermined US economic growth for more than 40 years, which he attributes to the role of speculative finance (financialisation) and the complicity of central banks in driving this process. This is why he recommends the reversal of the financialisation process and the restructuring of the financial system, which should have been done in the aftermath of the global financial crisis. One step in this direction is the restoration of the Glass–Steagall Act that calls for the separation of commercial banking from investment banking, as well as other constraints on banking activities along the lines followed during the Great Depression. Balder also recommends the restructuring and democratisation of the Fed to make it work collaboratively with the Treasury to finance recovery. Last, but not least, he recommends the creation of a 21st-century Reconstruction Finance Corporation (RFC) that can invest on behalf of the public in job creation, infrastructure, green technology, etc.

Mader et al. (2020b) compare the new normal that followed the global financial crisis and the anticipated new normal in a post-COVID world. The global financial crisis provided an opportunity to change, but what followed was a world characterised by a higher level of financialisation, alongside austerity, jobless growth, precarity, exploding inequality, tech takeover and authoritarianism. They warn of the possibility of a 'financialised recovery', which 'entails further bailouts for the shadow banking sector, new sanctions for the unemployed, housing and other social assets gobbled up by institutional investors seeking new safe havens, and crippling medical debts making the next pandemic wave even deadlier for the poor'.

Some of the ways whereby COVID could transform the status quo are suggested by the contributors to *The Routledge International Handbook of Financialization* (Mader et al., 2020a). The comments reflect the fear that the current response of central banks to the pandemic is further entrenching the disconnect between financial markets and the real economy, rescuing the owners of financial assets while ignoring unemployment, low wages and rising precarity. They also mention the fear that COVID-19 will become another major milestone in the long history of central bank-facilitated financialisation.

They raise concern about the fear that individualised and financialised solutions to medical and housing costs are sharpening social inequalities.

Mader et al. (2020b) are not optimistic about the future. They argue that the outlook for the performance of pension funds does not look good and that they are now in a far weaker position than following the global financial crisis, as they are forced to assume higher levels of risk because of ultra-low and negative interest rates. Their comments contain some recommendations about bailing out tenants (rather than banks), for universalised waiting lists, and for merging private and deficient public hospital capacities to provide better access to ICU beds. However, they believe that the outlook seems bleak, suggesting that 'uncertainty looms, but the financialisation of social policy looks set to continue' and that 'financialised capitalism is likely to live on, with developing countries remaining in a subordinate position'.

9.5   INEQUALITY

Inequality had been a critical issue long before the advent of COVID-19. Extreme inequality is out of control as hundreds of millions of people live in hideous poverty while those at the very top reap huge rewards, one way or another. While the number of billionaires has been rising and their wealth accumulating at an accelerating rate, the poor are getting poorer. The problem is that governments in 'democratic' countries fuel the inequality crisis by deliberate policy choices, including low income tax rates for corporations and the rich while underfunding public services that benefit the poor, such as healthcare and education, both of which have become private goods and a source of profitable business. In many countries, decent education or quality healthcare have become a luxury, which only the rich can afford, while taxes fall disproportionately on wage and salary earners – that is, the lucky ones who have jobs.

Governments in 'democratic' countries do not only aggravate inequality – they also hide it. In August 2019, *The Guardian* reported that the Australian Bureau of Statistics (ABS) removed references to wealth inequality reaching its peak in 2017–18 from a press release to 'help craft a "good media story"', according to internal documents' (Karp, 2019). *The Guardian* had access to 'emails and drafts' showing that 'the ABS issued a separate income inequality media release in July to create a narrative of "stable" inequality despite wealth inequality on the rise, with one email noting the ABS did not want to "draw attention" to a bad result for the poorest households'. Naturally, a spokesman for the ABS denied any interference by the Morrison government or the suggestion that it sought to misrepresent data (this, of course, means that the government did interfere and seek to misrepresent data).

The drivers of inequality include globalisation, skill-biased technological change and policy changes. Globalisation is conducive to inequality because of competition from foreign low-wage workers and the relocation of industry. Skill-biased technological change leads to job losses as demand for low-skill workers declines. Rapid policy changes in favour of the corporate sector and the rich are bound to aggravate inequality. Other drivers include the rise of the 'superstars' who are promoted by the corporate media and the culture of superstardom – otherwise, how can we explain a working class person paying $500 out of after-tax income to watch a tennis or a golf player (the first abuses umpires and the ball boys, while the second misses the hole from a distance of less than one metre 'because it is windy')? Another driver is financialisation, which has produced billionaires out of salaries and bonuses (the most notorious example being Jeffrey Epstein). Automation is yet another driver as workers are replaced with robots and computer algorithms for the purpose of boosting corporate profit. Ideology is also a driver as right-wing neo-cons take hold of governments, resulting in less progressive tax laws, anti-labour policies and slower expansion of the welfare state (see, for example, Krugman, 2007).

As bad as inequality is without COVID-19, the pandemic is likely to make it worse. In fact pandemics tend to aggravate inequality as the experience shows. Furceri et al. (2020) estimate the distributional impacts of five major events – SARS (2003), H1N1 (2009), MERS (2012), Ebola (2014) and Zika (2016) – over the five years following each event and find that on average, the Gini coefficient of income in affected countries went up steadily after those events. After five years, the net Gini coefficient (market incomes after taxes and trans-fers) is estimated to be above the pre-shock trend by around 1.25%, which is 0.5 percentage points higher than the increase in Gini in market income. They conclude that the impact on net Gini is larger than that on market Gini, which suggests that redistributive public programmes have been inadequate to miti-gate the distributional impacts of the shock on market incomes and may even have been regressive in the medium term.

COVID-19 is likely to aggravate inequality via several channels. To start with, the pandemic has pushed up the prices of essential goods and services, which is not reflected in the official CPI figures, simply because governments tend to lie about inflation (see, for example, Moosa, 2020a). The other channel is the rise in unemployment, with the biggest job losses affecting low-paid workers who are more represented in the sectors that have suspended activities such as hotels, restaurants and tourism services. Another form of interaction between inequality and the pandemic is that the pandemic has infected and killed the poor disproportionately. This is because the poor are in a weaker position to practise social distancing than the rich who can isolate themselves by hiding in their yachts and holiday homes. Furthermore, high-paid workers can work from home while low-paid blue-collar workers typically do not have this option. Then a higher share of low-paid workers are in essential services such as nursing, policing, teaching, cleaning, refuse removal, and store attendants where they are more likely to come into contact with people who are infected. This is why Stiglitz (2020) describes the Coronavirus by saying that it has not been 'an equal opportunity virus', arguing that it goes disproportionately after the poor, particularly in poor countries, and in advanced economies like the US where access to healthcare is not guaranteed.

With or without COVID-19, the way forward is to do something about inequality, not only because it is grotesque and morally reprehensible but also because it is bad for the economy. According to Stiglitz (2020), the starting point is to abandon the neoclassical economic model of competitive equilibrium whereby producers maximise profit, consumers maximise utility, and prices are determined in competitive markets where demand and supply are balanced, producing the 'optimal' outcome. This, however, is not how the economy works, which is why this model distorts understanding of the growth of inequality, or even innovation-driven growth.

What is required, according to Stiglitz, is a 'comprehensive rewriting of the rules of the economy' to contain corporate power, enforce the bargaining power of workers, and erode the rules governing the exploitation of consumers, borrowers, students and workers. The specific requirements of the new system are: (i) monetary policy that targets employment rather than just inflation; (ii) bankruptcy laws that are better balanced, rather than being too creditor-friendly; (iii) corporate governance laws that recognise the importance of all stakeholders, not just shareholders; (iv) rules governing globalisation that must do more than just serve corporate interests; (v) protection of workers and the environment; and (vi) labour legislation that protects workers and provides greater scope for collective action. Like Stiglitz, Hill and Narayan (2021) suggest actions to be taken to mitigate rising inequality, which requires 'a durable and inclusive recovery, while building resilience among the vulnerable against future crisis'. To that end, they suggest: (i) boosting investments in health and education, particularly at an early age and for children; (ii) levelling the playing field in the labour market by improving access to affordable childcare and parental leave policies; (iii) enhancing access to financial services and technology; and (iv) investing in safety nets and social insurance.

Stiglitz does not mention tax policy, which represents the best tool for income redistribution to alleviate inequality. Numerous suggestions have been made in this respect by the OECD, including the imposition of a wealth tax and financial transaction tax; the maintenance of the overall progressivity of the tax code and cross-country co-operation on international tax issues; boosting transparency and international co-operation on tax rules to minimise 'treaty shopping'; reducing social security contributions and payroll taxes on low-income workers; abolishing or scaling back a wide range of tax deductions, credits and exemptions that benefit high-income recipients disproportionately; taxing as ordinary income all remuneration, including fringe benefits and stock options; shifting the tax mix towards greater reliance on recurrent taxes on immovable property; taxing capital gains at the personal level at slightly progressive rates; broadening the income tax base to reduce avoidance opportunities; and developing policies to improve transparency and tax compliance (for a discussion of these measures and a comprehensive treatment of inequality, go to www.oecd .org/social/inequality.htm).

The importance of tax, both as a cause and solution to inequality is highlighted by Goldin and Muggah (2020), who contend that 'the spectacular accumulation of wealth in the hands of a small minority is ramping-up pressure to tax the rich and their heirs'. They point out that in 2020 alone, children of the super-rich inherited around $764 billion and paid an average of just 2.1% tax on this income, whereas the average tax rate for working people is 15.8%, seven times more.

The situation is simply shocking, to say the least. Inequality can no longer be ignored or brushed aside as a by-product of an efficient market system. Even if we were to believe that inequality should be accepted for the sake of efficiency, it can still be rejected on the basis of morality. The fact of the matter is that inequality is not desirable even in terms of macroeconomics as it causes under-consumption and retards growth. It is not even good for capitalism as the poor cannot buy the goods produced by firms, thus impeding the achievement of profit maximisation. The COVID-19 pandemic has shown that inequality is indeed evil.

9.6   MINIMUM WAGES AND ESSENTIAL WORKERS

COVID-19 has exerted downward pressure on real wages in most countries, but in some countries average wages went up artificially, largely as a reflection of the substantial job losses among lower-paid workers. In a crisis like COVID-19, average wages can be skewed significantly by sharp changes in the composition of employment. This is called the 'composition effect', which materialises when most of those who lose their jobs are low-paid workers, leading to an increase in the mean wages of the remaining employees. In countries where strong job retention measures have been introduced or extended to preserve employment, surges in unemployment have been moderated, such that the effects of the crisis may have been more apparent through downward pressure on wages than through massive job losses. The crisis disproportionately affected lower-paid workers, thereby increasing wage inequality.

The pandemic has forced a rethink of minimum wages and led to calls for raising minimum wages where they exist – both of these propositions are rejected by free marketeers. In the US, the federal minimum wage is just $7.25

an hour, which has been at this level since 2009. In accordance with the Raise the Wage Act of 2021, the minimum wage would be raised to \$9.50 in 2021, thereafter it would be raised gradually to \$15 an hour in 2025.

Minimum wage systems differ from one country to another and range from simple systems to complex ones. Simple systems require a single national minimum wage rate whereas complex systems involve multiple minimum wage rates, determined by sector, occupation, age and region. Minimum wages are intended to protect workers from unduly low pay that is tantamount to slave labour, and to reduce wage and income inequality. The extent to which a minimum wage may reduce inequality depends on (i) the effectiveness of minimum wages, (ii) the level at which minimum wages are set, and (iii) the characteristics of minimum wage earners. The first condition pertains to the extent of the legal coverage and the level of compliance (by employers). The second condition means that a higher level of the minimum wage reduces inequality unless the effect is offset by the resulting unemployment. The third condition pertains to the structure of a country's labour force, particularly whether workers with low incomes are wage workers or self-employed, and the characteristics of the beneficiaries of the minimum wage (in particular, whether or not they live in low-income families). According to the ILO (2020), the majority of wage earners paid at or below the minimum wage are located in the lower tail of the distribution of household incomes, but the characteristics of minimum wage earners vary by country and region.

The Minimum Wage Fixing Convention of the International Labour Organisation (No. 131) stipulates that setting an adequate minimum wage level should involve social dialogue and take into account the needs of workers and their families as well as economic factors. It is recommended that minimum wages are set, on average, at around 55% of the median wage in developed countries and at 67% of the median wage in developing and emerging economies. Furthermore, a sufficiently frequent adjustment is crucial to maintain minimum wages at an adequate level (particularly if inflation is high), and a very low level often reflects failure to adjust rates regularly over time. These considerations bring into focus two aspects of the minimum wage debate: whether or not to have a minimum wage and whether or not to increase the current level of the minimum wage as a result of COVID-19. The arguments for and against are similar.

Let us first consider the arguments for minimum wages. A minimum wage leads to an improvement in the standard of living of minimum wage workers, which would result in a higher level of morale, producing more tangible benefits for the firm, such as easy employee retention and lower hiring and training costs. Paying minimum wages could provide a boost to economic growth because the marginal propensity to consume of minimum wage earners is very high. This is a prediction of the theory of under-consumption, which states that recession and stagnation arise from an inadequate consumer demand relative to output. It also relates to the basic contradiction in capitalism resulting from the fact that workers are also the consumers of the goods produced by firms.

An additional advantage of minimum wages is that they can alleviate inequality and poverty, which have been aggravated by COVID-19. The availability of a minimum wage may also reduce crime. Minimum wages are conducive to the reduction of government spending on welfare. A minimum wage could go a long way towards the improvement of public health and reduction in premature deaths. People who make the minimum wage do not use public services as frequently as the unemployed would. This would have a positive impact on the fiscal balance and may reduce taxes. Minimum wages could be beneficial for employers, in the sense that a minimum wage can be used as a reference point for wage setting.

Opponents of minimum wages are typically free marketeers who believe that the wage rate, like any other price, should be determined by the market, not by the government. This is an issue that we have dealt with before as we considered why it may be necessary for the government to intervene in price setting and economic activity in general. The opponents also see minimum wages as leading to inflation and unemployment, where inflation results from the rise in the costs of production, while unemployment follows from the setting of the minimum wage above the market equilibrium level. Minimum wages may encourage overqualified workers to take minimum wage positions that would ordinarily go to young or otherwise inexperienced workers. Another argument against is that minimum wages may lead to the aggravation of poverty and inequality as employers may cut working hours and therefore the take-home pay. Minimum wages, the opponents claim, may cause corporate failure and redundancies. They may also lead to more automation, thus replacing service employees. The same outcome may be caused by outsourcing jobs to countries where wages are low. Furthermore, the opponents argue that minimum wages may reduce high school enrolment rates and other job benefits. It is, however, unlikely that earning a minimum wage of $15/hour as opposed to $10/hour will encourage youngsters to leave school. As for benefits, I cannot see what benefits those who earn $10/hour receive that they will not receive when they earn the minimum wage of $15/hour.

While some of the arguments made by the opponents may sound plausible, their plausibility is judged only in terms of the principles of neoclassical economics where there is no place for ethics and morality. If the corporate objective is to maximise profit without any consideration of social costs, then yes the arguments make sense. However, there is no reason why we should continue to be guided by the principles of neoclassical economics. This is exactly the point made by Stiglitz (2020) who suggests that the way forward is to abandon the neoclassical economic model of competitive equilibrium and advocates the institution of labour legislation that protects workers and provides greater scope for collective action. The claim that minimum wages could cause corporate failure is truly outrageous. If anything, those who get paid 2,000 times the minimum wage cause corporate failure through incompetence, greed or a lethal combination of both.

Those who oppose minimum wages because they are not market determined also reject maximum wages, again because they are not market determined. It seems that it is bad for economic efficiency if someone on $10/hour is paid a minimum wage of $15/hour, but it is good for efficiency if the CEO of an airline is paid $25 million a year. Even better, it is good for efficiency to pay a footballer $50 million a year even though the club is bankrupt, and it is fine to pay the CEO of a failed bank $200 million in a golden parachute payment. For some reason, $15/hour is above what is determined by the market but the $25 million, $50 million and $200 million are market-determined prices. Even if we forget about ethics and morality, this does not make sense. Rewarding lavishly a CEO who single-handedly causes the collapse of a bank (or whatever) is the same as rewarding an arsonist for starting a fire.

Let us then consider maximum wages, which can be used to finance minimum wages. A maximum wage is the highest level of compensation that a firm can pay an employee over a given period of time. Maximum wages may be imposed in economic crises as an austerity measure, or as a gesture of social good to reduce income inequality. The idea of a maximum wage can be traced back to Aristotle who believed that no one person in Greece should have more than five times the wealth of the poorest person (Hayes, 2019). Maximum wages represent an issue that is increasingly becoming a frequent subject of debate in the 21st century as more CEOs and top executives take home millions of dollars in earnings compared to the minimum wage earned by some (perhaps the majority) of the employees in the same companies.

A maximum wage can be implemented in two forms: a fixed sum or a ratio. In 1942, Franklin Roosevelt proposed a marginal tax rate of 100% for income over $25,000 in order to discourage war profiteering and encourage the rich to make sacrifices in earnings. If Congress had not rejected Roosevelt's proposal, $25,000 would have been an annual salary cap. In 2017, the former British leader of the opposition, Jeremy Corbyn, called for a CEO–worker pay ratio of 20:1. If Corbyn's proposal had been passed into law, top executives of companies seeking government contracts would not have been able to earn more than twenty times the annual income of the lowest paid workers. It is no wonder that Corbyn had to endure a conspiracy and a witch-hunt that saw him out of the leadership of the Labour Party and replaced with a more 'business-friendly' leader.

The proponents believe that a maximum wage is likely to bolster the economy because more money can be used to create incentives for existing employees and to create new jobs and hire more people. With more people working, more taxes can be collected, which in turn means that the government and society benefit from a reduction in the wages of top executives. Furthermore, if the earnings of the top earners of a company are tied directly to that of minimum wage employees in the same company (in the form of a ratio) top managers will have the incentive to raise the level of the minimum wage in order to get an increase in pay themselves. This creates another win–win situation where profits trickle down to the company, government and economy.

As in the case of minimum wages, the opponents of maximum wages argue that wages should be determined by the market, not by the government. The 'talent' argument is invoked in this case to suggest that by setting maximum wages, companies would have fewer talented leaders and employees, as the more valuable talents would be unwilling to work for a capped fee. To make it more dramatic, the opponents argue that maximum wage legislation could set the stage for human capital flight where the most talented individuals emigrate to where they are paid their worth. Therefore, the argument goes, such a policy would be detrimental to the economy.

Excessive pay is conspicuous in the financial sector more than in any other sector. Financial operations are typically fraudulent, which means that talented fraudsters deserve the millions they get paid until they destroy the institutions they work for and rip off their clients. This is what Harrington and Hjelt (2001) say in reference to a CEO who got a pay package worth some $151 million for running Citigroup in 2000:

> The great CEO pay heist executive compensation has become highway robbery – we all know that. But how did it happen? And why can't we stop it? The answers lie in the perverse interaction of CEOs, boards, consultants, even the Feds.

Yes, the whole scheme is fraud, including regulatory capture. Otherwise, it can be put mildly as in Clementi et al. (2009) who suggest that to the extent that the pay packages of senior management deviate materially from the long-term financial interests of shareholders, any overcompensation problem is a failure of corporate governance. Dowd (2009, p. 152) describes the talent argument sarcastically as follows:

> Again and again, we have business leaders whose sky-high remuneration was said to be based on their superior abilities, the heavy responsibilities they were bearing, and so forth. They then run their businesses onto the rocks, blame bad luck, and ask us to believe that they weren't responsible.

In reference to the bankruptcy of Lehman Brothers, Dowd (2009) suggests that senior executives had been working on their golden parachutes at the same time as they were pleading for federal rescue (meaning taxpayers' money) and it turned out that three departing executives had been paid bonuses just days before the firm collapsed. On this issue, Dowd concludes as follows:

> One can only wonder what these people were being paid so much for. Cases such as these give great offence to the public who must pay for them, and the system that gives rise to them is manifestly indefensible .... Indeed, I would go so far as to say that this type of irresponsible behavior on the part of so many senior executives has now become the single biggest challenge to the political legitimacy of the market economy itself.

Paying obscene salaries and bonuses to the few at the top is supposed to be good for low-paid workers because of the trickle-down effect – that is, those talented people will spend money and create jobs. In reality, and as a New Zealand Labour Party MP Damien O'Connor famously said, the trickle-down effect is the 'rich pissing on the poor'. In the 1992 presidential election, independent candidate, Ross Perot, called trickle-down economics 'political voodoo'. A 2012 study by the Tax Justice Network indicates that the wealth of the super-rich does not trickle down to improve the economy, but tends to be amassed and sheltered in tax havens with a negative effect on the tax bases of the home economy (Moosa, 2017).

In the near future, the economic and employment consequences of the COVID-19 crisis are likely to exert massive downward pressure on wages, which begs the question of how to move forward. The ILO (2020) recommends the adoption of 'adequate and balanced wage policies, arrived at through strong and inclusive social dialogue' to mitigate the impact of the crisis and support economic recovery. The ILO elaborates on this recommendation as follows:

> Adequately balanced wage adjustments, taking into account relevant social and economic factors, will be required to safeguard jobs and ensure the sustainability of enterprises, while at the same time protecting the incomes of workers and their families, sustaining demand and avoiding deflationary situations. Adjustments to minimum wages should be carefully balanced and calibrated.

The ILO believes that 'in planning for a new and better "normal" after the crisis, adequate minimum wages – statutory or negotiated – could help to ensure more social justice and less inequality'. Tomaskovic-Devey et al. (2020) see the way forward in high minimum wages, universal healthcare, and a strengthened labour movement.

If anything, the COVID-19 crisis has exposed the gap between the value created by essential frontline workers and the low wages they receive. It seems that most of the people who earn less than the minimum or at least adequate wage are essential workers. In addition to health workers, Tomaskovic-Devey et al. (2020) identify as essential workers agriculture, warehouse, port and transportation workers because of the vital role they play in maintaining supply lines of basic food and medical supplies. Taibbi (2020b) suggests that these workers are not receiving the help they deserve because 'there's no sudden universal health care, no guaranteed sick leave, no massive jobs plan, just Band-Aids', which is why 'they will die in massive numbers and emerge from this crisis, if and when it ends, poorer and more vulnerable than before'.

9.7   CONCLUDING REMARKS

The status quo, the prevailing socio-economic order, is shaped by neoliberalism, the prevailing ideology since the early 1980s. Actions taken by governments worldwide to save the day, predominantly fiscal measures, break the rules of neoclassical economics that govern the ideology of neoliberalism. The virus has forced a rethinking of neoliberalism and the role of the state in the economy, even by right-wing commentators and politicians.

Examples of this change of heart, no matter what motivates it, are more than ample. Evans-Pritchard (2020), who is a prominent right-wing commentator for the British conservative newspaper, the *Daily Telegraph*, advised Boris Johnson to 'embrace socialism immediately' in order to avert it. Johnson himself dared to contradict his mentor who rejects the concept of society, Margaret Thatcher, by recognising society as a fact of life when he declared that 'the coronavirus crisis had proved there really was such a thing as society' (*The Guardian*, 2020). George Saravelos, Deutsche Bank's global head of foreign exchange research, hardly a radical thinker, concludes that 'there is no such thing as a free market anymore' (Saravelos, 2020). *The Economist* (2020b), which is a firm believer in the power (and beauty) of the market, predicts that 'the state is likely to play a very different role in the economy'. In an interview with the *Financial Times*, Emmanuel Macron (a former banker and hardly a left-wing thinker – 'the president of the rich' as the French call him), said that it was 'time to think the unthinkable' and that 'while socialism in one country may not have worked, the unthinkable in all countries forces us to reinvent ourselves' (Macron, 2020). The newspaper of the City of London (hardly the socialist manifesto) notes that 'reversing the prevailing policy direction of the last four decades will need to be put on the table' (*Financial Times*, 2020). Writing in the billionaires' magazine, *Forbes*, Zitelmann (2020) says the following:

> Now is the time to be extra vigilant: 12 years ago, anti-capitalists succeeded in reframing the financial crisis – wrongly – as a crisis of capitalism. The false narrative that the financial crisis is a result of market failure and deregulation has since become firmly established in the minds of the population at large. And now

left-wing intellectuals are again doing their utmost to reframe the corona crisis to justify their calls for the all-powerful state. Unfortunately, the chances that they could succeed are very high indeed.

The virus seems to have dictated a consensus as reflected in the views that 'this time truly is different' (Reinhart, 2020); that 'the state is back with a vengeance against markets' (Golub, 2020; Hameiri, 2020; Rodik, 2020); and that we are witnessing the 'death of neoliberalism' (Avineri, 2020; Cherkaoui, 2020; Lent, 2020; Saad-Filho, 2020a; Wong, 2020).

Unfortunately, it is unlikely that the neoliberal era is (or will be) over just because governments around the world resorted to 'emergency Keynesianism' to deal with the economic consequences of the pandemic. Šumonja (2020) correctly argues that the state 'has actually been the organising force of neoliberal assault on all political obstacles to the profitability of capital accumulation'. Without the likes of Jeremy Corbyn in power, nothing is likely to change and the status quo will persist, albeit with some improvement. Boris Johnson is not killing neoliberalism but he is trying to save it by using 'emergency Keynesianism', as advised by Evans-Pritchard (2020).

10. Epilogue

10.1 RECAPITULATION

The title of this book is *The Economics of COVID-19: Implications of the Pandemic for Economic Thought and Public Policy*. At this stage it seems appropriate to ask what we have learned about those implications. Like any crisis, the pandemic represents both a challenge and an opportunity: a challenge because it has caused immense suffering and an opportunity because it gives us a chance to reflect on what should be done to alleviate suffering when the next crisis hits. It also provides an opportunity for governments to pass laws that would not pass otherwise, and for unscrupulous entrepreneurs to engage in behaviour that would not be possible otherwise.

The pandemic has provided the opportunity for bad things to happen and highlighted some of the existing problems that were typically swept under the carpet, such as poverty and inequality. The pandemic has led to deterioration in democracy and abuse of human rights as governments seize the opportunity to do what they like best: ruling by decree. The pandemic has allowed governments to use mass surveillance with impunity, when at one time the malpractice was denied until Edward Snowden told us otherwise. The pandemic has led to the rise of fascism, represented by the good performance of right-wing parties in parliamentary elections, just like what happened as a result of the Spanish flu 100 years ago. The pandemic has given glory to the military and how they have contributed to the relief effort, perhaps ushering in more military spending (and consequently more wars). Failure to contain the pandemic makes governments inclined to distract attention by fear mongering and spreading the myth of an external enemy, which is mostly China. The expectation that China's international status will be reinforced in a post-COVID world makes war with China more likely (after all, the Thucydides Trap tells us that war breaks out when a rising power challenges the incumbent power). The pandemic has also highlighted the critical socio-economic problems of poverty, inequality and homelessness.

The implication for economic thought is the change of heart away from neoclassical economics and the free market doctrine. As in the global financial crisis, Marx and Keynes have made a comeback as governments resorted to 'emergency Keynesianism' to deal with the economic fallout. The global financial crisis dealt a blow to the credibility of the Anglo-American model of public policy. Likewise, the COVID crisis has dealt a blow to the ability of the Anglo-American system to deal with health crises, whereas China appeared not only as a good performer in tackling the pandemic, but also as a medical aid provider on an international scale.

The change of heart away from neoliberalism is put forward strongly by Šumonja (2020) who suggests that COVID-19 is a 'neoliberal pandemic'. He rejects the proposition that the crisis is an 'exogenous shock to an otherwise functional system', a 'Black Swan-type event' or a 'meteorite of history which can only be ascribed to a foreign entity'. He presents three reasons as to why COVID-19 is a 'neoliberal pandemic'. The first, which comes from evolutionary biology, is that the increased appearance of corona viruses (such as SARS, MERS and COVID-19) in humans is an outcome of 'the agroindustry's devastating impact on natural ecosystems rather than a series of isolated incidents'. In this sense, deforestation has pushed the increasing capitalised wildlife deeper into the remaining primary ecosystems, which enabled 'the spillover of previously boxed-in pathogens to human communities that are forced to breach the natural barrier between them while working'. The second reason pertains to the spread of the virus, which was caused in part by globalisation and in part by 'epidemiological neoliberalism' as Frey (2020) calls it. The underlying principle here is to let the market work its magic, even if it means allowing people to get sick and die from 'just another flu'. The attitude of 'business as usual—just wash your hands and keep your distance' is intended to allow governments to abdicate their responsibilities during a health crisis. The third reason is forty years of the privatisation of public health institutions, resulting in a disastrous situation as private healthcare providers have no commercial interest in preparing for or preventing emergency situations. No wonder that rich countries like the US and UK are the worst performers in respect to fighting the pandemic (and so is Brazil, thanks mainly to Bolsonaro). The pandemic has brought to light the underlying weaknesses of the neoliberal model in terms of investment, productivity and growth, as well as the adverse socio-economic consequences. These issues were not addressed in the aftermath of the global financial crisis when they should have been.

In terms of public policy, the pandemic has taught us the necessity of government intervention in economic activity and that the market is not a magical device that restores equilibrium and prosperity after a shock. The use of Keynesian expansionary fiscal policy has been widespread. No one expresses this point better than Šumonja (2020) who opines:

> No neoliberal taboo was left unbroken: from a 1,200 dollars per person government giveaway in the United States; nationalisation of payrolls across Europe; different credit guarantee schemes, suspension of mortgage payments and additional funding

(48.5 billion pounds) for the NHS, public services and charities in the United Kingdom; expanded childcare benefits for low-income parents and basic income support for the self-employed in Germany; tax and utility bill holidays, and nationalisations of ailing companies in France; to government takeovers of Alitalia airline in Italy and hospitals in Ireland.

Likewise, Saxer (2020) makes the following remarks:

The age of neoliberalism, in terms of the primacy of market interests over all other social interests, is coming to an end … After four decades of neoliberal scepticism about the state, a long-forgotten fact is coming to the light: that nation states still have enormous creative power, if only they are willing to use it.

The pandemic has taught us that low or negative interest rates do not revive the economy and that quantitative easing does not work, except that it causes asset price inflation and perhaps consumer price inflation in the long run. The pandemic showed that even though governments and financial institutions have been preaching the avoidance of cash, people actually accumulated massive amounts of cash even though lockdowns made it necessary to use electronic means of payment. The pandemic has shown that the stock market does not reflect macroeconomic reality, in which case policies intended to revive the economy may end up creating stock price bubbles. The pandemic has taught us the hazard of excessive privatisation and deregulation, and the importance of universal healthcare and welfare. In fact, it has taught us that governments must work on a set of policies that resemble FDR's New Deal. In terms of preparation for the next pandemic, we have learned that the government must take the lead by purchasing (even better, producing) and storing PPE and other essential items to fight the pandemic and that the private sector is incapable of executing this task, even though it is portrayed as being more efficient than the public sector.

10.2   COVID-19 AS AN OPERATIONAL LOSS EVENT AND AN EXAMPLE OF NEGLECTED RISK

An operational loss event is caused by exposure to operational risk, which is defined by the Basel Committee on Banking Supervision as 'the risk arising from inadequate or failed internal processes, people and systems or from external events' (BCBS, 2004). It follows from this definition that operational risk can be decomposed into four components (Mestchian, 2003): (i) process risk, such as inefficiencies or ineffectiveness in the various business processes; (ii) people risk, such as employee error, employee misdeeds and employee unavailability; (iii) technology (or system) risk, such as the system failures caused by breakdown; and (iv) external risk, which is the risk of loss caused by the actions of external parties. Buchelt and Unteregger (2004) use this decomposition of operational risk to describe the sinking of the Titanic. The ship sank because of: (i) the myth that it was unsinkable, which created carelessness and complacency; (ii) the pressure put on Captain Smith to get to New York as quickly as possible, thus travelling too far north and too quickly for safety; and (iii) inadequate safety measures, such as the small number of lifeboats and poor emergency procedures. Thus, Buchelt and Unteregger argue, the ship sank because of the failure of people (the crew, passengers and the boss), systems (the ship and its equipment), processes (emergency plans and procedures) and external factors (the iceberg).

The same analogy can be made with respect to COVID-19, which is a catastrophic operational loss event. The failure of people can be seen in Donald Trump, Boris Johnson and Jair Bolsonaro. The failure of systems is represented by the inadequacy of healthcare systems after years of privatisation, outsourcing and austerity. The failure of processes can be seen in tactical response measures, such as contact tracing and the timing of lockdown. The external factor is the virus itself. In the operational risk terminology, the pandemic is a low frequency–high severity event.

Now the question is whether or not the pandemic is a case of neglected risk, which requires the determination of whether or not it was anticipated. Yes, a pandemic on this scale is a once-in-a-hundred-years event, but it has been a hundred years since the Spanish flu decimated humanity. The fact of the matter is that the virus was not unexpected. In November 2005, 15 scientists published a letter in *Nature Medicine* in which they warned of the possibility that a SARS-type bat coronavirus would appear in humans (Menachery et al., 2015). In *The Black Swan*, Nassim Taleb warned of 'the risk of an acute and very rare virus across the planet' (Taleb, 2010). The US National Intelligence Council (2004) warned that globalisation could be slowed down or stopped by a pandemic. In April 2015, Bill Gates warned that 'if anything kills over 10 million people in the next few decades, it is most likely to be a highly infectious virus rather than war' (Gates, 2015).

If a tiny virus can kill more people than the imaginary enemies can in combat, why is it that trillions of dollars of taxpayers' money are spent on saving the lives that could (allegedly) be taken by Russia, China, Iraq, Syria, Libya, Venezuela, etc., not the lives taken by the virus? Lives must be saved, no matter who or what the enemy is. This enemy had been anticipated but when it struck, countries were caught unprepared. In the 6th century BC, the following was said:

> Whoever prepares wisely to face the enemy that does not yet exist will be victorious. To use his rusticity as a pretext and not to foresee is the greatest of all crimes; to be ready outside of all contingencies is the best of virtues.

These are words of wisdom that came from Sun Tzu (a Chinese general, military strategist, writer and philosopher) more than 2,500 years ago (Nylan, 2020). Why is it that today's political leaders lack any vision of this sort?

10.3   CASES OF MISHANDLING THE CRISIS: US, UK AND BRAZIL

The pandemic was handled so badly in three neoliberal countries (US, UK and Brazil) that they ended up with the worst performance and the largest death tolls. In the UK, Prime Minister Boris Johnson got infected and had to be admitted to the ICU in a London hospital, apparently because he did not take the virus seriously. In April 2020, the *Sunday Times* suggested that the UK had failed to prepare adequately for the pandemic, both in the long term and in the weeks running up to the lockdown (Calvert et al., 2020). The paper reported that the prime minister failed to attend five meetings of the government's Cobra emergency committee concerning the virus in February and that preparations for the pandemic had been neglected for years as the government cut spending and focused on Brexit to the detriment of everything else. In late February 2020, the UK exported some of its stock of protective equipment to China while companies offering to make protective equipment and help with testing were not taken up on the offer until April.

In the same vein, Wall (2020) claims that the prime minister originally advocated a herd infection strategy, whereby 60% of the population would be infected, building up collective immunity and halting the virus. This course of action falls under the social-Darwinism principle of 'survival of the fittest'. Wall argues that when it was revealed that the herd strategy would lead to thousands of deaths and overwhelm the NHS, he 'belatedly introduced lockdown'. Wall goes on to argue that Britain lacks the amount of equipment needed to treat all of the COVID-19-stricken patients and that it has been challenging to get protective gear to health professionals. He also suggests that Britain lacks the capacity to track infected people and warns that 'any lifting of the lockdown will result in a massacre'.

On 17 March 2020, an article in the *National Review* described the UK's response to COVID-19 as 'an outlier' and the contrast with other countries as 'baffling' (Kearns, 2020). In reference to the original plan to suppress the virus through gradual restrictions, rather than trying to stamp it out entirely, O'Grady (2020) argues that 'while countries around the world began to lock down workplaces, schools, and public gatherings in response to the rapidly spreading coronavirus, the United Kingdom's initial strategy sent many into an uproar'. Anthony Costello (a former director of maternal and child health at the World Health Organization) told the ABC in an interview that 'the virus could ultimately claim more lives in the UK than any other European nation' because 'we basically allowed an exponentially-rising epidemic to get out of control when if we'd acted much earlier, like the Koreans, you would have suppressed it'. He added that 'Prime Minister Boris Johnson took action two weeks too late' (Hawley, 2020).

We saw in Chapter 2 that Brazil probably has the worst performance in terms of containing the virus, thanks primarily to the leadership of Jair Bolsonaro. On 20 June 2020, it was announced that Brazil was the second country, after the US, to record one million cases of COVID-19. Lipson (2020) refers to the 100,000 residents of Paradise City, Sao Paulo's second biggest 'favela', who have never had access to proper healthcare, education or sanitation. He describes the situation by saying that 'people continue walking in the streets as if the virus hasn't arrived in our community, as if the virus was only affecting rich people who travelled outside the country'.

Lipson seems to put the blame squarely on Bolsonaro (nicknamed 'Trump of the Tropics') for 'his populist zeal and anti-science approach to government' and his approach to the pandemic, which often echoed that of the US President. Bolsonaro downplayed COVID-19 for months, describing it as 'a little flu' that Brazilians were uniquely suited to overcome. He demanded all but the elderly ignore the state governments' social isolation restrictions, even attending anti-lockdown protests in person to insist that nothing was more important than the economy. Likewise, T. Phillips (2020) blames Bolsonaro, 'whose jumbled and dysfunctional handling of a pandemic he has called a "fantasy" has made Boris Johnson's widely panned response look sober and efficient'. We have learned from history how the actions of one person in power can put a whole country in a dire situation. It remains to say that Bolsonaro contracted the virus in July 2020 but, as president, he survived most likely by the exceptional healthcare provided to presidents and prime ministers, unlike the residents of Paradise City, Sao Paulo.

Donald Trump was no different from Bolsonaro. He also contacted the virus and his treatment is estimated to have cost taxpayers a humble one million dollars. An interesting article appeared in the 27 May 2020 issue of *The Atlantic* (updated subsequently), in which the author identifies President Trump's 'lies about the coronavirus', arguing that 'President Donald Trump has repeatedly lied about the coronavirus pandemic and the country's preparation for this once-in-a-generation crisis' (Paz, 2020). For example, on 27 February 2020, the president claimed that the outbreak would be temporary and that it was going to disappear, but a few days later Anthony Fauci, the director of the National Institute of Allergy and Infectious Diseases, warned that he was concerned that 'as the next week or two or three go by, we're going to see a lot more community-related cases'. On 11 March 2020, Trump said that private-health-insurance companies had 'agreed to waive all co-payments for coronavirus treatments, extend insurance coverage to these treatments, and to prevent surprise medical billing'. The truth is that insurers agreed only to absorb the cost of coronavirus testing – waiving co-payments and deductibles for getting the test. On 13 March 2020, Trump claimed that Google engineers were building a website to help Americans determine whether they need testing for the coronavirus and to direct them to their nearest testing site, but that was news to Google itself. On 24 March 2020, Trump claimed that the US had outpaced South Korea's testing, at a time when testing in the US was severely lagging behind that in South Korea.

Perhaps the most serious claims are those about the seriousness of COVID-19. On 17 March 2020, Trump said the following 'I've always known this is a real – this is a pandemic. I felt it was a pandemic long before it was called a pandemic … I've always viewed it as very serious'. The truth is that Trump has repeatedly downplayed the significance of COVID-19. On 27 March 2020, he claimed that the pandemic was 'something nobody thought could happen … Nobody would have ever thought a thing like this could have happened'. The truth is that the alarm had been sounded many times in the past decade about the potential for a devastating global pandemic (as we saw in the previous section). On 24 April, it was claimed that Trump was being 'sarcastic' when he suggested in a briefing on 23 April that his medical experts should research the use of powerful light and injected disinfectants to treat COVID-19. The truth is that Trump's tone did not sound sarcastic when he made the apparent suggestion to inject disinfectants. In fact, he said the following: 'I see the disinfectant, where it knocks it out in a minute'. On 4 July 2020, Trump claimed that '99%' of COVID-19 cases are 'totally harmless', but the truth is that the virus can cause tremendous (one of his favourite words) suffering if it does not kill a patient. And there is more where these came from.

10.4   CLOSING REMARKS

It is a miracle of evolution that SARS-CoV-2, a virus that measures one hundredth of a cell, could kill so many people and bring the world to a standstill. This virus is brutal because of easy transmissibility and a range of symptoms going from nothing at all to deadly. The struggle against the virus is described as a 'war', but the enemy cannot be dealt with by the army, air force or navy, and the spy agencies could not predict the attack. This enemy can only be dealt with by science, public health and good economics. Yet, governments keep on pouring money into the military and spy agencies and claim unaffordability when it comes to healthcare. This happens whether the people in charge are Republicans or Democrats in the US, Labour or Tories in the UK, and Labor or Liberals in Australia. The difference between Republicans and Democrats, Labour and Tories, and between Labor and Liberals is like the difference between *Tweedledum* and *Tweedledee*. This is what happens when political parties depend on donations from the private sector and when politicians aspire for highly paid jobs in the private sector when they are out of public service.

History tells us that despite the global vaccine roll-out, the end of the COVID-19 pandemic will be slow. The 'end' however, does not mean total eradication as in the case of smallpox – rather, it is more likely that the disease will become endemic and that it will be with us for the foreseeable future. In January 2021, *Nature* asked more than 100 immunologists, infectious-disease researchers and virologists working on the coronavirus whether it could be eradicated. Almost 90% of respondents think that the virus will become endemic. However, failure to eradicate the virus does not mean that our life-style during the pandemic will be unchanged and that masks, social distancing and recurring lockdowns will be the rule of the land. We will have to live with the virus, and how we cope with it depends on the type of immunity people acquire through infection or vaccination and on how the virus evolves. We have learned to live with influenza, which is endemic, and cope with it through a combination of annual vaccination and acquired immunity.

The silver lining is that the pandemic has taught us lessons, not only in public health but also in economics. We can no longer allow the invisible hand, which slaps us hard from time to time, to run the economy. We can no longer ignore inequality, poverty and homelessness. We can no longer carry on with business as usual in the privatise–liberalise–deregulate tradition. We can no longer indulge in complacency when it comes to preparation for a pandemic, just because preparation is not conducive to short-run profit maximisation. We can no longer engage in policies that do not work or work only for the benefit of a privileged minority. The pandemic has also taught us that it is time to break away from the economic doctrines that have shaped economic policy since the 1980s.

Hopefully, we will have some politicians who are brave enough to start a new New Deal, just like the brave and foresighted Franklin D. Roosevelt managed to take millions of people out of poverty through the original New Deal. Hopefully, politicians will start believing the teachings of great thinkers like Thomas Paine, not the 'teachings' of Ronald Reagan, Margaret Thatcher and their inspirers. One can only be optimistic that some positive change will emerge from the disaster of COVID-19.

References

ABC (2021) WHO Chief Warns of 'Moral Failure' as Coronavirus Vaccine Rollout Favours Wealthier Nations, ABC News, 19 January.

Acheson, R. (2020) COVID-19: Foreign Military Bases Spread Violence and Virus, Women's International League for Peace and Freedom, 14 May.

Acuto, M. (2020) COVID-19: Lessons for an Urban(izing) World, *One Earth*, 2, 317–319.

Adam, D. (2020) A Guide to R – The Pandemic's Misunderstood Metric, *Nature*, 3 July.

Afsahi, A., Beausoleil, E., Dean, R., Ercan, S.A. and Gagnon, J.P. (2020) Democracy in a Global Emergency, *Democratic Theory*, 7, 5–19.

Akon, M.S. and Rahman, M. (2020) Reshaping the Global Order in the Post COVID-19, *Chinese Journal of International Review*, 2, 1–5.

Albrow, M. and King, E. (1990) *Globalization, Knowledge and Society*, London: Sage.

Aldasoro, I., Fender, I. and Tarashev, N. (2020) Effects of Covid-19 on the Banking Sector: The Market's Assessment, *BIS Bulletin*, No. 12.

Aljazeera (2020) WHO: Travel Bans Cannot be Indefinite, Countries Must Fight Virus, 27 July.

Alvarez, F.E., Argente, D. and Lippi, F. (2020) Simple Planning Problem for COVID-19 Lockdown, NBER Working Papers, No. 26981.

Araujo, M.B. and Naimi, B. (2020) Spread of SARS-CoV-2 Coronavirus Likely to be Constrained by Climate, *medRxiv* (published online, 16 March).

Arnold, R.J., Sa, D., Gronniger, T., Percy, A. and Somers, J. (2006) A Potential Influenza Pandemic: Possible Macroeconomic Effects and Policy Issues, Report to the Congressional Budget Office, 27 July.

Assi, R., Calan, M.D., Kaul, A. and Vincent, A. (2020) Closing the $30 Trillion Gap: Acting Now to Manage Fiscal Deficits During and Beyond the COVID-19 Crisis, McKinsey and Company, 16 July.

Astore, W.J. (2018) Meet the New, Super-Expensive Stealth Bomber the US Doesn't Need, *The Nation*, 4 June.

Auer, R., Cornelli, G. and Frost, J. (2020) Covid-19, Cash and the Future of Payments, *BIS Bulletin*, No. 3.

Avineri, S. (2020) Coronavirus has Killed Neoliberalism. Even Trump Knows that, *Haaretz*, 30 March.

Bacchus, J. (2020) An Unnecessary Proposal: A WTO Waiver of Intellectual Property Rights for COVID-19 Vaccines, *Free Trade Bulletin*, No. 78.

Bainbridge, J. and Carrizales, T.J. (2017) Global Homelessness in a Post-Recession World, *Journal of Public Management and Social Policy*, 24, 71–90.

Balder, J.M. (2020) Reversing Financialization in the Post-COVID-19 World, 24 August. https://www.advisorperspectives.com/articles/2020/08/24/reversing-financialization-in-the-post-covid-19-world.

Bank for International Settlements (2019) Triennial Central Bank Survey of Foreign Exchange and Over-the-counter (OTC) Derivatives Markets in 2019, 8 December. https://www.bis.org/statistics/rpfx19.htm.

Barr, J.M. and Tassier, T. (2020a) Escape from New York? Density and the Coronavirus Trajectory, 20 April. https://buildingtheskyline.org/covid19-and-density/.

Barr, J.M. and Tassier, T. (2020b) Modeling the Impact of Density on the Spread of the Corona Virus, Working Paper, 3 April. https://buildingtheskyline.org/wp-content/uploads/2019/10/Theory-and-Empirical-Model-6April20.pdf.

Barrett, R. and Brown, P.J. (2008) Stigma in the Time of Influenza: Social and Institutional Responses to Pandemic Emergencies, *Journal of Infectious Diseases*, 197 (Supplement 1), S34–S37.

Barro, R., Ursua, J. and Weng, J. (2020) The Coronavirus and the Great Influenza Pandemic: Lessons from the 'Spanish Flu' for the Coronavirus' Potential Effects on Mortality and Economic Activity, NBER Working Papers, No. 26866.

Bartlett, B. (2013) Financialization as a Cause of Economic Malaise, *New York Times*, 11 June.

Barwick, E. (2020) Aged Care is a Public Good, not a Cash Cow, *Australian Alert Service*, 7 October, 5–6.

Bauer, L. (2020) Hungry at Thanksgiving: A Fall 2020 Update on Food Insecurity in the U.S., *Brookings*, 23 November.

BBC (2020a) Rich Countries Hoarding Covid Vaccines, Says People's Vaccine Alliance, BBC News, 9 December.

BBC (2020b) Coronavirus: Shops 'Exploiting' Pandemic by Profiteering, BBC News, 17 April.

BCBS (2004) *Basel II: International Convergence of Capital Measurement and Capital Standards: A Revised Framework*, Basel: Bank for International Settlements, June.

Beaumont, H. (2020) Universal Healthcare 'Critical' in COVID-19 Pandemic: Experts, Aljazeera News, 14 November.

Beckley, M. (2020) China's Economy is Not Overtaking America's, *Journal of Applied Corporate Finance*, 32, 10–23.

Bell, J. (2020) The U.S. and COVID-19: Leading the World by GHS Index Score, Not by Response, 21 April. https://www.nti.org/analysis/atomic-pulse/us-and-covid-19-leading-world-ghs-index-score-not-response/.

Bellofiore, R. (2013) Two or Three Things I Know about Her: Europe in the Global Crisis and Heterodox Economics, *Cambridge Journal of Economics*, 37, 497–512.

Bennhold, K. and Sanger, D.E. (2020) U.S. Offered 'Large Sum' to German Company for Access to Coronavirus Vaccine Research, German Officials Say, *New York Times*, 2 April.

Bernanke, B.S. (2004) The Great Moderation, 20 February. https://www.federalreserve.gov/boarddocs/speeches/2004/20040220/.

Bertossa, D. (2020) Fighting the Backlash: Covid Driven Health Privatisation Has Started, *Public Services International*, 5 October.

Black, W. (2011) How the Servant Became a Predator: Finance's Five Fatal Flaws, *Huffington Post*, 25 May.

Boldrin, M. and Levine, D.K. (2008) *Against Intellectual Monopoly*, Cambridge: Cambridge University Press.

Borger, J. (2019) Trump Contradicts Aides and Says Troops in Syria 'Only for Oil', *The Guardian*, 14 November.

Bregman, R. (2017) *Utopia for Realists and How We Can Get There*, London: Bloomsbury.

Brignall, M., Collinson, P. and Smithers, R. (2020) Coronavirus: Your Guide to Safer Shopping and Travel, *The Guardian*, 14 March.

Brinca, P., Duarte, J.B. and Castro, M.F. (2020) Measuring Labor Supply and Demand Shocks During COVID-19, Federal Reserve Bank of St Louis Working Papers, No. 2020-011F.

Brittain, A., Stanley-Becker, I. and Miroff, N. (2020) White House's Pandemic Relief Effort Project Airbridge is Swathed in Secrecy and Exaggerations, *Washington Post*, 8 May.

Brouder, P. (2020) Reset Redux: Possible Evolutionary Pathways Towards the Transformation of Tourism in a COVID-19 World, *Tourism Geographies* (published online, 6 May).

Brumfiel, G. and Wilburn, T. (2020) Countries Slammed their Borders Shut to Stop Coronavirus. But Is It Doing Any Good?, NPR, 15 May.

Buchelt, R. and Unteregger, S. (2004) Cultural Risk and Risk Culture: Operational Risk after Basel II, Financial Stability Report, No. 6.

Buettner, R., McIntire, M., Craig, S. and Collins, K. (2020) Trump Paid $750 in Federal Income Taxes in 2017: Here's the Math, *New York Times*, 29 September.

Bufalino, A. (2020) You Wouldn't Believe Who Got a Small Business Loan, *American Conservative*, 7 July.

Burns, A., van der Mensbrugghe, D. and Timmer, H. (2006) Evaluating the Economic Consequences of Avian Influenza, World Bank Working Papers, No. 47417.

Busby, J. (2020) What International Relations Tells us about COVID-19, *E-International Relations*, 26 April.

Butler, P. (2020) UK's Poorest 'Skip Meals and Go Hungry' During Coronavirus Crisis, *The Guardian*, 13 August.

Butler, S. (1933) Smedley Butler on Interventionism. https://fas.org/man/smedley.htm.

Calder, S. (2020) Coronavirus: 36,000 British Airways Staff to be Furloughed in Worst-Ever Crisis for Modern Aviation, *The Independent*, 2 April.

Calnitsky, D. and Latner, J.P. (2017) Basic Income in a Small Town: Understanding the Elusive Effects on Work, *Social Problems*, 64, 373–397.

Calvert, J., Arbuthnott, G. and Leake, J. (2020) Coronavirus: 38 Days when Britain Sleepwalked into Disaster, *Sunday Times*, 19 April.

Campbell, K.M. and Doshi, R. (2020) The Coronavirus Could Reshape Global Order, *Foreign Affairs*, 18 March.

Cassim, Z., Handjiski, B., Schubert, J. and Zouaoui, Y. (2020) The $10 Trillion Rescue: How Governments Can Deliver Impact, McKinsey and Company, June.

Çelik, S., Demirtaş, G. and Isaksson, M. (2020) Corporate Bond Market Trends, Emerging Risks and Monetary Policy, OECD Capital Market Series.

Chakraborty, B. (2020) China Cashes in off Coronavirus, Selling Spain $467 Million in Supplies, Some of Them Substandard, Fox News, 26 March.

Chatterjee, A., Gethin, A. and Czajka, L. (2020) Coronavirus: Why South Africa Needs a Wealth Tax Now, *The Conversation*, 28 April.

Chaudhry, R., Dranitsaris, G., Mubashir, T., Bartoszko, J. and Riazi, S. (2020) A Country Level Analysis Measuring the Impact of Government Actions, Country Preparedness and Socioeconomic Factors on COVID-19 Mortality and Related Health Outcomes, *Lancet Regional Health*, 1 August.

Cherkaoui, M. (2020) The Shifting Geopolitics of Coronavirus and the Demise of Neoliberalism, Al Jazeera Centre for Studies, 22 March.

Chewning, E., Chinn, D., McNally, E.Y. and Rutherford, S. (2020) Lessons from the Military for COVID-Time Leadership, McKinsey and Company, 20 May.

Chinazzi, M., Davis, J.T., Ajelli, M., Gioannini, C., Litvinova, M., Merler, S., Piontti, A., Mu, K., Rossi, L., Sun, K., Viboud, C., Xiong, X., Yu, H., Halloran, E., Longini, M. and Vespignani, A. (2020) The Effect of Travel Restrictions on the Spread of the 2019 Novel Coronavirus (COVID-19) Outbreak, *Science*, 368, 395–400.

Chuter, A. (2021) More Nukes and a Regional Pivot: Britain Unveils its Long-Awaited Defense Review, *Defense News*, 16 March.

City A.M. (2020) Editorial: Vaccine Success is a Shot in the Arm for the Free Market, 17 November. https://www.cityam.com/editorial-vaccine-success-is-a-shot-in-the -arm-for-the-free-market/.

Clementi, G.L., Cooley, T.F., Richardson, M. and Walter, I. (2009) Rethinking Compensation in Financial Firms, *Financial Markets, Institutions and Instruments*, 18, 160–162.

CNN (2021) Qatar Airways to Retire Half of its A380 Planes, 15 January.

Cohen-Setton, J. (2016) The New Washington Consensus, 3 June. https://www.bruegel .org/ 2016/06/the-new-washington-consensus/.

Colchester, M. and Norman, L. (2021) Vaccine-Export Fight Hastens Decline in EU–U.K. Relations, *Wall Street Journal*, 17 March.

Collins, C. and Clemente, F. (2020) It is Time to Levy a One-Time Pandemic Wealth Tax on Billionaires' Windfall Gains, *Market Watch*, 20 August.

Collis, H. (2020) WTO Members Reject IP Rules Waiver for Coronavirus Technologies, *Politico Pro*, 16 October.

Colvin, C. and McLaughlin, E. (2020) Coronavirus and Spanish Flu: Economic Lessons to Learn from the Last Truly Global Pandemic, *The Conversation*, 11 March.

Congressional Research Service (2021) Global Economic Effects of COVID-19 (updated 10 March). https://fas.org/sgp/crs/row/R46270.pdf.

Connolly, K. (2008) Booklovers Turn to Karl Marx as Financial Crisis Bites in Germany, *The Guardian*, 15 October.

Constable, S. (2020) How COVID-19 Killed the Stock Buyback Program, *Forbes*, 8 April.

Contractor, S. and Kakar, I.S. (2020) Covid-19 and Unregulated Private Hospitals: Lessons for Private Sector Engagement, *International Health Policies*, 18 June.

Cordelli, C. (2020) The Covid Crisis has Shown How Privatisation Corrodes Democracy, *The Guardian*, 25 December.

Correa-Martínez, C.L. et al. (2020) A Pandemic in Times of Global Tourism: Superspreading and Exportation of COVID-19 Cases from a Ski Area in Austria, Letter to the Editor, *Journal of Clinical Microbiology*. https://jcm.asm.org/content/ 58/6/e00588-20.

Correia, S., Luck, S. and Verner, E. (2020) Pandemics Depress the Economy, Public Health Interventions Do Not: Evidence From the 1918 Flu. SSRN: https://ssrn.com/ abstract=3561560.

Council for Trade-Related Aspects of Intellectual Property Rights (2020) Waiver from Certain Provisions of the TRIPS Agreement for the Prevention, Containment and Treatment of COVID-19: Communication from India and South Africa, World Trade Organization, IP/C/W/669, 2 October.

Creighton, A. (2021) Coronavirus: Health Fascism has Consumed Human Rights, *The Australian*, 21 February.

Crotty, J. (1990) Owner–Manager Conflict and Financial Theories of Investment Instability: A Critical Assessment of Keynes, Tobin, and Minsky, *Journal of Post Keynesian Economics*, 12, 519–542.

Crotty, J. (2009) Structural Causes of the Global Financial Crisis: A Critical Assessment of the 'New Financial Architecture', *Cambridge Journal of Economics*, 33, 563–580.

Culhane, D., Treglia, D., Steif, K., Kuhn, R. and Byrne, T. (2020) Estimated Emergency and Observational/Quarantine Bed Need for the US Homeless Population Related to COVID-19. https://escholarship.org/uc/item/9g0992bm.

Cushen, J. (2013) Financialization in the Workplace: Hegemonic Narratives, Performative Interventions and the Angry Knowledge Worker, *Accounting, Organizations and Society*, 38, 314–331.

Dahinten, J. and Wabl, M. (2020) Germany Faces Backlash from Neighbors Over Mask Export Ban, Bloomberg, 10 March.

Darius, R. (2021) COVID-19 Has Exacerbated Anti-Globalisation Sentiments, Australian Institute of International Affairs, 8 January.

De Maio, G. (2020) The Impact of COVID-19 on the Italian Far Right: The Rise of Brothers of Italy, *Brookings*, 30 November.

Desai, D.D. (2020) Urban Densities and the Covid-19 Pandemic: Upending the Sustainability Myth of Global Megacities, ORF Occasional Papers, No. 244.

Diamond, J. (2009) *Guns, Germs, and Steel: The Fates of Human Societies*, New York: Norton.

Diamond, L. (2020) Democracy Versus the Pandemic, *Foreign Affairs*, 13 June.

Dick, S. (2020) It isn't Illegal to Rip off Australians in a Crisis. But that Soon May Change, *The New Daily*, 15 May.

Dixon, E. (2020) Fascists are Using COVID-19 to Advance their Agenda. It's Up to Us to Stop Them, *Truthout*, 11 April.

Dowd, K. (2009) Moral Hazard and the Financial Crisis, *Cato Journal*, 29, 141–166.

Dowd, K. (2017) Killing the Cash Cow: Why Andy Haldane is Wrong about Demonetisation, *Adam Smith Institute Briefing Papers*, April.

Dowd, T. (2020) Snowden Warns Governments are Using Coronavirus to Build 'The Architecture of Oppression', *Vice*, 9 April.

Dowda, J.B., Andrianoa, L., Brazela, D.M., Rotondia, V., Blocka, P., Dinga, X. and Millsa, M.C. (2020) Demographic Science Aids in Understanding the Spread and Fatality Rates of COVID-19, PNAS, 5 May.

Drezner, D.W. (2014) *The System Worked*, Oxford: Oxford University Press.

Drezner, D.W. (2020) The Song Remains the Same: International Relations After COVID-19, *International Organisation*, 74 (Supplemental Issue), August.

Dyer, O. (2021) Covid-19: 'Shkreli Awards' Go to Pandemic's top Profiteers, 5 January. https://www.bmj.com/content/372/bmj.n16.

Economist, The (2011) Cash Machines: Calls to Boost Manufacturing Ignore the Gains to be Made from Services, 2 April.

Economist, The (2014) Patents that Kill, 8 August.

Economist, The (2020a) A Sea of Debt, 12 March.

Economist, The (2020b) Rich Countries Try Radical Economic Policies to Counter Covid-19, 26 March.

Edmund Rice Centre (2020) Save Lives or Destroy Them – Militarism and COVID-19, *Just a Comment*, 22 (1).

Eichenbaum, M.S., Rebelo, S. and Trabandt, M. (2020) The Macroeconomics of Epidemics, NBER Working Papers, No. 26882.

Epstein, G.A. (2002) Financialization, Rentier Interests, and Central Bank Policy, Working Paper, Department of Economics and Political Economy Research Institute (PERI), University of Massachusetts Amherst.

Euronews (2020) Experts Play Down Likelihood of Banknotes Spreading Coronavirus, 6 March.

Evans, M., Berzon, A. and Hernandez, D. (2020) Some California Hospitals Refused Covid-19 Transfers for Financial Reasons, State Emails Show, *Wall Street Journal*, 19 October.

Evans-Pritchard, A. (2020) Boris Must Embrace Socialism Immediately to Save the Liberal Free Market, *Daily Telegraph*, 20 March.

Fan, V., Jamison, D. and Summers, L. (2016) The Inclusive Cost of Pandemic Influenza Risk, NBER Working Papers, No. 22137.

Fang, W. and Wahba, S. (2020) Urban Density is Not an Enemy in the Coronavirus Fight: Evidence from China, World Bank Blogs, 20 April.

FAO (1996) Rome Declaration on Food Security and World Food Summit Plan of Action, World Food Summit, 13–17 November, Rome.

FAO (2006) Food Security, FAO Policy Brief, Issue 2, June.

FAO (2019) State of Food Security and Nutrition in the World 2019. http://www.fao.org/state-of-food-security-nutrition.

Farha, L., Bohoslavsky, J.P., Barry, K.B., Heller, L., Schutter, O.D. and Carmona, M.S. (2020) Covid-19 Has Exposed the Catastrophic Impact of Privatising Vital Services, *The Guardian*, 19 October.

Fattah, E.A. (2020) A Social Scientist's Look at a Global Crisis: Reflections on the Likely Positive Impact of the Corona Virus, Special Paper: School of Criminology, Simon Fraser University.

Fazal, T.M. (2020) Health Diplomacy in Pandemical Times, *International Organisation*, 74 (Supplemental Issue), September.

Feffer, J. (2020) The Black Death Killed Feudalism. What Does COVID-19 Mean for Capitalism?, *Foreign Policy In Focus*, 14 May.

Felson, M., Jiang, S. and Xu, Y. (2020) Routine Activity Effects of the COVID-19 Pandemic on Burglary in Detroit, *Crime Science*, 9 (10).

Ferguson, N.M. et al. (2020) Impact of Non-Pharmaceutical Interventions (NPIs) to Reduce COVID-19 Mortality and Healthcare Demand, Imperial College COVID-19 Response Team, Report 9.

Fernyhough, J. (2019) Scrap Medicare, Mandate Private Health Cover: NIB Boss, *Financial Review*, 23 July.

Ferretti, L. et al. (2020) Quantifying SARS-CoV-2 Transmission Suggests Epidemic Control with Digital Contact Tracing, *Science*, 8 May.

Financial Times (2020) Virus Lays Bare the Frailty of the Social Contract, 3 April.

Florida, R. (2020) The Geography of Coronavirus, Bloomberg, 4 April.

Fondeville, N. and Ward, T. (2011) Homelessness During the Crisis, European Commission, Research Note 8/2011, November.

Food Security Information Network (2020) Global Report on Food Crises. http://www.fightfoodcrises.net/food-crises-and-covid-19/en/.

Forbes, S. (2016) Why Big Government is Waging War against Cash, *Forbes*, 21 March.

Fornaro, L. and Wolf, M. (2020a) Coronavirus and Macroeconomic Policy, *VOXEU*, 18 April.

Fornaro, L. and Wolf, M. (2020b) Covid-19 Coronavirus and Macroeconomic Policy: Some Analytical Notes, Unpublished Manuscript.

Fraser, C. et al. (2009) Pandemic Potential of a Strain of Influenza A (H1N1): Early Findings, *Science*, 324 (5934), 1557–1561.

Frey, I. (2020) 'Herd Immunity' is Epidemiological Neoliberalism, *The Quarantimes*, 19 March.

Friedman, D. (2002) No Light at the End of the Tunnel, *LA Times*, 16 June. https://www.latimes.com/archives/la-xpm-2002-jun-16-op-friedman-story.html.

Friedman, M. (1966) The Case for Negative Income Tax: A View from the Right, Hoover Institution, 9 December.

Friedman, M. and Friedman, R. (1962) *Capitalism and Freedom*, Chicago: University of Chicago Press.

Friedman, M. and Friedman, R. (1980) *Free to Choose: A Personal Statement*, New York: Harcourt Brace and Company.

Fukuyama, F. (2020) The Pandemic and Political Order, *Foreign Affairs*, 99, 26–32.

Furceri, D., Loungani, P., Ostry, J. and Pizzuto, P. (2020) Will Covid-19 Affect Inequality? Evidence from Past Pandemics, *Covid Economics*, 12, 138–157.

Gali, J. (2009) *Monetary Policy, Inflation, and the Business Cycle: An Introduction to the New Keynesian Framework*, Princeton: Princeton University Press.

Gaspar, V. (2020) Facing the Crisis: The Role of Tax in Dealing with COVID-19, IMF Views & Commentaries, 16 June.

Gates, B. (2015) The Next Outbreak? We're Not Ready, Ted Talk. https://www.ted.com/talks/bill_gates_the_next_outbreak_we_re_not_ready?language=dz.

Giddens, A. (1990) *The Consequences of Modernity*, Cambridge: Polity Press.

Gifford, C. (2020) Universal Basic Income Gains Support During the Pandemic, *World Finance*, 14 September.

Gilding, P. (2020) Covid-19 and the Death of Market Fundamentalism, *Renew Economy*, 16 April.

Giles, C., Arnold, M., Jones, S. and Smyth, J. (2020) Finance Ministers 'Ready to Take Action' on Covid-19, *Financial Times*, 3 March.

Giuliani, E. (2020) Piketty, Thunberg, or Marx? Shifting Ideologies in the COVID-19 Bailout Conditionality Debate, *Journal of International Business Policy*, 3, 443–450.

Glennie, J. (2011) What Comes after the Washington Consensus?, *The Guardian*, 9 February.

Glenza, J. (2020) Trump Enjoys Top Covid Care that Could Cost Ordinary Americans Millions, *The Guardian*, 8 October.

Global Preparedness Monitoring Board (2019) *A World at Risk: Annual Report on Global Preparedness for Health Emergencies*, September.

Goldin, I. and Muggah, R. (2020) COVID-19 is Increasing Multiple Kinds of Inequality. Here's What we Can Do About It, World Economic Forum, 9 October.

Golub, P. (2020) Bringing the State Back in During Covid-19, *Le Monde Diplomatique*, 18 March.

Gonzalez-Eiras, M. and Niepelt, D. (2020) On the Optimal 'Lockdown' During an Epidemic, Working Papers, Swiss National Bank, Study Center Gerzensee, No. 20.01.

Google (2020) COVID-19 Community Mobility Reports. https://www.google.com/covid19/mobility/.

Gössling, S., Scott, D. and Hall, C.M. (2020) Pandemics, Tourism and Global Change: A Rapid Assessment of COVID-19, *Journal of Sustainable Tourism* (published online, 27 April).

Grass, C. (2020) The COVID Crisis Supercharged the War on Cash, *Mises Wire*, 30 June.

Gray, J. (2009) *False Dawn: The Delusions of Global Capitalism* (revised edition), London: Granta Publications.

Gray, J. (2020) Why This Crisis is a Turning Point in History, *New Statesman*, 1 April.

Gros, C., Valenti, R., Schneider, L., Valenti, K. and Gros, D. (2020) Containment Efficiency and Control Strategies for the Corona Pandemic Costs. https://www.nature.com/articles/s41598-021-86072-x.

Guardian, The (2020) There is Such a Thing as Society, Says Boris Johnson from Bunker, 29 March.

Haagh, L. (2019) The Political Economy of Governance Capacity and Institutional Change: The Case of Basic Income Security Reform in European Welfare States, *Social Policy and Society*, 18, 243–263.

Hai, W., Zhao, Z., Wang, J. and Hou, Z.G. (2004) The Short-term Impact of SARS on the Chinese Economy, *Asian Economic Papers*, 3, 57–61.

Halbfinger, D.M., Kershner, I. and Bergman, R. (2020) To Track Coronavirus, Israel Moves to Tap Secret Trove of Cellphone Data, *New York Times*, 18 March.

Halliday, T.C. and Osinsky, P. (2006) Globalization of Law, *Annual Review of Sociology*, 32, 447–470.

Hameiri, S. (2020) Covid-19: Time to Bring Back the State, *Progress in Political Economy*, 19 March.

Hanrahan, P. (2020) Deregulation Needs to be a Priority in COVID Recovery, Australian Institute of Company Directors, 1 July.

Hansen, S. (2020) Here's How the Coronavirus Recession Compares to the Great Recession, *Forbes*, 8 May.

Harcourt, B.E. (2011) *The Illusion of Free Markets: Punishment and the Myth of Natural Order*, Cambridge, MA: Harvard University Press.

Harrington, A. and Hjelt, P. (2001) The Great CEO Pay Heist, *Fortune*, 25 June.

Harvey, A. (1989) *Forecasting, Structural Time Series Models and Kalman Filter*, Cambridge: Cambridge University Press.

Hasell, J. (2020) Which Countries have Protected both Health and the Economy in the Pandemic?, 1 September. https://ourworldindata.org/covid-health-economy.

Haug, N., Geyrhofer, L., Londei, A., Dervic, E., Desvars-Larrive, A., Loreto, V., Pinior, V.B., Thurner, S. and Klimek, P. (2020) Ranking the Effectiveness of Worldwide COVID-19 Government Interventions, *Nature Human Behaviour*, 4, 1303–1312.

Hawley, S. (2020) British Government Accused of Allowing Coronavirus to Get out of Control, ABC News, 21 April.

Hayes, A. (2019) Maximum Wage, *Investopedia*, 12 June.

Held, D., Goldblatt, D., McGrew, A. and Perraton, J. (1999) *Global Transformations*, Cambridge: Polity Press.

Hill, R. and Narayan, A. (2021) What COVID-19 Can Mean for Long-Term Inequality in Developing Countries, *World Bank Blogs*, 7 January.

Homer, M. and Benito, M. (2021) Gov. Abbott Announces End to Statewide Mask Mandate, Allows Texas Businesses to Open at 100%, *KHOU*, 2 March.

Homer, M. and Rouege, C. (2021) 'Premature and Misguided': Houston Leaders Criticize Gov. Abbott's Decision to Lift COVID Restrictions, *KHOU*, 3 March.

House of Lords (2020) *Employment and COVID-19: Time for a New Deal*, 3rd Report of Session 2019–2021, 14 December.

Hu, H., Nigmatulina, K. and Eckhoff, P. (2013) The Scaling of Contact Rates with Population Density for the Infectious Disease Models, *Mathematical Biosciences*, 244, 125–134.

Human Rights Watch (2021) Brazil: Institutions Stand Up to Bolsonaro, 13 January. https://www.hrw.org/news/2021/01/13/brazil-institutions-stand-bolsonaro.

ILO (2020) COVID-19 and the World of Work: Impact and Policy Responses. https://www.ilo.org/wcmsp5/groups/public/---dgreports/---dcomm/documents/briefingnote/wcms_738753.pdf.

Ilyushina, M. (2020) How Russia is Using Authoritarian Tech to Curb Coronavirus, CNN, 29 March.

IMF (2000) Globalization: Threat or Opportunity?, 12 April. https://www.imf.org/external/np/exr/ib/2000/041200to.htm.

IMF (2009) *World Economic Outlook*, Washington, DC: International Monetary Fund.

International Crisis Group (2015) *The Politics Behind the Ebola Crisis*. https://www.crisisgroup.org/africa/west-africa/politics-behind-ebola-crisis.

International Currency Association (2020) ICA Information on Cash and Pandemic, 29 April. https://currencyassociation.org/article/ica-references-on-cash-pandemic/.

Isaković, N.P. (2020) COVID-19: What has COVID-19 Taught us about Neoliberalism? https://www.wilpf.org/covid-19-what-has-covid-19-taught-us-about-neoliberalism/.

Islam, N., Sharp, S.J., Chowell, G., Shabnam, S., Kawachi, I., Lacey, B., Massaro, J.M., D'Agostino, R.B. and White, M. (2020) Physical Distancing Interventions and Incidence of Coronavirus Disease 2019: Natural Experiment in 149 Countries, *BMJ*, 370, m2743.

Jacoby, K., Stucka, M. and Phillips, K. (2020) Crime Rates Plummet amid the Coronavirus Pandemic, But Not Everyone is Safer in Their Home, *USA Today*, 4 April.

James, P. (2005) Arguing Globalizations: Propositions Towards an Investigation of Global Formation, *Globalizations*, 2, 193–209.

Jamison, D.T., Lau, L.J., Wu, K.B. and Xiong, Y. (2020) Country Performance against COVID-19: Rankings for 35 Countries, *BMJ Global Health*, 5 (12), e003047.

Jerving, S. (2020) How Effective are Travel Restrictions? A Look at Approaches to Contain Coronavirus, *Devex*, 28 February.

Johnson, C. and Lyons, S. (2020) Superspreaders and the Role they Play in Transmitting Coronavirus to Others, *ABC Health & Wellbeing*, 15 July.

Jones, G.S. (2017) In Retrospect: *Das Kapital*, *Nature*, 547, 401–402.

Joyce, R. and Xu, X. (2020) Sector Shut-Downs during the Coronavirus Crisis Affect the Youngest and Lowest Paid Workers, and Women, the Most, Institute for Fiscal Studies, 6 April. https://www.ifs.org.uk/publications/14797.

Kahl, C. and Berengaut, A. (2020) Aftershocks: The Coronavirus Pandemic and the New World Disorder, *War on the Rocks*, 10 April.

Kalkman, J.P. (2020) Military Crisis Responses to COVID-19, *Contingencies and Crisis Management*, 29, 99–103.

Kaplan, R.D. (2020) Coronavirus Ushers in the Globalization We Were Afraid of, Bloomberg, 20 March.

Karabell, Z. (2020) Stocks are Recovering while the Economy Collapses: That Makes More Sense than You'd Think, *Time*, 29 April.

Karp, P. (2019) ABS Drops Reference to Worsening Wealth Inequality to Craft a 'Good Story', *The Guardian*, 28 August.

Karp, P. (2020) Australian Universities Facing $16bn Black Hole as Covid-19 Student Numbers Plummet, *The Guardian*, 3 June.

Kavoussi, B. (2012) U.S. Could End Homelessness With Money Used to Buy Christmas Decorations, *Huffington Post*, 12 December.

Kearns, M. (2020) Why is the U.K.'s Response to COVID-19 Such an Outlier?, *National Review*, 17 March.

Kelly, J. (2020) Senators Accused of Insider Trading, Dumping Stocks After Coronavirus Briefing, *Forbes*, 2 March.

Kenwick, M.R. and Simmons, B.A. (2020) Pandemic Response as Border Politics, *International Organisation*, 74 (Supplemental Issue), August.

Keogh-Brown, M.R., Wren-Lewis, S., Edmunds, W.J., Beutels, P. and Smith, R.D. (2010) The Possible Macroeconomic Impact on the UK of an Influenza Pandemic, *Health Economics*, 19, 1345–1360.

Khan, A. (2021) What is 'Vaccine Nationalism' and Why is it so Harmful?, Aljazeera, 7 February.

Khan, I. (2020) Here's How a Revamped Wealth Tax Could Fuel the COVID-19 Recovery, *Brink News*, 16 August.

Khan, J. (2020) The Reopening Dilemma: Saving Lives vs. Saving the Economy is a False Tradeoff, Economists Say, *Fortune*, 5 May.

Kiersz, A. and Reinicke, C. (2020) 5 Charts Show How the Coronavirus Crisis Has Dwarfed the Great Recession in Just 2 Months, *Business Insider Australia*, 23 May.

Kılıç, S. (2020) Does COVID-19 as a Long Wave Turning Point Mean the End of Neoliberalism?, *Critical Sociology* (published online, 11 December).

Kinlaw, K. and Levine, R. (2007) Ethical Guidelines in Pandemic Influenza, 15 February. https://www.cdc.gov/os/integrity/phethics/docs/panFlu_Ethic_Guidelines .pdf.

Kinsella, S. (2010) When Patents Kill: Genzyme's Patent-Protected, Life-Saving Drug, *Christian Science Monitor*, 13 December.

Kirk, D. (2020) Korea Reveals 'New Deal' Designed to Boost Jobs, Revive Sagging Economy, *Forbes*, 14 July.

Kirshner, J. (2014) *American Power after the Financial Crisis*, Cornell: Cornell University Press.

Kliff, S. (2020) How Much would Donald Trump's Coronavirus Treatment Cost Most Americans?, SBS News, 8 October.

Knaus, C. (2020) Dozens of Australian Companies Fined for Trying to Unlawfully Profit from Covid Crisis, *The Guardian*, 6 September.

Kolakowski, M. (2019) Why the Corporate Debt Bubble May Burst Sooner than You Think, *Invetopedia*, 20 February.

Koopman, S.J., Harvey, A.C., Doornik, J.A. and Shephard, N. (2006) *Structural Time Series Analyser, Modeller and Predictor*, London: Timberlake Consultants Ltd.

Krugman, P. (2007) *The Conscience of a Liberal*, New York: Norton.

Lapointe, D. (2020) Reconnecting Tourism after COVID-19: The Paradox of Alterity in Tourism Areas, *Tourism Geographies* (published online, 5 May).

Lavoie, M. (2012) Financialization, Neo-Liberalism, and Securitization, *Journal of Post Keynesian Economics*, 35, 215–233.

Lechini, G. (2008) Introduction, in G. Lechini (ed.), *Globalization and the Washington Consensus: Its Influence on Democracy and Development in the South*, Buenos Aires: Consejo Latinoamericano de Ciencias Sociales.

Lederer, E.M. (2020) Crime Rates Plummet Around the World as the Coronavirus Keeps People Inside, *NESA*, 11 April.

Lee, J.W. and McKibbin, W. (2004) Estimating the Global Economic Costs of SARS, in S. Knobler, A. Mahmoud, S. Lemon, A. Mack, L. Sivitz and K. Oberholtzer (eds), *Learning from SARS: Preparing for the Next Outbreak*, Washington, DC: National Academies Press.

Lent, J. (2020) Coronavirus Spells the End of the Neoliberal Era. What's Next?, *Patterns of Meaning Blog*, 2 April.

Leonhardt, M. (2020) Uninsured Americans Could be Facing Nearly $75,000 in Medical Bills if Hospitalized for Coronavirus, CNBC, 1 April.

Lepecq, G. (2020) Who is Framing Cash?, *Cash Essentials*, 25 August.

Li, R., Richmond, P. and Roehner, B. (2018) Effect of Population Density on Epidemics, *Physica A*, 510, 713–724.

Lincicome, S. (2021) Manufactured Crisis: 'Deindustrialization', Free Markets, and National Security, *Policy Analysis*, No. 907.

Lindorff, D. (2018) The Pentagon's Massive Accounting Fraud Exposed, *The Nation*, 27 November.

Lipscy, P.Y. (2020) COVID-19 and the Politics of Crisis, *International Organisation*, 74 (Supplemental Issue), October.

Lipson, D. (2020) This is Where They Went Wrong, ABC News, 20 May.

Long, H. (2020) G-7 Leaders Promise to Help Economy as COVID-19 Spreads, But They Don't Announce Any New Action, *Washington Post*, 3 March.

Lorenzoni, G. (2009) A Theory of Demand Shocks, *American Economic Review*, 99, 2050–2084.

Lowy Institute (2021) Covid Performance Index: Deconstructing Pandemic Responses, January. https://interactives.lowyinstitute.org/features/covid-performance/.

Lund, S. (2018) Are We in a Corporate Debt Bubble?, McKinsey Global Institute, 21 June.

Lynch, D. (2019) Corporate Debt Nears a Record $10 Trillion, and Borrowing Binge Poses New Risks, *Washington Post*, 30 November.

Macron, E. (2020) Time to Think the Unthinkable, *Financial Times*, 17 April.

Mader, P., Mertens, D. and van der Zwan, N. (eds) (2020a) *The Routledge International Handbook of Financialization*, London: Routledge.

Mader, P., van der Zwan, N. and Mertens, D. (2020b) 9 Ways Coronavirus Could Transform Capitalism, *Tribune*, 2 June.

Makin, T. (2020) Coronavirus: It's Keynes's Fault – Again We Go into Debt to 'Stimulate' the Economy, *The Australian*, 17 June.

Maney, K. (2015) How Patents Kill Innovation and Hold Tech Companies Back, *Newsweek*, 25 February

Martinelli, L. (2017) *Assessing the Case for a Universal Basic Income in the UK*, Bath: Institute for Policy Research.

Martinez, M.A. (2009) *The Myth of the Free Market: The Role of the State in a Capitalist Economy*, Sterling, VA: Kumarian Press.

Matthews, J. (2017) No Need to Agree: Founding Fathers Considered Dissent a Form of Patriotism, *Daily Reporter*, 2 October.

Mattick, P. (1969) *Marx and Keynes: The Limits of the Mixed Economy*, Boston: Porter Sargent.

Mayer, J. (2018) The Origin of the Word 'Quarantine', 4 September. https://www.sciencefriday.com/articles/the-origin-of-the-word-quarantine/.

Mazzucato, M. (2020) The Covid-19 Crisis is a Chance to Do Capitalism Differently, *The Guardian*, 19 March.

McCoy, T. (2014) Why the Brutal Murder of Several Ebola Workers May Hint at More Violence to Come, *Washington Post*, 19 September.

McEvoy, J. (2021) Washington Pressured Brazil not to Buy 'Malign' Russian Vaccine, *Brasil Wire*, 14 March.

Medical Technology Association of Australia (2020) Revealed: Private Health Insurers Profiteering From COVID-19, 18 August. https://www.mtaa.org.au/news/revealed-private-health-insurers-profiteering-covid19.

Mellor, J. (2020) Did Nanny Make the Call? Rees-Mogg Compares Scramble for PPE with Contacting Plumber, *The London Economic*, 19 November.

Menachery, V.D. et al. (2015) A SARS-like Cluster of Circulating Bat Coronaviruses Show Potential for Human Emergence, *Nature Medicine*, 21, 1508–1513.

Messler, D. (2021) Why Oil Will Keep Rising in 2021, *Oilprice.com*, 14 January.

Mestchian, P. (2003) Operational Risk Management: The Solution is in the Problem, in *Advances in Operational Risk: Firm-wide Issues for Financial Institutions*, London: Risk Books.

Michael, L. (2020) Human Rights at Risk During COVID-19 Response, *Probono Australia*, 15 April.

Miller, R. and Boston, C. (2020) Coronavirus Exposes the Danger of Corporate America's Debt Binge, *Bloomberg Business Week*, 10 March.

Milligan, G.N. and Barrett, A.D.T. (2015) *Vaccinology: An Essential Guide*, Chichester: Wiley Blackwell.

Molina, G.G. and Ortiz-Juarez, E. (2020) *Temporary Basic Income, Protecting Poor and Vulnerable People in Developing Countries*, New York: UNDP.

Moosa, I.A. (2017) *Contemporary Issues in the Post-Crisis Regulatory Landscape*, Singapore: World Scientific.

Moosa, I.A. (2018) Does Financialization Retard Growth? Time Series and Cross-Sectional Evidence, *Applied Economics*, 50, 3405–3415.

Moosa, I.A. (2020a) *Controversies in Economics and Finance: Puzzles and Myths*, Cheltenham, UK and Northampton, MA, USA: Edward Elgar Publishing.

Moosa, I.A. (2020b) The Effectiveness of Social Distancing in Containing Covid-19, *Applied Economics*, 52, 6292–6305.

Moosa, I.A. and Khatatbeh, I.N. (2020) International Tourist Arrivals as a Determinant of the Severity of Covid-19: International Cross-Sectional Evidence, *Journal of Policy Research in Tourism, Leisure and Events* (published online, 17 December).

Moosa, I.A. and Khatatbeh, I.N. (2021a) Robust and Fragile Determinants of the Infection and Case Fatality Rates of Covid-19: International Cross-Sectional Evidence, *Applied Economics*, 53, 1225–1234.

Moosa, I.A. and Khatatbeh, I.N. (2021b) The Density Paradox in Covid-19, Working Paper.

Moosa, I.A. and Khatatbeh, I.N. (2021c) Robust and Fragile Determinants of the Severity of Covid-19 in Developing and Developed Countries: A Comparative Analysis, Working Paper.

Moosa, N. (2020) *The Financing of Healthcare: Theoretical, Empirical and Practical Considerations*, PhD Thesis, University of South Australia, September.

Mozur, P., Zhong, R. and Krolik, A. (2020) In Coronavirus Fight, China Gives Citizens a Color Code, With Red Flags, *New York Times*, 1 March.

Mundell, D. (2020) The Threat of Hunger and Malnutrition as a Result of Covid-19 is Greater than the Virus itself, *The Telegraph*, 16 October.

Naim, M. (1999) Fads and Fashion in Economic Reforms: Washington Consensus or Washington Confusion?, *Foreign Policy Magazine*, 26 October.

National Intelligence Council (2004) *Mapping the Global Future*, Pittsburgh: Government Printing Office. https://www.dni.gov/files/documents/Global%20Trends_Mapping%20the%20Global%20Future%202020%20Project.pdf

Niewiadomski, P. (2020) COVID-19: From Temporary De-Globalisation to a Re-Discovery of Tourism?, *Tourism Geographies* (published online, 5 May).

Núñez, A.C. (2020) Here are Some of the Most Outrageous Capitalist Responses to the Pandemic, 21 May. https://inthesetimes.com/article/covid-19-profiteers-are-making-a-killing.

Nye, J. (2011) *The Future of Power*, New York: Public Affairs.

Nylan, M. (2020) *The Art of War*, New York: Norton.

O'Grady, C. (2020) The U.K. Backed off on Herd Immunity, *National Geographic*, 20 March.

O'Hare, B.A. (2019) International Corporate Tax Avoidance and Domestic Government Health Expenditure, *Bulletin of the World Health Organization*, 97, 746–753.

O'Reilly, K.M., Auzenbergs, M., Jafari, Y., Liu, Y., Flasche, S. and Lowe, R. (2020) Effective Transmission Across the Globe: The Role of Climate in COVID-19 Mitigation Strategies, *Lancet Plenary Health*, 4, E172, 1 May.

OECD (2018) *Putting Faces to the Jobs at Risk of Automation*, Policy Brief on the Future of Work, Paris: OECD.

OECD (2020) Exploitative Pricing in the Time of COVID-19, 26 May. https://www.oecd.org/competition/Exploitative-pricing-in-the-time-of-COVID-19.pdf.

Office of the United Nations High Commissioner for Human Rights (2020) Statement by UN Human Rights Experts: Universal Access to Vaccines is Essential for Prevention and Containment of COVID-19 around the World, 9 November.

Olsen, N. and Zamora, D. (2020) Pandemics Show How the Free Market Fails us, *Jacobin*, 26 March.

Ornelas, E. (2020) Managing Economic Lockdowns in an Epidemic, *Vox*, 28 March.

Oxfam (2020) Pandemic Profits Exposed, *Oxfam Media Briefing*, 22 July.

Packer, G. (2020) We Are Living in a Failed State, *The Atlantic*, 15 June.

Paine, T. (1791) *Rights of Man*, London: J.S. Jordan.

Paine, T. (2018) *Public Good: Being an Examination Into the Claim of Virginia to the Vacant Western Territory, and of the Right of the United States to the Same*, Scotts Valley, CA: CreateSpace Independent Publishing Platform.

Parker, D. (2020) The Covid-19 Vaccines: Free Market Triumph, or Policy Success?, *Frontier Economics*, Article i7887.

Paz, C. (2020) All the President's Lies About the Coronavirus, *The Atlantic*, 27 May (updated on 3 November). https://www.theatlantic.com/politics/archive/2020/11/trumps-lies-about-coronavirus/608647/.

Pearce, K. (2020) What is Social Distancing and How Can it Slow the Spread of COVID-19?, *The Hub*, Johns Hopkins University, 13 March. https://hub.jhu.edu/2020/03/13/what-is-social-distancing/.

Persico, C. and Johnson, K.R. (2020) Deregulation in a Time of Pandemic: Does Pollution Increase Coronavirus Cases or Deaths?, IZA Discussion Papers, No. 13231.

Peterson Institute for International Economics (2018) What is Globalization? And How has the Global Economy Shaped the United States? https://www.piie.com/microsites/globalization/what-is-globalization.

Phillips, D. (2020) Bolsonaro Ignored by State Governors Amid Anger at Handling of Covid-19 Crisis, *The Guardian*, 1 April.

Phillips, N. (2021) The Coronavirus is Here to Stay – Here's what that Means, *Nature*, 16 February.

Phillips, T. (2020) The Country is Adrift: Echoes of Spanish Flu as Brazil's Covid-19 Catastrophe Deepens, *The Guardian*, 14 June.

Piachaud, D. (2018) Basic Income: Confusion, Claims and Choices, *Journal of Poverty and Social Justice*, 26, 299–314.

Pietrawska, B., Aurand, S.K. and Palmer, W. (2020) Covid-19 and Crime: CAP's Perspective on Crime and Loss in the Age of Covid-19: Crime in Los Angeles and Chicago During Covid-19, *CAP Index*, Issue 19.3.

Pillinger, M. (2020) Virus Travel Bans are Inevitable but Ineffective, *Foreign Policy*, 23 February.

Pipes, S. (2020) COVID-19 Reveals the Power of Deregulation, *Forbes*, 8 June.

Pollard, C.M. and Booth, S. (2019) Food Insecurity and Hunger in Rich Countries – It is Time for Action against Inequality, *International Journal of Environmental Research and Public Health*, 16 (10), 1804.

Potter, J. (2020) In Australia, COVID-19 Has Exposed a Litany of Privatization Disasters, *Jacobian*, 23 August.

Powell, J.H. (2020) Coronavirus and CARES Act, Testimony before the Committee on Banking, Housing and Urban Affairs, US Senate, 19 May.

Price-Smith, A.T. (2009) *Contagion and Chaos: Disease, Ecology, and National Security in the Era of Globalization*, Cambridge, MA: MIT Press.

Pullella, P. (2020) Pope Says Free Market 'Trickle-Down' Policies Fail Society, Reuters, 4 October.

Rahman, J., Mumin, J. and Fakhruddin, B. (2020) How Frequently Do We Touch Facial T-Zone: A Systematic Review, *Annals of Global Health*, 86, 1–9.

Ralph, A. (2020) Can Coronavirus Vaccine Success Cure Big Pharma's Ailing Reputation?, *The Times*, 11 November.

Ram, N. and Gray, D. (2020) Mass Surveillance in the Age of COVID-19, *Journal of Law and the Biosciences*, 7, 1–16.

Ramo, J.C. (2004) *The Beijing Consensus*, London: Foreign Policy Centre.

Rapp-Hooper, M. (2020) China, America, and the International Order After the Pandemic, *War on the Rocks*, 24 March.

Rasmussen, H.F. (2020) A Free-Market Agenda for Rebuilding from the Coronavirus, Acton Institute, 24 April.

Rawson, T., Brewer, T., Veltcheva, D., Huntingford, C. and Bonsall, M.B. (2020) How and When to End the COVID-19 Lockdown: An Optimization Approach, *Frontiers in Public Health* (published online, 10 June).

Razzak, W.A. (2020) Does Testing for Coronavirus Reduce Deaths?, Massey University, Discussion Papers, No. 20.05.

Reagan, R. (1961) Radio Address on Socialized Medicine. https://www.americanrhetoric.com/speeches/ronaldreagansocializedmedicine.htm.

Reinhart, C (2020) This Time Truly is Different, *Project Syndicate*, 23 March.

Reinsch, W.A., Caporal, J. and Tuljapurkar, S. (2020) Compulsory Licensing: A Cure for Distributing the Cure?, Center for Strategic and International Studies, 8 May.

Repucci, S. and Slipowitz, A. (2020) Democracy under Lockdown: The Impact of COVID-19 on the Global Struggle for Freedom, *Analysis and Policy Observatory*, 2 October.

Reuter, T. (2013) An Isolationist United States? If Only That Were True, *Forbes*, 10 October.

Richtel, M. (2020) Frightened Doctors Face off with Hospitals over Rules on Protective Gear, *New York Times*, 13 April.

Roach, S. (2021) The Dollar's Crash is only just Beginning, Bloomberg, 25 January.

Robb, G. (2021) U.S. PPI up 1% in March, up 4.2% Year-over-Year, Haver Analytics Says, *Market Watch*, 9 April.

Robertson, R. (1992) *Globalization: Social Theory and Global Culture*, London: Sage.

Rodik, D. (2020) Making the Best of a Post-Pandemic World, *Project Syndicate*, 12 May.

Romney, M. (2012) Romney Outlines How He Would 'Replace Obamacare', 13 June. https://khn.org/news/romney-hits-obama-on-health-law-calls-for-consumer-market/.

Roosevelt Institute (2020) A True New Deal: Building an Inclusive Economy in the COVID-19 Era. https://rooseveltinstitute.org/wp-content/uploads/2020/08/RI -TrueNewDealReport_202008.pdf.

Rozsa, M. (2020) Economist Richard Wolff: Capitalism is the Reason COVID-19 is Ravaging America, *Salon*, 4 October.

Rubio, M. (2020) We Need a More Resilient American Economy, *New York Times*, 20 April.

Saad-Filho, A. (2020a) Coronavirus, Crisis, and the End of Neoliberalism, *Socialist Project*, 17 April.

Saad-Filho, A. (2020b) From COVID-19 to the End of Neoliberalism, *Critical Sociology*, 46, 477–485.

Sajadi, M.M., Habibzadeh, P., Vintzileos, A., Shokouhi, S., Miralles-Wilhelm, F. and Amoroso, A. (2020) Temperature, Humidity and Latitude Analysis to Predict Potential Spread and Seasonality for COVID-19. https://ssrn.com/abstract=3550308.

Saravelos, G. (2020) The End of the Free Market: Impact on Currencies and Beyond, Deutsche Bank, 17 April. https://www.dbresearch.com/servlet/reweb2.ReWEB ?rwsite =RPS_EN.

Sard, B. (2009) Number of Homeless Families Climbing Due to Recession, Center on Budget and Policy Priorities, 8 January.

Sarin, N. and Summers, L. (2020) Increasing Tax Compliance in the United States, *Vox*, 24 April.

Sauter, M.B. and Stebbins, S. (2020) How the Current Stock Market Collapse Compares with Others in History, *USA Today*, 21 March.

Saxer, M. (2020) How Corona Broke the System, *International Politics and Society*, 23 March.

Sayeh, A. and Chami, R. (2020) The COVID-19 Pandemic Threatens to Dry up a Vital Source of Income for Poor and Fragile Countries, *Finance and Development*, June.

Scherbina, A. (2020) Determining the Optimal Duration of the COVID19 Suppression Policy: A Cost–Benefit Analysis, AEI Economics Working Papers, No. 2020-03.

Scott, B. (2016) The War on Cash, *The Long and Short*, 19 August.

Shah, S. (2020) Developing Countries Push to Limit Patent Protections for Covid-19 Vaccines, *Wall Street Journal*, 17 September.

Shayegh, S. and Malpede, M. (2020) Staying Home Saves Lives, Really!, RFF-CMCC European Institute on Economics and the Environment. https://papers.ssrn.com/sol3/ papers.cfm?abstract_id=3567394.

Sheiner, L. (2020) How Does the Coronavirus Pandemic Compare to the Great Recession, and What Should Fiscal Policy Do Now?, *Brookings Blogs*, 12 March.

Sinapi, C. (2014) The Role of Financialization in Financial Instability: A Post-Keynesian Institutionalist Perspective, Working Paper, Burgundy School of Business.

Siu, J.Y.M. (2015) Influence of Social Experiences in Shaping Perceptions of the Ebola Virus among African Residents of Hong Kong during the 2014 Outbreak: A Qualitative Study, *International Journal for Equity in Health*, 14, 88.

Skinner, V. and Carnemolla, P. (2020) If We Realised the True Cost of Homelessness, We'd Fix it Overnight, *The Conversation*, 22 September.

Skopeliti, C. (2021) 'Kill the Bill' Protest in Bristol Condemned as 'Thuggery and Disorder', *The Guardian*, 22 March.

Smith, R.D., Keogh-Brown, M.R., Barnett, T. and Tait, J. (2009) The Economy-Wide Impact of Pandemic Influenza on the UK: A Computable General Equilibrium Modelling Experiment, *British Medical Journal*, 339. https://www.bmj.com/content/339/bmj.b4571.

Smithson, M. (2020) Data from 45 Countries Show Containing COVID vs Saving the Economy is a False Dichotomy, *The Conversation*, 26 November.

Sonenshine, J. (2020) Stock Buybacks Have Fallen off a Cliff: Why They're Set to Make a Comeback, *Barrons*, 8 December.

South African Reserve Bank (2020a) Media Statement, 16 March.

South African Reserve Bank (2020b) The SARB Warns the Public that it is NOT Withdrawing Banknotes and Coin Because of COVID-19, 16 March. https://www.resbank.co.za/en/home/publications/publication-detail-pages/media-releases/2020/9779.

Spence, M. and Hlatshwayo, S. (2011) The Evolving Structure of the American Economy and the Employment Challenge, Working Paper, Council on Foreign Relations.

Stallman, R.M. (2018) Did You Say 'Intellectual Property'? It's a Seductive Mirage, Free Software Foundation, 15 December.

Standing, G. (2017) *Basic Income: And How we Can Make it Happen*, London: Pelican.

Stanhope, J. and Weinstein, P. (2020) Travel Restrictions and Evidence-Based Decision Making for Novel Epidemics, *Medical Journal of Australia*, 213 (9).

Stankiewicz, K. (2019) PayPal CFO: We've been Talking about the Death of Cash for Years – and Now 'it's here', CNBC, 24 October.

Stankiewicz, K. (2021) Sen. Warren on Wealth Tax: 'I Think Most People Would Rather be Rich' and Pay 2 or 3 Cents, CNBC, 2 March.

Stayner, G. (2017) Cost of Homelessness: Governments will Save Money by Spending on Accommodation Services, Study Finds, ABC News, 16 March.

Steger, M. (2009) *Globalization: A Very Short Introduction*, New York: Oxford University Press.

Stewart, E. (2020) The Economy is in Free Fall. So Why Isn't the Stock Market?, *Vox*, 6 May.

Stickle, B. and Felson, M. (2020) Crime Rates in a Pandemic: The Largest Criminological Experiment in History, *American Journal of Criminal Justice* (published online, 16 June).

Stiglitz, J.E. (2000) *Globalization and Its Discontents*, New York: Norton.

Stiglitz, J.E. (2010) *Free Fall: America, Free Markets, and the Sinking of the World Economy*, New York: Norton.

Stiglitz, J.E. (2020) Conquering the Great Divide, *Finance and Development*, September, 17–18.

Stokols, E. (2021) Biden Signs $1.9-Trillion COVID-19 Relief Bill, a Day Earlier than Expected, *Los Angeles Times*, 11 March.

Sumdani, H., Frickle, S., Le, M., Tran, M. and Zaleta, C.K. (2014) Effects of Population Density on the Spread of Disease, Technical Report 2014-05, University of Texas at Arlington.

Summers, L. (2020) COVID-19 Looks Like a Hinge in History, *Financial Times*, 14 May.

Sumner, A., Hoy, C. and Ortiz-Juarez, E. (2020) Estimates of the Impact of COVID-19 on Global Poverty, WIDER Working Papers, No 2020/43.

Šumonja, M. (2020) Neoliberalism is Not Dead – On Political Implications of Covid-19, *Capital and Class* (published online, 28 December).

Susskind, D. (2020a) *A World Without Work: Technology, Automation and How We Should Respond*, London: Allen Lane.

Susskind, D. (2020b) Universal Basic Income is an Affordable and Feasible Response to Coronavirus, *Financial Times*, 18 March.

Taibbi, M. (2020a) Big Pharma's Covid-19 Profiteers, *Rolling Stone*, 13 August.

Taibbi, M. (2020b) How the COVID-19 Bailout Gave Wall Street a No-Lose Casino, *Rolling Stone*, 13 May.

Tait, P. (2020) As Australia Slips Toward Fascism, Where Does the Public Health Community Stand?, *Croakey*, 29 May.

Taleb, N.N. (2010) *The Black Swan: The Impact of the Highly Improbable*, New York: Random House.

Talmazan, Y. and Smith, P. (2021) Unlikely that Covid Came from Wuhan Lab, WHO Says, NBC News, 9 February.

Tant, E. (2020) Study Shows Pandemics Can Give Rise to Fascism, *Flagpole*, 27 May.

Tarwater, P.M. (1999) The Effects of Population Density on the Spread of Disease, Texas Medical Center Dissertations. https://digitalcommons.library.tmc.edu/dissertations/AAI9929469/.

Tarwater, P.M. and Martin, C.F. (2001) Effects of Population Density on the Spread of Disease, *Complexity*, 6, 29–36.

Tau, B. (2020) Government Tracking How People Move Around in Coronavirus Pandemic, *Wall Street Journal*, 28 March.

Taylor, C. (2020) 1918 Flu Pandemic Boosted Support for the Nazis, Fed Study Claims, CNBC, 6 May.

Tediosi, F., Lönnroth, K., Pablos-Méndez, A. and Raviglione, M. (2020) Build Back Stronger Universal Health Coverage Systems after the COVID-19 Pandemic, *BMJ Global Health*. https://gh.bmj.com/content/5/10/e004020.

Thomas, D. (2020) Scramble to Secure PPE Cost UK Taxpayer Extra £10bn, *Financial Times*, 24 November.

Thomas, M.R., Smith, G., Ferreira, F.H.G., Evans, D., Maliszewska, M. et al. (2015) The Economic Impact of Ebola on Sub-Saharan Africa: Updated Estimates for 2015, World Bank Working Papers, No. 93721.

Thompson, D. (2020a) COVID-19 Cases are Rising, so Why are Deaths Flatlining?, *The Atlantic*, 9 July.

Thompson, D. (2020b) The Technology that Could Free America from Quarantine, *The Atlantic*, 7 April.

Thompson, W.R. (2008) Measuring Long-term Process of Political Globalization, in G. Modelski, T. Devezas and W.R. Thompson (eds), *Globalization as Evolutionary Process: Modeling Global Change*, London: Routledge.

Tomaskovic-Devey, D., Dominguez-Villegas, R. and Hoyt, E. (2020) The COVID-19 Recession: An Opportunity to Reform our Low Wage Economy? Center for Employment Equity, University of Massachusetts Amherst.

Toole, M.J. and Waldman, R.J. (1990) Prevention of Excess Mortality in Refugee and Displaced Populations in Developing Countries, *Journal of the American Medical Association*, 263, 3296–3302.

Tudora, A. and Zamfir, T. (2020) Fascists Enter Parliament as COVID-19 Devastates Romania, *World Socialist*, 29 December.

Turse, N. (2018) The Pentagon Sent $500 Million Abroad for International Drug Wars. What Happened Next is a Mystery, *The Nation*, 8 February.

UK Mission to the WTO (2020) UK Statement to the TRIPS Council: Item 15 Waiver Proposal for COVID-19, 16 October.

UN News (2020) UN Chief Calls for Domestic Violence 'Ceasefire' Amid 'Horrifying Global Surge', 6 April. https://news.un.org/en/story/2020/04/1061052.

UN Office of the High Commissioner on Human Rights (2020) COVID-19: States Should Not Abuse Emergency Measures to Suppress Human Rights – UN Experts, 16 March.

UNDP (2015) Socio-Economic Impact of Ebola Virus Disease in West African Countries: A Call for National and Regional Containment, Recovery and Prevention, February.

UNESCO (2020) Adverse Consequences of School Closures. https://en.unesco.org/covid19/educationresponse/consequences.

United Nations (2020a) COVID-19 and Universal Health Coverage, Policy Brief, October.

United Nations (2020b) The Impact of COVID-19 on Food Security and Nutrition, Policy Brief, June.

UNOCHA (2020) Global Humanitarian Overview 2020. https://www.unocha.org/global-humanitarian-overview-2020.

UNWTO (2021) World Tourism Barometer, January. https://www.unwto.org/unwto-world-tourism-barometer-data.

Van Parijs, P. and Vanderborght, Y. (2017) *Basic Income: A Radical Proposal for a Free Society and a Sane Economy*, Cambridge: Harvard University Press.

Vardi, S. (2020) Are Governments Violating Human Rights and Civil Liberties in Coronavirus Response?, American Friends Service Committee, 10 September.

Velasco, A. (2020) We are all Keynesians Again, *Financial Review*, 27 August.

Vlandas, T. (2020) A Pandemic 'Misery Index': Ranking Countries' Economic and Health Performance During Covid-19, *LSE Blog*, 4 December.

Vos, R., Martin, W. and Laborde, D. (2020a) As COVID-19 Spreads, No Major Concern for Global Food Security Yet. https://www.ifpri.org/blog/covid-19-spreads-no-major-concern-global-food-security-yet.

Vos, R., Martin, W. and Laborde, D. (2020b) How Much will Global Poverty Increase Because of COVID-19? https://www.ifpri.org/blog/how-much-will-global-poverty-increase-because-covid-19.

Wall, D. (2020) Britain: As COVID-19 Deaths Mount, Why is Boris Johnson Still Popular?, 21 April. https://www.greenleft.org.au/content/britain-covid-19-deaths-mount-why-boris-johnson-still-popular.

Wallach, P.A. (2019) On Deregulation, Trump Has Achieved Little, *National Review*, 19 December.

Wallach, P.A. and Weissmann, S. (2020) Taking Stock of COVID-19 Deregulation, *Brookings*, 17 June.

Walt, S.M. (2020) The Coronavirus Pandemic has Killed America's Reputation, *Foreign Policy*, 23 March.

Wang, J., Tang, K., Feng, K. and Lv, W. (2020) High Temperature and High Humidity Reduce the Transmission of COVID-19. https://arxiv.org/abs/2003.05003.

Warrell, H. and Fildes, N. (2020) Cyber Criminals Exploit Coronavirus Disruption, *Financial Times*, 16 March.

Wells, C.R., Sah, P., Moghadas, S.M., Pandey, A., Shoukat, A., Wang, Y., Zheng, W., Meyers, L.A., Singer, B.H. and Galvani, A.P. (2020) Impact of International Travel and Border Control Measures on the Global Spread of the Novel 2019 Coronavirus Outbreak, *PNAS*, 117, 7504–7509.

Whitehead, J.W. (2020) COVID-19 and the War on Cash: What is Behind the Push for a Cashless Society?, Scoop Independent News, 15 April.

Williamson, J. (1990) What Washington Means by Policy Reform, in J. Williamson (ed.), *Latin American Adjustment: How Much Has Happened?*, Washington: Peterson Institute for International Economics.

Williamson, J. (2000) What Should the World Bank Think about the Washington Consensus?, *World Bank Research Observer*, 15, 251–264.

Willsher, K., Holmes, O., McKernan, B. and Tondo, L. (2020) US Hijacking Mask Shipments in Rush for Coronavirus Protection, *The Guardian*, 3 April.

Winters, M.S. (2020) History Warns us: Crises Like COVID-19 Can Give Rise to Great Evil, *National Catholic Reporter*, 3 April.

Witko, C. (2016) The Politics of Financialization in the United States, 1949–2005, *British Journal of Political Science*, 46, 349–370.

Wolf, M. (2020) The World Economy is Now Collapsing, *Financial Times*, 15 April.

Wolff, R. (2020) *The Sickness is the System: When Capitalism Fails to Save us from Pandemics or Itself*, New York: Democracy at Work.

Wolfson, J.A. and Leung, C.W. (2020) Food Insecurity During COVID-19: An Acute Crisis with Long-Term Health Implications, *American Journal of Public Health* (published online, 12 November).

Wong, F. (2020) The Post-Neoliberal World is Already Here, *Democracy: A Journal of Ideas*, 7 May.

Woodward, A. (2021) 'Neanderthal Thinking': Biden Criticises Texas and Mississippi Governors for Dropping Coronavirus Restrictions, *The Independent*, 4 March.

Woolston, C. (2020) Bleak Financial Outlook for PhD Students in Australia, *Nature*, 9 July.

World Bank (2014) The Economic Impact of the 2014 Ebola Epidemic: Short and Medium Term Estimates for Guinea, Liberia, and Sierra Leone, World Bank Working Papers, No. 90748.

World Bank (2020) Food Security and COVID-19, 14 December. https://www .worldbank.org/en/topic/agriculture/brief/food-security-and-covid-19.

World Food Programme (2020) On World Food Day, We Need to Consider How we Can Help to Tackle the Global Scourge of Food Insecurity, WFP Global Update on COVID-19, November.

World Health Organization (2010) *Health System Financing: The Path to Universal Coverage*, Geneva: WHO.

World Health Organization (2019a) Emergencies: International Health Regulations and Emergency Committees, WHO Q&A, 19 December.

World Health Organization (2019b) Universal Health Coverage (UHC). https://www .who.int/news-room/fact-sheets/detail/universal-health-coverage-(uhc).

World Health Organization (2020a) Transmission of SARS-CoV-2: Implications for Infection Prevention Precautions, *Scientific Brief*, 9 July.

World Health Organization (2020b) COVID-19: Virtual Press Conference, 13 May.

World Health Organization (2020c) Impact of COVID-19 on People's Livelihoods, their Health and our Food Systems: Joint statement by ILO, FAO, IFAD and WHO, 13 October.

Wright, S. (2020) Suitcases of Cash Added to the Mountains of Loo Paper and Canned Goods, *Sydney Morning Herald*, 9 April.

Yang, J., Zhang, Q., Cao, Z., Gao, J., Pfeiffer, D., Zhong, L. and Zeng, D.D. (2020) The Impact of Non-Pharmaceutical Interventions on the Prevention and Control of COVID-19 in New York City. https://www.medrxiv.org/content/10.1101/2020.12 .01. 20242347v1.

Yap, J. and Huan, A. (2018) The Good, the Bad and the Ugly of Globalisation, *Sid Directors Bulletin*, Third Quarter.

Yu, W. and Keralis, J. (2020) Controlling COVID-19: The Folly of International Travel Restrictions, *Health and Human Rights Journal*, 6 April. https://www.hhrjournal.org/2020/04/controlling-covid-19-the-folly-of-international-travel-restrictions/.

Zitelmann, R. (2020) Left-Wing Intellectuals are Thrilled: Corona and Dreams of the End of Capitalism, *Forbes*, 31 March.

Index